BRUCE SPRINGSTEEN

THE DAY I WAS THERE

Neil Cossar

THIS DAY BOOKS
IN MUSIC
www.thisdayinmusic.com

A catalogue record for this book is available from the British Library

This edition © This Day In Music Books 2018
Text © This Day In Music Books 2018

ISBN: 978 1 999592 71 4

Picture research Liz Sanchez
Cover design by Oliver Keen
Book design by Robot Mascot
Printed in the UK by CPI

THIS DAY IN MUSIC BOOKS

This Day In Music Books
2B Vantage Park
Washingley Road
Huntingdon
PE29 6SR

www.thisdayinmusic.com
Email: editor@thisdayinmusic.com

Exclusive Distributors:
Music Sales Limited
14/15 Berners St
London
W1T 3JL

Contents

CONTENTS

1992

RICHFIELD COLISEUM
185

22 AUGUST 1992
RICHFIELD, OHIO

THE SPECTRUM
188

28 AUGUST 1992
PHILADELPHIA,
PENNSYLVANIA

1993

SECC
189

31 MARCH 1993
GLASGOW, UK

NATIONAL BOWL
194

22 MAY 1993 MILTON
KEYNES, UK

MEADOWLANDS ARENA
195

24 JUNE 1993 EAST
RUTHERFORD, NEW
JERSEY

1995

TRADEWINDS
196

22 JULY 1995 SEA
BRIGHT, NEW JERSEY

1996

NEWCASTLE CITY HALL
198

2 MARCH 1996
NEWCASTLE-UPON-
TYNE, UK

ROYAL ALBERT HALL
198

17 APRIL 1996 LONDON,
UK

BRIXTON ACADEMY
199

24 APRIL 1996 LONDON,
UK

LOWELL MEMORIAL AUDITORIUM
200

14 NOVEMBER
1996 LOWELL,
MASSACHUSETTS,
NEW ENGLAND

1997

PALACE THEATRE
203

15 FEBRUARY 1997
MELBOURNE, AUSTRALIA

1999

CONVENTION HALL
206

18 MARCH 1999 ASBURY
PARK, NEW JERSEY

EARLS COURT
206

21 MAY 1999 LONDON, UK

CONTINENTAL ARENA
209

20 JULY 1999 EAST
RUTHERFORD NEW
JERSEY

MEADOWLANDS ARENA
210

29 JULY 1999 EAST
RUTHERFORD, NEW
JERSEY

MEADOWLANDS ARENA
211

6 AUGUST 1999 EAST
RUTHERFORD, NEW
JERSEY

UNITED CENTER
213

27 SEPTEMBER 1999
CHICAGO, ILLINOIS

2000

NASHVILLE ARENA
215

12 APRIL 2000
NASHVILLE, TENNESSEE

2001

CLEARWATER FESTIVAL
215

18 AUGUST 2001 ASBURY
PARK, NEW JERSEY

2002

ISLE OF WIGHT FESTIVAL
216

14 JUNE 2002 SEACLOSE
PARK, ISLE OF WIGHT

2003

TELSTRA DOME
217

20 MARCH 2003
MELBOURNE, AUSTRALIA

OLD TRAFFORD CRICKET GROUND
218

29 MAY 2003
MANCHESTER, UK

RDS ARENA
219

31 MAY 2003 DUBLIN,
IRELAND

PNC PARK
222

6 AUGUST 2003
PITTSBURGH,
PENNSYLVANIA

LINCOLN FINANCIAL FIELD
223

8 AUGUST 2003
PHILADELPHIA,
PENNSYLVANIA

SKYDOME
224

10 SEPTEMBER 2003
TORONTO, CANADA

KENAN STADIUM
225

14 SEPTEMBER 2003
NORTH CAROLINA

SHEA STADIUM
225

3 OCTOBER 2003 NEW
YORK CITY

CONTENTS

FOREWORD

'You gotta see him live!' was the buzz on the East Coast of the U.S. in the early Seventies. They were talking about some kid named Bruce Springsteen from Asbury Park, New Jersey. I first got to 'see him live' for the first time in 1973 and have seen about a hundred and fifty shows since. (Many Springsteen fans can give you the exact number of shows they've been to, but I didn't realize I should've been counting until many years later.) Like Elvis, James Brown, and now Beyonce, he is a once-in-a-generation performer who gives his all every night. Along with the amazing E Street Band, a Bruce show leaves you simultaneously exhausted and screaming for more.

Still performing four-hour shows in his late sixties with setlists that change every night, Bruce and the band are the gold standard in what live rock and roll should be: joyous, angry, moving, unpredictable, funny, heart-breaking, hopeful, and always drenched in sweat.

In this book, Neil Cossar has collected concert memories of Springsteen fans from the past forty plus years and why a particular show stood out for them. If you've never seen him live, a book can't really do the experience justice, but it will have to do until the next tour – unless you're not a fan, in which case I don't know why you're wasting your time reading the foreword to a book you're clearly going to hate.

To everyone else, enjoy!

Mike Scully
The Simpsons
Parks and Recreation

INTRODUCTION

His authority in rock music is unshakeable. In his lyrics he focuses on the little man's winding path through life with a certain melancholy and profound compassion. In a world of music where styles are fluctuating all the time, Bruce Springsteen stands with both feet firmly planted on the ground of rock 'n' roll.

Bruce Springsteen was born of Irish-Italian ancestry on September 23, 1949, in Freehold, New Jersey, the son of Douglas and Adele Springsteen. Freehold during his whole career would be a significant symbol of his musical work, writing about the everyday life and ordinary people from his hometown, representing the average American town and its ordinary, 'real' people.

Springsteen grew up hearing fellow New Jersey singer Frank Sinatra on the radio. He found inspiration in music when he saw Elvis Presley on *The Ed Sullivan Show* at the age of seven. He bought his first guitar at 13, and after witnessing The Beatles performing on *Ed Sullivan*, Springsteen has stated that he 'locked himself up in his room for many months trying to learn how to play'. After his first paid gigs in The Rogues he joined The Beatles-influenced Castiles and began playing gigs in New Jersey and New York, and headlined in Café Wha? in Greenwich Village.

Called for conscription in the United States Armed Forces when he was 18, Springsteen failed the physical examination and did not serve in the Vietnam War. He had suffered a concussion in a motorcycle accident when he was 17, and this together with his 'crazy' behaviour at induction gave him a classification of 4F (unfit for military service) which made him unacceptable for service.

Springsteen's next group was Earth, a Cream-style power trio. Then while in college, Springsteen formed Child with some local musicians, including drummer Vini 'Mad Dog' Lopez and keyboardist Danny Federici (re-named Steel Mill). The group was later joined by guitarist Steve Van Zandt. Springsteen disbanded Steel Mill in early 1971.

Other acts followed over the next two years; Dr. Zoom & the Sonic Boom with Southside Johnny on harmonica (early to mid-1971), The Sundance Blues Band (mid-1971), and the Bruce Springsteen Band (mid-1971 to mid-1972). With the addition of pianist David Sancious, the core of what would later become the E Street Band was formed, with occasional temporary additions such as horn sections, the Zoomettes (a group of female backing vocalists for Dr. Zoom).

Springsteen had also been playing solo shows in New York City in the beginning of the Seventies and during this time met his first manager, Mike Appel, who arranged an audition for legendary Columbia Records talent scout John Hammond, who had signed Bob Dylan to Columbia.

When John Hammond auditioned Bruce Springsteen in his office in 1972, hearing some original songs only on guitar and piano, his response was simply 'You've got to be on Columbia Records'.

Springsteen gathered his previous back up band for the recording of his debut album *Greetings from Asbury Park, N.J.* released in 1973. The album was well received but sales were disappointing (initially selling about 25,000 copies). Like Dylan, Bruce Springsteen remains at Columbia to this day, and his recordings must rank as among the most exciting spectacles in the living fabric of American culture. When Springsteen then decided to use a tenor saxophone on the songs 'Blinded by the Light' and 'Spirit in the Night,' he called upon Clarence Clemons (who he had previously met in September 1971).

British act Manfred Mann's Earth Band would take the lead off track, 'Blinded by the Light', from *Greetings from Asbury Park, N.J.* into a number one hit in 1976. Springsteen's second album *The Wild, the Innocent & the E Street Shuffle* released in September 1973 also failed to sell despite very good reviews. The album includes the song 'Rosalita (Come Out Tonight),' the band's most-used set-closing song for the first ten years of its career.

Born to Run, the songwriter's third, was his make or break album. The massive Phil Spector sound on almost every song on *Born to Run* touched on the central mythical image of the rock 'n' roll era - Springsteen has said that he wanted *Born to Run* to sound like 'Roy Orbison singing Bob Dylan, produced by Spector'. It took Bruce and his band months in total to record the title track, with versions including string section overdubs, a choir on the chorus and one with a double-tracked lead vocal. Bruce's friend, guitarist Steve Van Zandt, a veteran of early Springsteen bands and who joined the E Street Band during the album sessions, now laughs at the thought of it. 'Anytime you spend six months on a song, there's something not exactly going right. A song should take about three hours.'

Born to Run was released in 1975. Advance sales put the album on the chart a week before its release date, and it made the Top Ten shortly afterward going gold in a matter of weeks, cementing Springsteen's success for many years ahead. 'Born to Run' gave Springsteen his first hit single and as he embarked on his first national tour *Time* and *Newsweek* ran simultaneous cover stories on Springsteen.

Springsteen bought a 1950 Corvette with his first royalty cheque from 'Born to Run', the first car he ever owned, it now resides in a Rock 'n' Roll Hall Of Fame exhibition.

Despite this breakthrough, Springsteen was unable to follow up his ground breaking third album due to legal disputes with former manager Appel. He brought in rock critic Jon Landau as his new manager but was unable to record new material until the dispute was settled. During this period he wrote 'Because the Night' with American singer-songwriter, poet Patti Smith, which became a Top hit for her in the spring of 1978 while The Pointer Sisters hit number two in 1979 with Springsteen's unreleased track 'Fire'.

Darkness on the Edge of Town (which had the working title *American Madness*) saw Springsteen's return in June 1978. The album marked the end of a three-year gap between albums brought on by legal battling with former manager Mike Appel. His 'Heartland' soul rock sound with a social undertone and positive reviews helped put

Springsteen back on top with the album spending 97 weeks on the US chart.

In March 1979 Springsteen attended a Ramones show in Asbury Park, New Jersey and met Joey Ramone who asked him to write a song for the band. Springsteen composed 'Hungry Heart' that night, but decided to keep it for himself on the advice of his producer and manager, Jon Landau. When released 'Hungry Heart' gave Springsteen his first Top Ten hit. The track was also used in the Tom Cruise movie *Risky Business,* the first time a Springsteen song was used in a film.

Springsteen fully consolidated his status with his following release and Springsteen's only double album, *The River,* in October 1980.

The album was Springsteen's first to go number one on the *Billboard* chart and spent four weeks at the top - going on to sell over five million copies worldwide.

Nebraska, released on 30 September, 1982 was a stripped down acoustic solo album. Recorded on a four-track machine at his home it marked a major turn for the rock icon. The music captured on the record is what he originally recorded as demos on acoustic guitar and harmonica in January 1982. Because of the album's sombre content, Springsteen chose not to tour in support of the album, making it Springsteen's only major release that was not supported by going out on the road.

Born in the U.S.A. released on 4 June, 1984 became Springsteen's most successful album ever, with seven Top 10 hits ('Dancing in the Dark', 'Cover Me', 'Born in the U.S.A', 'I'm on Fire', 'Glory Days', 'I'm Goin' Down' and 'My Hometown') and became one of the highest-selling records ever, having sold 30 million copies by 2012. The album received a nomination for Album of the Year at the 1985 Grammy Awards.

Born in the U.S.A. arrived at a time when American politicians with Ronald Reagan as their leader wanted to create a new form of patriotism after the war and tragedies in Vietnam. However, 'Born in the U.S.A.' was in part a tribute to Springsteen's friends who had experienced the Vietnam War, some of whom did not come back and addresses the harmful effects of the War.

In 1984 Springsteen met model and actress Julianne Phillips, and the couple married in May 1985. The marriage quickly began to fall apart, however, and Springsteen began an affair with E Street Band backup singer Patti Scialfa, who shared his working-class New Jersey background. Phillips filed for divorce in 1989. Springsteen moved in with Scialfa and they had two children together before officially marrying in 1991. Their third and last child was born in 1994.

His eighth studio album *Tunnel of Love* released in October 1987 saw Springsteen record some of his most personal songs and playing most of the parts himself, often with drum machines and synthesizers. The album went triple Platinum in the US, with 'Brilliant Disguise' being one of his biggest hit singles.

Springsteen dissolved The E Street Band in 1989 and worked on the two albums *Human Touch* and *Lucky Town*, released simultaneously in 1992. He also wrote the title song for the Jonathan Demme film *Philadelphia* (1993), one of the first bigger Hollywood productions about AIDS. The song 'Streets of Philadelphia' won the Best Original Song Academy Award that year, and Springsteen became the first rock artist to win an Oscar in this category.

> ❮ When I was growing up, there were two things that were unpopular in my house. One was me, and the other was my guitar ❯

The 1995 album *The Ghost of Tom Joad* became Springsteen's second acoustic album and won the 1997 Grammy Award for Best Contemporary Folk Album. The character of Tom Joad entered the American consciousness in John Steinbeck's 1939 Pulitzer Prize-winning novel, *The Grapes of Wrath*, set against the economic hardships of the Great Depression.

The four disc box set *Tracks*, a career-spanning collection that included 56 previously unreleased recordings a number of single B-sides, as well as demos and alternate versions of already-released material released in 1998 became the first box set ever to debut at number one on the charts.

Springsteen's twelfth studio album *The Rising* released in July 2002 debuted at number 1 on the *Billboard* 200 chart. It was his first with the E Street Band in 18 years and is widely believed to have been based on Springsteen's reflections during the aftermath of the 11

September, 2001 attacks. Springsteen told journalist Mark Binelli that a stranger in a car had stopped next to him, rolled down his window and said: 'We need you now.' *The Rising* is predominantly based upon themes of relationship struggles, existential crisis and social uplift. The album won a Grammy Award for Best Rock Album in 2003.

His third acoustic album the 2005 *Devils & Dust* contained twelve songs of assorted vintage and a narrative setting (Springsteen wrote the title song in 2003, after the start of the Iraq War) became his seventh number one on the US *Billboard* album chart. He received five Grammy Award nominations for this work, three for the song 'Devils & Dust', Song of the Year, Best Rock Song, and Best Solo Rock Vocal Performance, and two for the album as a whole.

The 2006 *We Shall Overcome: The Seeger Sessions* won the Grammy Award for Best Traditional Folk Album at the 49th Grammy Awards. The first and so far only album of entirely non-Springsteen material contains his interpretation of thirteen folk music songs made popular by activist folk musician Pete Seeger.

In 2008 keyboardist Danny Federici who had followed the band and forged its sound since the beginnings passed away of melanoma aged 58. After his illness was diagnosed he set up the Danny Federici Melanoma Fund to raise money for research at the Sloan-Kettering hospital in New York City. On the news of his death Springsteen said: 'He was the most wonderfully fluid keyboard player and a pure, natural musician. I loved him very much.'

Magic his fifteenth studio album released in September 2007 was his first with The E Street Band since 2002. It became Springsteen's seventh number one in the UK and debuted at number one on the US chart, becoming Springsteen's eighth number one album in the US. *Magic* was nominated for the Grammy Award for Best Rock Album but lost to the Foo Fighters' *Echoes, Silence, Patience & Grace* and the album ranked number two on *Rolling Stone's* list of the Top 50 Albums of 2007.

2009 saw the release of *Working on a Dream* the last to feature new work of founding E Street Band member Danny Federici. The album reached number one in 17 countries around the world, and reached the Top 10 almost everywhere else. Later in November 2014, Springsteen released a graphic novel titled *Outlaw Pete*, which is based on the opening track from *Working on a Dream*.

In June 2011 another founding member, Clarence Clemons, whose saxophone sound had followed Springsteen since day one and created his particular rock groove suffered a stroke and died a few days later. Clemons had been a strong pillar in the E Street sound playing an essential role in Springsteen's songs, particularly in the first years on 'Jungleland,' 'Incident on 57th Street' and 'Rosalita (Come Out Tonight)'. The Big Man, who stood at 6 feet 4 inches tall and built like the football player he might have been was by far the E Street Band's flashiest dresser, in eye-popping suits and broad-brimmed hats.

The 2012 album *Wrecking Ball* was named best album of 2012 by *Rolling Stone* and along with the album's first single, 'We Take Care of Our Own', was nominated for three Grammy Awards. *Wrecking Ball* became Springsteen's tenth number one album in the US, tying him with Elvis Presley for third-most number one albums of all-time.

Springsteen's eighteenth studio album *High Hopes* features Springsteen's regular backing band, The E Street Band, plus Rage Against the Machine and Audioslave guitarist Tom Morello. Contributions from deceased E Street Band members Clarence Clemons and Danny Federici are also included. *High Hopes* became his eleventh US number one placing him third all-time for most number one albums only behind The Beatles and Jay-Z. *Rolling Stone* named it the second-best album of 2014 on their year-end list.

To date Springsteen has released 18 studio albums, 70 singles, 8 extended plays, 23 live albums, 7 box sets, 8 compilation albums, 57 music videos and 17 home videos. World wide albums sales stand at over 122 million.

❝ I looked at myself and I just said, 'Well, you know, I can sing but I'm not the greatest singer in the world. I can play guitar very well but I'm not the greatest guitar player in the world, so I said, 'Well, if I'm going to project an individuality, it's going to have to be in my writing. **❞**

Bruce Springsteen

1966 – 1969

After playing a handful of shows as a member of The Rouges, Bruce Springsteen joined The Castiles (their name taken from a popular shampoo). The Castiles played at high school graduation dances, including Springsteen's own Class of '67 dance on June 9 1967.

Springsteen's first recording session took place on 18 May 1966 at Mr. Music in Bricktown, New Jersey. The Castiles spent their recording time recording two songs written by Springsteen and George Theiss; 'Baby I' and 'That's What You Get', both of which had been performed in concert regularly during 1966 and early 1967. Only a few copies where pressed on acetate. They were eventually released in 1993 on the bootleg *The Bruce Springsteen Story Vol. 2*.

'For the first recording session, things were very primitive. The engineer who was the owner of the studio had a little room, and we pulled all our amps and drums in there and he had a hard time handling any volume whatsoever. The amps were faced towards the wall to muffle them. It was a big deal. It was the first time you heard yourself coming back on tape. The guy sent you the acetate, it looked like a record - it spun round and round and round. We put a needle on and music came off which we thought was incredible at the time!'
– Bruce Springsteen

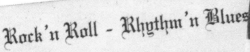

MONMOUTH COLLEGE

1969 NEW JERSEY

I WAS THERE: MITCH DIAMOND

I was going to Monmouth College in the late Sixties. We saw Child and Steel Mill quite a lot as they played the local gigs and also opened occasional shows in the college. At the time, I was very impressed with 'the guitar player'. I remember talking to a couple of friends in between acts at a show. I believe it was Steel

Mill. The consensus was that the band absolutely stunk except for that frontman/guitarist. He was special, we decided.

WEST END PARK

5 MAY 1969 LONG BRANCH, NEW JERSEY

I WAS THERE: JAY DREAMING

I had been to the Sunshine Inn many times and also played at the Upstage Club owned by Margaret Potter and her husband. The West End bar, as it was called, was actually the Brighton Bar, on Brighton Avenue in West End, Long Branch. Bruce played there many times.

On the back of *The Wild, the Innocent, and the E-Street Shuffle* is a picture of the band in front of an old storefront. This was around the corner from the Brighton Bar and used to be a little bike repair shop / candy store called Tommy Reed's.

I grew up around the corner on West End Avenue. My friends and I used to see Bruce a lot in those days when he was living in a little house on West End Court, a block away from the Brighton. He used to tell us stories when we were on the boardwalk at night at the end of West End Avenue. I'd see him a lot at the local clubs.

This was actually before Steel Mill and the band was still called Child, which had to be changed due to the name being used by someone else. This was the first concert by Bruce's band, doing mostly original material.

I WAS THERE: RANDALL KENT WHITED

I met the band called Child and Bruce Springsteen in 1969 through Carl 'Thinker' West. I had gone to Alaska in 1968 and was checking out the area. I wrote to Tinker to tell him how I was, and he said, 'Appear here immediately' and sent me a plane ticket. I arrived in New Jersey shortly thereafter in the Spring/Summer of 1969.

I had been hired to work in the Governor's office by the Secretary of State, Keith Miller, who became governor of Alaska after Wally Hickel was made Secretary of Interior of the United States by Richard Nixon. Wally's claim to fame was that he was fired by Nixon, which some say is an honor. I was in charge of the state ballots.

Tinker together with some other surfers and I had built a surf truck in 1966, put about 20 boards in the super-rack on top, and headed for the East Coast where we felt there was a better market for selling surfboards. We had originally been Challenger Surfboards, located in Mission Beach (San Diego) California. But the west coast sales were not sufficient, so we decided to do the East coast trip. We became Challenger Eastern Surfboards after that trip, and located the shop near Asbury Park, New Jersey (spring of 1967). On that trip we travelled from New York to Florida to Texas and back to southern California. We decided to place the shop in New Jersey because it was a fairly central location.

The surf shop in New Jersey is where Bruce and his band Child would practice. Tinker knew lots of people in the music business, and they would stop by and even practice in the shop (it was a huge building where we made about 40 custom boards a week). The drummer even slept in the band room (a room where they kept their equipment and practiced).

What I remember about Bruce is that he was kind and considerate and did not party like the rest of us from California. He did not drink or smoke as I recall. Quite the healthy one - which was not the norm in those wild Sixties.

I remember going to some of the local bars or taverns where the band would play. Child was contemplating going on the road with Cotton's Blues band and they wanted me to be the road manager. I declined since I could not spend much time away from surfing (the beach and ocean) in those days. Tinker said, 'These guys are going to be big' and I said I don't care, the surf is going to be big. Tinker was literally a rocket scientist at JPL a few years before I met him, and he was right on in his calculations usually. He was right that the starving band would eventually make it big. At the end of that season I returned to Alaska. I lost contact with all the Jersey folk, got married, and raised kids. One day I looked at a *Time* magazine (early Nineties or late Eighties) and Bruce was on the cover. The article mentioned Tinker and that he and Bruce had a falling out. I hadn't known about that. I think they must have resolved it because, in his Rock and Roll Hall of Fame speech, he mentioned Tinker as the fourth person (after Dad, Mom, and a fella that supported him at age 15) in the hierarchy of those who helped him make it.

FREE UNIVERSITY

20 NOVEMBER 1969 RICHMOND, VIRGINIA

I WAS THERE: TOM YOLTON

Morning Disaster, advertised to play, couldn't make it so my group Mercy Flight filled in. This was in the old Free University, an alternative to traditional universities for free-thinking individuals and a place to try to qualify for a student different from the Vietnam War. Upstairs was a concert hall. Steel Mill had just changed their name from Child. There was some other band in New Jersey with the same name.

Going down in the late afternoon we arrived on the scene just as the band was heaving Danny Federici's Hammond B-3 organ up the precarious flight of stairs leading to the Free University's second floor hall. I remember Springsteen and the rest of the band celebrating after the job was done, apparently a regular ritual, as no one look forward to hauling that thing around.

Tinker West, their manager and sound guy, was directing the set-up. He owned a surfboard factory back in Asbury Park, New Jersey. Surfboards and Springsteen. It doesn't get any weirder than that. I remember marvelling at the large sound system Steel Mill had. They had big speaker cabinets with big amps and lots of wattage. At this time Steel Mill was Springsteen, Danny Federici, Vinnie Lopez on drums and Little Vinnie - I don't know his real name - on bass. Little Vinnie, during the performance, would just hop around in his little spot on stage constantly. The energy was amazing. Mercy Flight played their set. We were a brand-new band. I came home from class one day finding a note on my dorm room door saying this band was looking for a lead guitar player so come down and practice with them if I'm interested. Our set that night must have sounded all right. Steel Mill was impressed and began expressing an interest in having us open their shows.

Turning the stage over to Steel Mill was an experience. They tore into their songs with explosion. Mind you, this was original stuff that had balls. Each song just as good as the last. I remember going goddamn.... goddamn...each time they would crack out a chorus or a guitar part or some vocal impossibility. They had great harmonies. Something hard to find in local bands. They had dynamics. One minute the band could be hush soft, to let the singer accentuate a particular phrase or word, then crash into a volume rise that would catch everyone off guard.

'Who was that guy?'

'Well his name was Bruce'

'Oh'

'And the band is from New Jersey - Asbury Park - we should come up there some time and play.'

'Well that would be cool. And whose songs are those?'

'Oh, Bruce writes all our stuff.'

'Damn, those are hellacious.'

'Oh well, Bruce just sits around and writes songs all day - he writes tons of songs.'

'What's his name again?'

' Bruce...Bruce Springsteen.'

Well the concert raged on and the crowd was loving it. I think everyone was a little jealous at the adulation Springsteen was receiving but somehow I thought it was meant to be. He could pour on the charisma. A sweaty, beer-soaked crowd at the end of the night heard the band announce from stage they were looking for a place to crash. Something hard to fathom now, but after the tour de force that night Steel Mill had plenty of offers.

1970-1971

CLEARWATER SWIM CLUB

11 SEPTEMBER 1970 ATLANTIC HIGHLANDS, NEW JERSEY

I WAS THERE: THOMAS BLATZ

Steel Mill played that night, Bruce on guitar (I think it was a Les Paul), Steve Van Zandt on his clear Danny Armstrong bass, Danny Federici on the Hammond B-3. and the drummer with a Viking-horned helmet atop the bass drum, whose name escapes me. Bruce and Steve were out front, sporting tie-dye

CLEARWATER SWIM CLUB PRESENTS

STEEL MILL

With Task, Sid's Farm, Jeannie Clark

FRIDAY, SEPTEMBER 11th, 5 to 10 P.M

DONATION $2.50

RT 36   ATLANTIC HIGHLANDS

sleeveless t-shirts, bellbottoms, long hair and great tans, and Bruce with his signature underbite and flawless delivery and phrasing, hypnotizing the crowd of at least 500 fans with a wonderful litany of intensely original music, including: 'Hail Resurrection', 'Garden State Parkway Blues', and a piece called 'Heavy Louise' that was extraordinary in its quiet, contemplative narrative that drew the listener to a place they'd never been before, but longed to return to. Bruce had the charisma and power of an evangelist, and the complete attention of every member of the crowd. His guitar work in those days was cutting edge, and the polyphony and synchronicity between him and Van Zandt was spellbinding. They just rocked, to put it mildly.

Carl West (Tinker) was doing the sound, as he always did, his gleaming Macintosh amplifiers churning out the amperes that powered the towers of black voice of the theater cabinets and horns, and the evening was in full swing, until the Middletown police arrived. They had been summoned, by an irate neighbor, to stop the 'noise', and apparently pulled the plug on the electricity. The band was in the middle of a number, and suddenly, all one could hear was drums, and then quiet. Tinker, a former boy scout, was always prepared, and fired up his generator in short order. Within minutes the band continued their performance, and cheers erupted from the throngs of happy fans.

At this point, the police returned, and began climbing up to the rear of the stage to pull the plugs from the amplifiers, and it was then, I believe, that Mr. Federici unwittingly toppled his rather large amplifier over, on top of one of the officers on the ground. Needless to say, the music stopped, and a tumult ensued, resulting in the crowd being told to leave. The rumor was that Mr. Federici retreated to his native Flemington, NJ, where his family owned the Dy-Dee laundromat, to hide out, until the heat died down. The heat did not die down, and eventually Danny faced the music, as it were, the Middletown police were infamous for their intolerance of those with long hair, in those days.

I WAS THERE: DAVE HAZLETT

Mercy Flight had opened up for Steel Mill several times and we had gotten to know all of the guys pretty well. Brucey asked me to come to New Jersey and fill in, so I packed up and left for the N.J. shore, beach, girls, fun, surfing!

The great thing about this was that their manager Tinker owned Challenger Surfboard Co. so I just knew that I would be playing in a great rock & roll band at night and riding the waves during the day. (Wrong!) The next job was in about two weeks at Clearwater Swim club, I was sleeping in a sleeping bag and Brucey had a mattress in the office of the surfboard factory. We would get up in the mornings and go to the beach to check out the sights and then mid-afternoon everyone would start showing up. Practice was held in the back room of the surfboard factory, where Tinker kept this old 1948 Woody station-wagon that he was restoring (it was so cool). You could see the surfboards he was sanding and making (dust everywhere) and I loved every minute of it. We would get in there for hours running over the songs, until we had all of the stops and beginnings just right. Brucey was always spontaneous on stage, so things were subject to change at any minute.

After lots of loving work to get ready for the Clearwater Swim Club job, we were set and ready to go. What I didn't know was that there was a curfew imposed from the audience in this town. I guess the clue for me was the police/national guard bus parked across the road behind the band, full of people in riot suits it seemed. I kept on thinking, is this what this little town does for every job, knowing in my mind that if it wasn't and if they started shooting, my back was as big as anyone's.

The band started playing and the people started grooving and dancing and screaming and all of a sudden, I didn't give a damn about the cops, I was in that world that most musicians go into when everything is happening. The crowd was everywhere and Brucey was working them just like he does so well. We played the set and everyone was going crazy.

When the time for the band to quit playing came so did the cops.

They started getting out of the bus about fifteen minutes before it was time for the band to quit. We were rocking and so was the crowd. They kept on shouting, 'Bruce! Bruce! Bruce!' Every musician in the world dies for this, there is no better complement to an artist than to have the crowd loving you, and the natural and proper thing to do is to play a few more songs. If you have ever owned a radio or any electronic product everyone knows that you've got to have the juice and that's exactly what they did to cut it off.

Tinker was really good at hooking things up, so suddenly like magic the juice came back on and the band was in business. There were people on the stage and I can remember standing there with Brucey. This one girl kept on asking if I was his brother, because of some resemblance.

Then the cops moved in. They were in front of the stage, on the sides of the stage and trying to get on the stage from behind. Danny and I jumped up, and the amps on the back of the stage fell over backwards and all hell broke loose. I looked at Danny, and the next thing was to get out of there, so I took off under the stage and ran into other members of the band, I guess it was the path of least resistance, and also it would be hard for a cop to hit you on the head under there. We all started loading the equipment as fast as we could.

I was told later that the cops were going to confiscate the equipment, so not knowing if they were going to come to the surfboard factory and take the equipment, we had a good friend take it over to his parents' house, without saying a word to anyone for fear of losing all that we owned, for safe-keeping until things cooled down.

I can remember riding back to the surfboard factory in that old truck Tinker had, the same one they had when I first met them. The back was covered with canvas and they wouldn't think twice about loading it up and driving wherever they could to play music. Riding back that night was very different - it was Tinker, Brucey and myself on the bench-seat of the old truck. I remember just how much confusion there was that night, and Tinker saying to Bruce I was the guy for the job, Bruce asking me what I wanted to do, and them not really knowing what was going to happen to them.

I stayed for a few days after that night and went back to Richmond, still not sure what was going to happen to any of us, but always remembering the love that I've shared with those guys from that day on.

SUNSHINE INN

14 MAY 1971 ASBURY PARK, NEW JERSEY

I WAS THERE: ALBEE TELLONE

Dr Zoom & The Sonic Boom was a fun band that Bruce threw together when the owner of the Sunshine Inn in Asbury Park, NJ, wanted to hire him but his new 10-piece band wasn't ready. One day Bruce came over to our apartment to talk to us about helping him play a show. I was sharing an apartment in Asbury Park with Steve Van Zandt, 'Southside' Johnny Lyon and John 'Hotkeys' Waasdorp. He told us he just wanted to have fun with his friends and maybe make a little money. We were all starving young musicians back then. He tried to include as many of his friends as he could. That's why Kevin Connair was MC and Danny Gallagher played a game of Monopoly onstage with three friends. Almost every night of the week we played Monopoly all night at my dining room table in our apartment in Asbury Park, which was just up the street from Palace Amusements. Monopoly reflected what we did at night during the week. There was nothing else to do. We actually had four of our friends sitting onstage at a card table playing Monopoly during the show.

We opened for the Allman Brothers, but the place was packed with Bruce's fans, who had never heard of them. Steven loved the Allmans and that's why we had two drummers, to show them they weren't the only band with two. It was a lot of fun.

Bruce got all of his musician friends from Asbury for this. We had a band called Albee and the Hired Hands, because I was into country-rock at the time. Southside Johnny played bass, Steven on lead and Hotkeys on piano; Bobby Williams on drums; me on acoustic guitar and vocals. A lot of people don't know that after Dr Zoom & the Sonic Boom, Bruce was invited by Steve and Johnny to play guitar in the Sundance Blues Band, after second guitarist Joe Hagstrom quit. Sundance was Steve's idea. It was basically Bruce's bandmates, with Southside Johnny as lead vocalist. They got the name from the movie, *Butch Cassidy and the Sundance Kid*, which was their favourite at the time.

Dr Zoom's MC Kevin Connair was a singer-songwriter friend of ours whom Bruce liked very much. That is why Bruce asked Kevin to be the master of ceremonies to introduce the band and some of the songs. He also sang in the Zoom Chorus with the Zoomettes. The other Kevin - Kevin Kavanaugh was later my piano player in Albee and the Hired Hands when Steve left and John Waasdorp took over lead guitar (who also sang in the Zoom Chorus with the Zoomettes). At first, we had separate men and women's choruses, but it became the Zoomettes later. Kevin Kavanaugh later played piano in the original Jukes with Southside Johnny. John Waasdorp was a terrific lead guitarist who played with the Jukes in the beginning but left the band before recording. He suffered from severe depression and committed suicide a few years later.

We went to a second-hand clothes store and got hats and things to wear for the gig. Southside got an old suit to wear and a fedora hat because he wanted to look like a Chicago blues cat. We rehearsed at Tinker's surfboard factory, where Bruce and Vini Lopez lived. When we got there Bruce looked at Johnny and said 'Hey man, it's Chicago Johnny,' to which John replied, 'From the Southside' (of Chicago). We all called him Southside Johnny after that. I don't remember why, but Steve started calling me Al-bany Al-bee during rehearsals. It became Albany Al after a while, even though I have never been to the city of Albany, NY in my life. So, whenever I played the sax I took on the character of Albany Al.

Dr Zoom & the Sonic Boom was not an important or missing link in the overall picture of Bruce's career. It was just friends having fun playing music together. Just like any musicians do when they have jam sessions.

THE STUDENT PRINCE

SUMMER 1971 ASBURY PARK, NEW JERSEY

I WAS THERE: ROBERT D. SALZMANN

The Student Prince gigs truly were a piece of rock history and I consider myself very fortunate to have been a witness to it. In 1971, the band's personnel did change frequently, often during the course of an evening. Southside Johnny would step up to the microphone while Bruce and his band members took a break. At other times, the band would come around, grab some 'suds' and speak with us at the bar and tables. If they were frustrated or disappointed by the evening's turnout, they did a great job of hiding it from us.

They were particularly good at covering the blues, Rolling Stones and Chuck Berry. As a matter of fact, they played the Stones cover version of Buddy Holly's 'Not Fade Away' and were better than the Stones themselves.

They knew that it was the music that held us all together in those days of social-generational turmoil. It was the music that got you through the coming week and eased the mundane routines waiting on Monday. They were truly in tune with their audience at the time: NJ long-haired, freaks that weren't really welcome in many other clubs or places. The Student Prince was dingy but typical of the bars open to my generation and we gladly tolerated the grunge in exchange for the music. We were a small army of rock 'n' roll gypsies dressed in jeans, denim jackets and flannel shirts, and the Bruce Springsteen band grew to become one of our preferred escapes from our menial jobs and daily lives.

Each week, as the Student Prince gigs progressed, there seemed to be more and more people coming to hear the group, building the momentum for fame. I remember that on my first visit there were probably 12 - 15 people total. In hindsight, I guess we were spoiled by these earliest of days. As the scene outgrew the Student Prince, many of us faded into the background and watched from a distance.

THE STUDENT PRINCE

4 SEPTEMBER 1971 ASBURY PARK, NEW JERSEY

I WAS THERE: CLARENCE CLEMONS

I knew this girl singer from The Joyful Noyze, Karen Cassidy, who kept on saying to me that I had to meet this guy called Bruce. It took a few months because I was always working and he was always working, but she kept saying you have to meet this guy. We then happened to be playing at this place in Asbury Park at the same time. I was playing a matinee show and he was playing at the Wonder Bar, a few blocks from my gig. This storm was blowing in, it was thunder and lightning and I walked into the club and as I opened the door the wind actually tore the door out of my hand and blew it down the street. So all the bouncers went running down the street to go after the door. I'm standing there with this thunder and lightning behind me and I walk in. This is a black guy walking into a white club, and it was like, wow, wait a minute. I walked over and found out who this Bruce was, and said to him I want to sit in, and he said, 'Sure, do whatever you want to do'. So I sat in and it was a magical moment. I swear I will never forget that moment. It was like all the things I had been struggling for and all the things I wanted to do was right there. It felt so natural to me; it felt just like I was supposed to be there. It was a very magical moment. He looked at me, I looked at him, and we fell in love.

THE LEDGE

17 DECEMBER 1971 RUTGERS UNIVERSITY, NEW JERSEY

I WAS THERE: MALLORY ROBINSON

I was 20-years-old and hanging with friends at the Rutgers Student Center, where I saw a poster for the Bruce Springsteen Band and Southern Conspiracy at the Ledge in Rutgers. I paid 50 cents and went in and saw all the young blonde Rumson boys. By the third song I knew this guy was going to be the biggest thing ever. I've been following them ever since. For 40 years I have been collecting everything and anything Bruce. There can never be any song like 'Jungleland.' I think we're lucky now to be able to go online and see almost any concert at any time.

1972 Springsteen began recording his debut album *Greetings from Asbury Park, N.J.* at 914 Sound Studios in Blauvelt, New York in July 1972. During breaks from recording, he jammed with saxophonist Clarence Clemons and The Joyful Noyze on at least two occasions at The Shipbottom Lounge in Point Pleasant, New Jersey.

When then-CBS President Clive Davis heard the 10 tracks slated for the album he didn't think there was a hit single on it. Springsteen went back to work and composed two more songs with more commercial potential, 'Blinded by the Light' and 'Spirit in the Night'. Problems arose when keyboard player David Sancious and bassist Garry Tallent weren't able to return to the studio to record the new songs. Also, Bruce wanted to incorporate saxophone into both songs, but didn't have a sax player. He got in touch with Clarence Clemons, who came to the studio for a session. The two songs were recorded with the one-off line-up of Clemons on sax, Vini 'Mad Dog' Lopez on drums, and Springsteen.

Both tracks were released as singles by Columbia, but neither reached the US charts. By October of 1972 Springsteen was ready to tour and promote the album. He put together a band featuring Clemons, Tallent, keyboardist Danny Federici and drummer Vini 'Mad Dog' Lopez.

HOLLINGER FIELD HOUSE

28 OCTOBER 1972 WEST CHESTER, PENNSYLVANIA

I WAS THERE: MAUREEN HUGHES

I thought I was going to see The Persuasions, who were opening for comedy duo Cheech and Chong. There was another band on the schedule, Bruce Springsteen and the E Street Band. I don't remember everything they played except for 'Pretty Flamingo'. Several months later I saw them play at the Main Point in Bryn Mawr, Pennsylvania, after *Greetings from Asbury Park, NJ* was released.

I probably saw 100 or more shows at the Main Point in Bryn Mawr, following him throughout the Northeast. Saw him play at University of Maryland with Chuck Berry. Saw him in Philly at the Spectrum the night John Lennon died. Finally got to meet him in person at the Hershey hotel before the show in 2016. Finally after all these years I got to shake his hand and say thank you. And lucky me, I snag tickets to see Springsteen on Broadway, July 12th, 2018. I think the circle is complete.

1973

In January 1973, Springsteen played the opening night of 12 shows at Max's Kansas City, a favourite hangout of Andy Warhol and his entourage, as well as various New York musicians, poets, artists and politicians. Opening for headliner American comedian and singer-songwriter Biff Rose Springsteen played two shows a night, starting with two solo numbers before bringing out the band.

Songs played included; 'Mary Queen of Arkansas', 'Bishop Danced', 'Wild Billy's Circus Story', 'Spirit in the Night', 'Does This Bus Stop at 82nd Street?' and 'Thundercrack.'

MAX'S KANSAS CITY

31 JANUARY 1973 NEW YORK CITY

I WAS THERE: DAVID BOWIE

The first time I saw him was at the back room in Max's Kansas City and he was playing on his own. He was just playing piano and then brought the band on about half-way through. I was going to leave. I went there to see Biff Rose, I used to like him in the Sixties and I found he was playing in town. He was the headline act and Springsteen was on as well. I thought it was another Dylan copyist when he came on and started his acoustic set. Then the band came on

Upstairs at max's kansas city

FINAL SHOWS TONIGHT!

BRUCE SPRINGSTEEN

SPECIAL GUESTS

THE WAILERS

Tickets on sale now at Max's

213 Park Ave. South at 17th St. For Res. Call: 777-7870

and I think it was the best rock band I've seen in my life for about half an hour and I wish he'd done that more then. I thought 'he might go somewhere' and went out and bought his album, *Greetings from Asbury Park, NJ* and thought this is a great songwriter.

CIVIC CENTER

10 JUNE 1973 SPRINGFIELD, MASSACHUSETTS

I WAS THERE: MIKE SCULLY

I first heard the *Greetings* album in January of 1973 on our local FM AOR station, WHVY (Heavy FM), Springfield, Massachusetts, and instantly loved it. When I heard he was opening for Chicago in June of that year at the Springfield Civic Center, a friend and I bought tickets. I don't even think his name was on the ticket or marquee. Most of the crowd didn't seem to know who the band was when they took the stage. I'll never forget a girl sitting behind us saw Clarence's sax and assumed it was Chicago. She said to her boyfriend, 'I didn't know Chicago had a black guy.'

They probably played about 45 minutes and, for some reason, I remember a scruffy Bruce playing a guitar solo with his back to the crowd. I could be completely imagining that, however. We stayed for Chicago but had got what we came for - our first glimpse of Bruce Springsteen live. I wish I could remember more specific details, but I was 16 and didn't realize how Bruce's music was going to become such an influence in my life and how much time and money I would devote to seeing him over the next 45 years. I just thought I was seeing a new guy whose album I liked.

MY FATHER'S PLACE

31 JULY 1973 ROSLYN, LONG ISLAND, NEW YORK

I WAS THERE: RIK SHAFER

I went there so many times and had so much fun, it was unbelievable.

I remember seeing Springsteen when the first album came out. He was so loud that the rafters rattled.

Bruce Springsteen played a three-night run at The Childe Harold, a cozy, wood-lined saloon in Dupont Circle in early December 1973. In its heyday many up and coming acts appeared here including Emmylou Harris, The Ramones and Bonnie Raitt. Music fans filled every nook and cranny, the bathrooms reeked of marijuana, and everyone talked for years after about whom they saw perform there. Springsteen's payday for three nights: a grand total of $750.

THE CHILDE HAROLD

6 DECEMBER 1973 WASHINGTON, DC

I WAS THERE: PETE CARROLL

The first time I saw Bruce Springsteen was when I'd gone to The Childe Harold, a small venue in Washington, DC, to see Mike Aldridge and the Seldom Scene but a chalk-written notice on a blackboard outside the venue stated the scheduled gig was cancelled, - replaced by Bruce Springsteen. Earlier that year he'd released his debut album *Greetings from Asbury Park* with a bit of 'the new Dylan' hype. I knew very little about him and didn't realise the guys sat next to me having food at the back of the venue prior to the gig were the band until I saw them climb on stage. David Sancious, Vini Lopez, Danny Federici, Garry Tallent and Clarence Clemons were tightly squeezed

on to a very small stage, about a foot above a very sparse audience, leaving virtually no space for Bruce; there were possibly 80 people in the house. I remember watching and thinking he was more Van Morrison than Bob Dylan.

The impact drove me into a record store and I've continued buying his records. The next time I saw Bruce was November 18th, 1975, at Hammersmith Odeon in London with the fully-fledged E Street Band; Roy Bittan, Max Weinberg and Steve Van Zandt completing the classic line-up. Tickets were two pounds (including booking fee). I bought six from the box office on Shaftesbury Avenue. I've still got the receipt and my ticket - seated J17, Circle, Block 5.

The performance that night was intense and full of drama. Bruce was static in '73 at The Childe Harold. He now prowled, proclaimed and owned the stage in a woolly knitted hat, pumping out garage rock and soul; Clarence Clemons, the big man in a sharp white suit and hat now occupied a pivotal role as Bruce's foil. I have since seen him many times – all of which have been memorable, standouts including shows at Manchester Apollo and Birmingham Arena in 1981 when he rolled out *The River*. I've also seen several shows in Australia. I was working for Sony Music when I met him backstage at the Palais Theatre in Melbourne in 1997 during his solo Ghost of Tom Joad tour. And 45 years after I first saw Bruce, it's incredible to watch his three-hour energy packed show with an audience of thousands and reflect on those lean, tough uncertain early years, the band finding its voice.

1974

THE MOSQUE

25 JANUARY 1974 RICHMOND, VIRGINIA

I WAS THERE: CHRIS CHARLESWORTH

The first time I saw Bruce Springsteen & the E Street Band was for

two shows in the US East Coast state of Virginia, the first at the
Mosque in Richmond on January 25 and the second a night later
at the Chrysler Theatre in Norfolk. They were small old-fashioned
theatres, and both are still operating today, though The Mosque is
now called The Landmark. I don't think they were sold out.

I stayed in the same hotel as the band and remember chatting with
Bruce in the coffee shop on the morning after the first show. He was
eating a burger and fries washed down with coke, and wasn't very
talkative, shy almost, maybe a bit tongue-tied. He was thin then, with
a whispery beard, and intense, like he had a lot on his mind. I didn't
press him, just told him how much I'd enjoyed the show the night
before, and he was grateful for the compliment, humble, courteous,
like I imagine the young Elvis would have been.

The two concerts blur together a bit 40 odd years later so I
can't actually remember which one it was (and it might have
been both) where Bruce and his band played 'Pretty Flamingo',
Manfred Mann's best song and a 1966 UK chart-topper, but what
I remember as clear as day was Bruce's long, witty and gloriously
uplifting monologue that prefaced it. As it was my introduction
to Bruce live, his monologues were quite new to me, surprising,
captivating and unique.

The 'Pretty Flamingo' story began with Bruce telling us how he
once lived on a street in Jersey which a beautiful girl would walk
down every day at five o'clock, so he and his buddies from the block
would gather there at a quarter to five every day just to watch her
stroll by. While the band ticked over in the background, idling like a
car in neutral, Bruce conjured up in a few pithy sentences the image
of a shapely heartbreaker that he and his buddies, and by inference
they included some of the band, were too afraid to approach. They
were desperate to know her name but too shy to ask, even some crazy
guy in Bruce's gang who often did really brave stuff because he was
far too crazy to care about the consequences.

And so it went on, with the girl walking by for weeks, maybe
months, Bruce and his buddies still watching her every day, and no
one knew what she was called. By this time we in the audience were

all hopelessly in love with her, just as Bruce and his pals obviously were, and they'd coined a nickname for her. 'And then… like I moved away,' said Bruce, disappointment clouding his face. 'We never found out what her name was. We used to call her something. What was it that we called her Clarence? Can you remember? What did we call her, Steve? I remember. Should I tell 'em?'

Then, louder, repeated, his right arm raised. 'Should I tell 'em?'

'Yeah,' called Steve and Clarence in unison. 'Tell 'em Bruce.' 'Should I tell 'em?' He was screaming now. 'Yeah!'

Bruce brought his arm down. A chord. 'On our block all of the guys called her Flamingo.' Guitars and drums exploded. Perfect. Just fucking perfect. The incredible tension of the build-up was finally released and like a great tidal wave crashing through the theatre Bruce and his band launched deliriously into this great song. The crowd went nuts. But he wasn't finished with us. Two, maybe three, minutes in, just after the first verse, after Flamingo had brightened up the neighbourhood like she just could, he brought the band down again, let them tick over again, and he had us captive again.

'What can I do, Clarence?' he asked, even more passionate than before. 'I gotta find that girl. I'm gonna hire a detective, someone good, like Charlie Chan.' He was laughing now, full of fun, and we were holding on to every word. 'And when I get her I know what I'm gonna tell her. I know what I'm gonna tell her. I'm gonna tell her I'm in a band. I'm in a band!' Off they went again, careering downhill like men possessed. 'Some sweet day, I'll make her mine, Pretty Flamingo.' In a band. The best place in the world. I was hooked and have been ever since.

ICE HOCKEY ARENA

27 APRIL 1974 UNIVERSITY OF CONNECTICUT

I WAS THERE: LYN BAUMGARTEL

The first time was in the spring of 1974, an outdoor concert at my school, also including Aerosmith and Fairport Convention. I wasn't really familiar with Bruce or his music. Needless to say, I was blown away by his set so much that I went right out and bought *Greetings from Asbury Park, NJ* the next day. After Bruce's set, a friend of mine came along. He stopped for a minute to chat, then held up a beer and said 'I've gotta go - I'm bringing this to Bruce.' Of course I went with him to see Bruce standing off the side of the stage. Wayne gave him the beer and I said, 'Great show, Bruce!' He said, 'Yeah, thanks' and that was it. If I'd known then what I know now.

I was 22 at the time and I wasn't particularly a fan at the time of the show. I don't remember who I was looking forward to seeing that day, but I wasn't really that familiar with Bruce. I was at school at the University of Connecticut, and the show was an outside show on a Saturday afternoon somewhere on campus - I think it was actually in a parking lot. What I remembered most about the show was 'Spirit in the Night'. Clarence's sax really got to me, and of course the whole band performance. From then on I was a fan.

Unfortunately, I don't have any pictures from that time. There must have been tickets, but if there were, mine is long gone.

I've seen him one other time since then - it was in September 2003 during The Rising tour. I went with my son, who was around 22 at the time. We were both blown away by the show.

CIVIC AUDITORIUM

25 JULY 1974 SANTA MONICA, CALIFORNIA

I WAS THERE: TOM STEFL

My buddies and I went to see Dr. John. While waiting in line we happened to notice that second billed on the marquee was some Jewish kid we'd never heard of named Springsteen. Oh well.

After Springsteen opened up, he burned down the house, totally exhausted the audience, and did three (I think) encores, which were not standard, or in the contract back in '74. Now even further drained, nobody was really interested in sticking around for Dr. John. As a matter of fact, before Dr. John even started to play, the house

ONE NIGHT ONLY

BRUCE SPRINGSTEEN
AND THE E STREET BAND

ALL STAR SHOW

ALL STAR SHOW

PLUS OPENING ACT

YOUR NAME GOES HERE

SAN FRANCISCO
COW PALACE - JUNE 26, 1974

SHOW STARTS AT 7:00 PM
RESERVED TICKETS ON SALE AT THE COW PALACE BOX OFFICE

began to empty, which prompted someone to come on stage and basically plead with the crowd to hang around. I actually felt sorry for Dr. John and often wonder if anyone ever got fired for putting Springsteen on the bill.

Springsteen placed an advert in Village Voice in late-summer 1974, seeking a replacement for departed E Street Band drummer Ernest 'Boom' Carter. The ad asked for someone who could play with power and economy rather than showy style. Max Weinberg was one of over 50 drummers who auditioned and was hired on $110-a-week.

I WAS THERE: MAX WEINBERG

In the audition everybody got half an hour to play, no matter how good or how bad they were. At the time I was playing in Broadway show Godspell up on 76 Street, The Promenade Theatre. It was a Monday night, a dark night, I didn't want to bring an entire drum set, so brought a bass drum, a snare drum, and the cymbals that go up and down, the hi-hats. I wasn't trying to make any minimalist statement, it was just more convenient to bring a small drum set, and that made quite an impression.

The first night I played with Bruce and the E Street Band we had two three-hour shows. I remember asking Bruce, 'How do you pace yourself?' He said, 'Max, the trick is to not pace yourself.'

RITZ MUSIC HALL

8 NOVEMBER 1974 CORPUS CHRISTI, TEXAS

I WAS THERE: CONNIE BEHRHORST

In 1974, I was a 16-year old girl living in Corpus Christi Texas. It's a small coastal town, with not much going on unless you wanted to hang out with wannabe surfers. The one thing we did have was an old movie theatre, turned into a music venue, the Ritz Music Hall. It was the era of redneck rock in Texas. Willie Nelson, Waylon Jennings and the boys. That fateful night I was all alone. Unusual because at that age we ran in packs. Still, I had nothing to do and five bucks burning in my pocket. I ventured downtown and hoped Willie was playing and there would be some cute older guys to hang with.

When I arrived at the Ritz that night, Willie was not playing. The guy at the ticket window said some guy from New York City was playing. I had never heard of Bruce Springsteen and didn't want to part with my hard-earned money. The guy offered to let me in for free (I was cute back then). I accepted his offer with the hopes of hanging with some cute guys. I went in and went straight up to the stage. There were not more than 50 people there. This scraggly guy in a loose-knit beret came out and broke into 'Incident on 57th Street.' I had never heard or seen anything like this. By the time he played 'Lost in the Flood', I was transformed. I felt like I was hearing music for the first time in my young life. I didn't even care who else was there.

I woke up the next day and wondered if that had really happened to me and went to the local record store to get his album. They didn't have any, but specially ordered *The Wild, the Innocent & the E Street Shuffle*. It took a month to come in. I hoped it would be as I remembered. I tried telling all my friends about that experience, but you know how that went. I played that record over and over. Every time I was transported back to that night and that experience. It was like they say about 'chasing that first high', but in this case it worked every time. A big part of my life was written that day. I have been chasing him ever since.

MEMORIAL GYMNASIUM

17 NOVEMBER 1974 CHARLOTTESVILLE, VIRGINIA

I WAS THERE: SETH DAVIDSON

I saw Bruce Springsteen and the E Street Band for the first time at the Memorial Gym at the University of Virginia, Charlottesville.

Although Bruce's first two studio albums had been out for over a year and it was six months since Jon Landau had declared Bruce to be 'the future of rock and roll', I had never heard any of his music.

The afternoon before the show I stopped by a friend's apartment and he played *The Wild, the Innocent & the E Street Shuffle* for me. I thought it was a good album, but it didn't prepare me in the slightest for the amazing live performance I was about to see.

Memorial Gym only held around 2,500 people and I don't think it was sold out. Despite my lack of familiarity with Bruce's work, I was transfixed from start to finish. I remember commenting to a friend that it was as if Bruce had reached out into the audience and grabbed us by the neck and said, 'You're going to like me. You will have no choice.' That concert was held in the fall of my final year of college. The following August I moved to New York City for law school. I arrived the same week that *Born to Run* was released. Bruce posters were plastered all over the city, some for the album, and some for his August gigs at the Bottom Line. Not long after that, he was on the cover of Time and Newsweek and we all know what's happened since. Over the years, I've seen Bruce a number of times in venues of all sizes. But nothing will top that first time in Charlottesville.

1975

THE MAIN POINT

5 FEBRUARY 1975 BRYN MAWR, PENNSYLVANIA

I WAS THERE: BILL SCARBOROUGH, CLUB OWNER

I think that the booking of a singer named Bruce Springsteen is the best example I can give you of personal taste. Here was a new act out of nowhere, who happened to sign with a major label (Columbia), and put out an album that reminded me of the best of Dylan. I decided to book him as a headliner, even though he was barely known. We did all right with him, but not as well as we hoped.

I WAS THERE: TOM GREMSCHEID

I'm from Philadelphia originally, so I've been a Springsteen fan from the very beginning. My favourite show was my first, at a club called The Main Point which held maybe 300 people. The band played most of the songs from the first two albums, including the first live performance of 'Thunder Road' and some terrific covers, including Johnny Rivers' 'Mountain of Love', Bob Dylan's 'I Want You', and some great new songs that blew the crowd away. They would turn out to be the *Born to Run* album, released in the summer of 1975.

Two years later, living in Hawaii, I found a bootleg album of that show in a small record store, including the introduction by a Philly DJ. 'This is Bruce's last appearance in the Delaware Valley before he goes off to conquer America and the world.' How prophetic!

WIDENER COLLEGE

6 FEBRUARY 1975 CHESTER, PENNSYLVANIA

I WAS THERE: KEITH BROFSKY

I grew up in Claymont, Delaware, a suburb just north of Wilmington and south of Philadelphia, within walking distance of the Pennsylvania state line.

My buddies and I started listening to Bruce's first two albums when we were about 15. We'd play pool at a friend's house, put *The Wild, the Innocent & the E Street Shuffle* album on, and turn up the volume. Even at that age, we knew this guy was talented.

One friend had an older brother who managed to get him into the bars in New Jersey, which had an 18-year old drinking age. His height helped. Meanwhile, the rest of us were envious as hell he had seen Bruce play a number of times and raved about him like it was the second coming.

So when we heard Bruce was playing at a nearby college gymnasium, we jumped at the tickets. It was Widener College in Swarthmore, in the dark days of winter. We heard a new album was in the works, but for us, 'Spirit in the Night' was our anthem. When the day arrived, we were psyched. I remember waiting outside in the cold for quite some time, and the excitement of Bruce's arrival. He worked his way through the fans as a teaser. There was a long wait to get in, building our anticipation and impatience.

As it turned out, Bruce ordered that eight-foot sheets of acoustic foam rubber be hung from the ceiling to improve the sound in the echoey hall.

It was a testament to his perfectionism, even back then. When he finally came on stage, The energy and excitement was palpable. Here it is, 44 years later, and that hasn't changed.

He played with his heart out, wearing the big floppy-knit cap and leather jacket. Spirit In The Night was the highlight for me, but so many of the songs resonated and had us dancing in the dark.

At the end of the show, we were pumped and having a hard time calming down. Someone suggested we take a sheet of foam rubber for a souvenir. It was up high and would be a feat to reach, but I climbed on my tallest friend's shoulders, made a leap to grab the foam, and came crashing down to the floor with the sheet, which didn't exactly land under me. It was a thud but at 16-years-old, no biggie. That foam rubber ended up in the back of my VW Super Beetle, serving nicely as a bed for me and my first love. I couldn't think of a more appropriate use of my Springsteen memorabilia. Me and crazy Sharon, making love in the bug, singing our birthday songs.

> This music is forever for me.
> It's the stage thing, that rush moment
> that you live for. It never lasts, but
> that's what you live for.
>
> Bruce Springsteen

Three years later, in 1978, what seemed like a lifetime since the Widener show, I saw Bruce at Red Rocks Amphitheater, Denver, Colorado. I was there for college and beyond thrilled that Bruce was back. *Darkness on the Edge of Town* was an epic album, and I knew that seeing it live was going to be amazing. I convinced a group of Denver pals this was a show not to be missed. They'd only vaguely heard of him but said okay. We were there early, about three rows from the stage, hanging out in the afternoon waiting patiently for the show that night. The promoters placed two-fold brown brochures on the seats, introducing the patrons to who Bruce was. I recall reading it bemused, as though he needed such a formal introduction.

I was sitting there with my camera in hand, when I noticed a cool looking, dark-haired dude hanging out by the side of the stage, leaning against a stage flat. I looked through my telephoto lens and realized to my astonishment, I was looking at the man himself. He was gazing out at the amazing view at what is probably one of the most inspiring of venues, with its towering red rock walls. Bruce was clean-cut and almost hard to recognize from the early days, but I exclaimed to my buddies, 'That's Bruce!' They couldn't believe he'd be so accessible and visible, but I was convinced. I walked down to the front of the stage, feeling way too conspicuous, aimed right at Bruce not 40ft away, and took a few shots. He remained cool, as he always is in front of a camera. I was wearing my T-Shirt with the first album art on the front, my indication that I was an early fan. Our eyes met, I smiled slightly, he nodded and I turned and sheepishly walked back to my seat. The show was probably one of the most amazingly pure rock concerts I'd ever seen… like watching history in the making. My friends were forever converted to the man and his music.

UNIVERSITY AUDITORIUM

19 FEBRUARY 1975 PENNSYLVANIA

I WAS THERE: DENNIS LOCKARD

Bruce Springsteen saved my life. OK, I'm exaggerating. A little.

It was the mid-Seventies. My mother had died a few years earlier and I lived with my Dad. I was just out of high school and aimless, drifting and unsure of what to do next. I buried myself in pop culture – music, television and *One Flew Over the Cuckoo's Nest*.

Music was mostly a morass. The Beatles broke up the same week my mother died, the significance of which is not lost on me. Both left a void of differing degrees.

Listening to Santana, Chicago and Jethro Tull out of necessity instead of choice, I noticed an ad in *Crawdaddy* magazine containing the quote, 'I have seen the future of rock'n'roll and its name is Bruce Springsteen.'

This had me heading out to Joe Nardone's Gallery of Sound in my '74 Torino very quickly on a last-chance power drive. Even though there were two Springsteen albums available, I only bought the one mentioned in the ad, *The Wild, the Innocent, and The E Street Shuffle*. $4.99 was a lot of money in those days. But the return on that small investment was, in the end, incalculable. I still recall putting the album on for the first time in my darkened bedroom. The first side was good, certainly different from 'Thick as a Brick.'

But the second side was positively epochal, fusing the visionary romance of the New York City streets with the sounds of girl groups, Jay and the Americans and frat rock, and ending with an ode to a singing junkman, this was the music I was searching for. To this day, I still get goose-bumps listening to it.

I listened even more closely to his subsequent work. In his vast catalogue, I heard freedom, the importance of having dreams and working hard to achieve them, the significance of finding joy in the smallest and seemingly trivial things and places, and the promise of redemption.

Springsteen opened other doors too. When I was growing up, I mostly dismissed the founding fathers of rock'n'roll with the derisive (to me) term 'oldies.' Guys like Little Richard, Chuck Berry and Buddy Holly were his heroes, and when Springsteen closed with Elvis's 'Wear My Ring Around Your Neck' the first time I saw him at Penn State, all the walls came crashing down. Hey, not only were these songs and artists important to Bruce, but they were great too. His influences became my education.

As I've got older, Bruce's music has followed me. I can't really say that about anyone else. Springsteen and me: 35 years, still burnin' down the road, still teaching (and learning) life lessons along the way.

Bruce Springsteen, always the coolest guy in the room.

CARTER BARRON AMPHITHEATRE

28 JULY 1975 WASHINGTON DC

I WAS THERE: TIM GARVIN

We were given free tickets to see this CBS recording artist. This was before *Born to Run* came out. When we asked what Springsteen was like, we were told he sounded like Dan Fogelberg, which couldn't be more different.

This scrawny guy with a really bad beard walks out onto the stage in Chuck Taylor high tops and performed for two and a half hours. My world was changed. I went back to Connecticut and got a record of Bruce Springsteen and The E-Street Band. It was the most glorious sounding music. Each song was about ten minutes long. It was just incredible.

I WAS THERE: JOHN PRINE, SINGER, SONGWRITER

When he saw me, he got a folding chair and put it by the side of the stage, and then he went out to do the show. Then four songs into it - back then, there was no stopping in between songs. Bruce would hit the stage, do four or five songs with no breath for the audience - he leaned over at one point because he was working his way back to the side of the stage where I was. I'm sitting in the folding chair, and he goes, 'How am I doing?' and the place was coming apart!

All of a sudden, he was not this introspective singer, songwriter; he was Chuck Berry, Little Richard, Elvis, Bob Dylan, all of these rolled into one, and he reminded everybody of what rock 'n' roll was like.

THE BOTTOM LINE

16 AUGUST 1975, NEW YORK CITY

I WAS THERE: ANDY MURRAY

A couple of years ago I happened to be on a boat outing down the
Thames organised by David Hepworth and Mark Ellen, for their
'Word In Your Ear' event series. As someone who knew them slightly,
I was hauled up on stage, to talk about my favourite show of all
time. I gave it a small amount of thought and decided it was Bruce

*Andy Murray on the Sands of Morar
in the Scottish Highlands*

Springsteen at the Bottom
Line Club, New York,
August '75.

I'd been aware of Bruce's
first album in 1973, because
I had been in the US when
Columbia Records had been
touting him as 'the New
Dylan', and doing what big
record labels do, i.e. over-
hyping new talent. Since I
wasn't particularly in the
market for a new Dylan,
I didn't give it very much
more attention. But later
that year, back studying at
Leeds Polytechnic, I went

into Leeds University's record shop and casually asked the bloke behind
the counter: 'What's new?' He said, 'You have to listen to this', and
proceeded to play the entire second side of *The Wild, the Innocent, and
The East Street Shuffle*. Bruce's second album had got a particularly good
review in the Sheffield University students' newspaper, but albums were
expensive in those days – about four times the price of a gig ticket, or a
day's worth of student grant (kids, ask your parents) – so I wasn't about
to rush out and get it on the basis of one good review.

Andy peeled this poster off a wall in Manhattan when the glue was still wet.

Anyway, he dropped the needle on 'Incident On 57th Street', which segued into 'Rosalita', followed by the triple lock of 'New York City Serenade', by which time I was grabbing the disc out of the guy's hands. I thought it was the most fantastic album side I had heard in a long time, so bought it straightaway and I loved it so much that for about six months I never played side one; it took me a while before I discovered 'The E Street Shuffle', 'Kitty's Back' and 'Wild Billy's Circus Story.'

The summer of 1975 saw me staying with my then-girlfriend's family in New Jersey, and they of course were Bruce fans already, since his fame as a live act had spread all up The East Coast out of the Jersey Shore in the south, across to Philly and all the way up to Cambridge, Massachusetts, where Jon Landau gave Bruce his prescient thumbs up review in the *Real Paper*.

By early 1975, a version of *Born to Run* had been leaked to some East Coast radio stations, and there was a short string of dates ending in March, at which some new material was aired, but the Born to Run dates, as a precursor to the third album release, started properly in July.

The *Born to Run* album was due to be released at the end of August and to preview it Bruce embarked on his now-legendary 10-show (two shows a night for five nights) stint at the Bottom Line, a small venue on West 4th Street in Greenwich Village, Manhattan. The Bottom Line was absolutely the place to go for up-and-coming artists - it held about 400 people, with long tables and chairs filling up the entire space in front of a wide but distinctly shallow stage, the principle being, I assume, that the promoters stood to make as much money from the food and drinks that they sold to the hungry patrons as they did from the entrance fee. We're not talking big production values, either - I can't recall any special lighting at all, though there must have been some. But there was distinct shortage of smoke, lasers or LEDs. It couldn't have made Bruce very much money, the E Street Band then being a seven-piece line-up. But it was an amazing space in which to see any performer close-up.

A bit of context: on 3rd November 1974, long-time supportive radio station WMMR in Philadelphia had a surprise for listeners: the radio premiere of *Born to Run*. With an astonishing nine months to go before the album saw the light of day, and with no confirmed album release date, various radio stations in the US began to play *Born to Run*. Their early endorsement had two effects: when the official single was finally universally available, radio programmers jumped on it and it became an instant smash; and Columbia Records became convinced that their signing had the capability of creating hits, becoming much more supportive of Bruce and the band.

Come July, Bruce had finally finished the album, 14 months in the making, and it was scheduled for a late August release. Columbia obviously figured that their chance of hitting the big time with Bruce had arrived, because they bought some hundreds of show tickets for media and retail folk, as well as plastering 60 x 40 posters around the streets of New York advertising the dates and the forthcoming album, with a picture from the *Born to Run* sessions - a back view of Bruce, 'Wild & Innocent' superimposed on his leather jacket, and sneakers dangling from the headstock of his Fender Esquire.

New York FM radio station WNEW had been initially put off by Columbia's hype, but had finally come around, with the realisation that Bruce was sincere, and, as importantly, was popular with their gig-going listeners. Furthermore, he was plainly headed in an upward trajectory, with or without their support. WNEW accordingly had committed to broadcasting one of the shows, settling on the early show from Friday night, which would have been Bruce's fifth show since Wednesday, by which time one could assume that he would have worked out any technical glitches as well as having a reasonable reserve of energy. The show went out live as it happened, over the airwaves down the Eastern seaboard and, as widely bootlegged, gives a pretty accurate picture of what the shows were like - exciting, dynamic, humorous, heartfelt, long.

As soon as the shows were announced, I knew there would be no chance of getting any advance tickets, so my only hope was to queue up for one of the 50 standing tickets available each night. As I listened to Friday night's show live on the radio, I became increasingly worried that anyone who hadn't previously been a Bruce fan would be so converted by the broadcast that there would be riots in the street outside the venue for the last few remaining tickets per day. So with some trepidation I got the train into Manhattan on Saturday morning, August 16, and positioned myself across the street from the Bottom Line at the corner of Mercer Street, where the standing room-only queue started. There were only two others at the spot, so I ended up third in the queue by 10.15am.

The building itself, although with a Dylanesque address on West 4th Street, was the corner part of a good solid Manhattan stone building rather akin to a bank. 1975 would have been one of the last

years that you could see a really popular artist in a club, since the tiny
Bleecker Street venues had long ceased to be economically viable,
and it would take the rise of punk and new wave, courtesy of CBGB
in The Bowery, some blocks away downtown, to stimulate a club
culture again.

The style of the Bottom Line is something that could probably
never be repeated nowadays - patrons were entirely seated at tables,
with six chairs or so to each table and no space at the front for
dancing. There was definitely no mosh pit, but it did mean that the
keenest fans were seated right in front of the artist, so there certainly
was a connection between performer and audience that helped
induce a cohesive performance. The 50 or so last-minute attendees,
who had queued to get tickets on the day, were allowed to stand 10
deep between the furthest tables and the bar, but the whole place was
so small it was reminiscent of the old Marquee Club in London's
Wardour Street, a rocking sweatbox from top to bottom.

Its intimacy would have been very suitable for the singer-
songwriters the venue was showcasing at the time and in some ways
might have suited Columbia's initial view of Bruce as an acoustic
troubadour, except of course that by mid '75 the E Street Band
had really honed their craft live by nationwide touring. Bruce and
ensemble had been emboldened by his decision never to open a show
for anyone again, after they suffered in large venues as the opener
for Chicago, where the size of the places acted as a dampener on the
energy that Bruce and the band were putting out.

Back out on the corner, it was an entertaining eight hours with no
drink, no food, but a certain amount of chat, because by lunchtime
the queue was halfway round the block and by show time it was
all the way round. I have no idea how many of those queuing got
in, but it can't have been more than maybe 100, because there just
wasn't the room to fit more than that number in the club, jammed up
against the bar.

The other overriding aspect to seeing Bruce on his home turf was
that it was hot – a hot, sticky, humid, August such that Britain rarely
sees, but which was the perfect complement to the urban poetry of

much of Bruce's material at the time. The E Street Band had
of course, since the *E Street Shuffle* album, lost keyboard genius
David Sancious and slightly quixotic drummer Vini 'Mad Dog'
Lopez, whose sense of timing wasn't quite in sync with the
grooves laid down by the other original members. Ernest 'Boom'
Carter helped out for six months, laid down the drums on *Born
to Run's* title track, then left to hook up with the already-departed
Sancious. The other songs featured replacements 'Professor' Roy
Bittan on piano and 'Mighty' Max Weinberg on drums, but in
terms of live gigs, August '75 was still a relatively early outing
for the new incarnation of the band.

The radio broadcast the previous night had introduced new
guitarist Miami Steve Van Zandt, who we now know as Bruce's
guitar buddy from way back, but at the time was just an additional
member of the band. A very welcome addition, since his staccato
and slide-riff additions to the slow version of 'The E Street Shuffle'
made it into an entirely different song; the rendition from the
Bottom Line is to me still the most effective and engaging version
of that song.

To put in context what Bruce was up against at the time, the No.1
album in Britain in August 1975 was *Horizon* by The Carpenters.
Number One singles included 'Give A Little Love' by The Bay City
Rollers, followed by 'Barbados' by Typically Tropical. Big albums
early that summer in the US were slightly more rocking: *Captain
Fantastic* by Elton John, followed by *Venus and Mars* by Wings, *One of
these Nights* by The Eagles and Red Octopus by Jefferson Starship, but
even so, No.1 singles in the US charts included 'Love Will Keep Us
Together' by the Captain and Tennille, 'Listen To What The Man
Said' by Wings and 'The Hustle' by Van McCoy.

Even before the E Street Band struck up a note, the theatricality
of the front line's appearance was pure attitude. Each member had
a persona, partly related to their semi-jocular nicknames, as invented
by Bruce: Clarence Clemons (the 'Big Man', the 'Big Kahuna',
'Master of the Universe') was a majestically imposing figure in a
sharp suit, echoed, in a slightly more Damon Runyon-esque way by

Miami Steve, complete with fedora. Bruce himself (bear in mind that
this was at least a year before the Ramones album hit the streets) was
in the prototypical New York street punk outfit of T-shirt, leather
jacket, skinny jeans with turn ups, sneakers and, on some nights, grey
peaked cap. Organist Danny Federici was a little more understated,
while Roy Bittan and Max Weinberg sported neatly-trimmed beards.
Beards! This was not the done thing, except of course Bruce himself
was also bearded at the time - he only shaved it off the following year,
never to return to that look.

The full impact of the live band experience is quite hard to
explain, partly because Bruce has since become so successful that
people have got some idea for themselves of how his particular
influences show through in his mixture of Elvis, British Invasion,
Motown and Tin Pan Alley. Perhaps you just have to take my word
that such an exuberant show was a heady tonic in the oh so cool
world of Rock, mid-Seventies.

And, it was a great, great show. To see a band at the top of its
game at close proximity, blasting through exciting songs in the
company of 400 enthusiastic devotees was a really exhilarating
experience. It started with the band version of 'Tenth Avenue
Freeze-out', followed by 'Spirit In The Night', then and now, one of
the Bruce anthems. In contrast to the way shows seem to go these
days in large halls, there was an amazing amount of dynamics in the
performance. For instance, 'Spirit In The Night' started as a full-tilt
swinging ensemble piece, heavy on Clarence Clemons' saxophone
riff, with the audience, unbidden, chiming in on 'all night' in the
choruses. In the middle breakdown section, though, as Bruce laid out
his tale of drunken frolics by a midnight Jersey lake, he muted the
band and intoned the lyrics, dropping to a whisper - yes, a whisper -
before the band roared back in.

That then turned in to an homage to pop/R&B's finest
songwriters, as Bruce tips them a hat in one of his renditions of
various classics. On the radio the previous night it had a been a
suitably Spector-esque 'And Then (S)he Kissed Me', repeated in the
Saturday early show, with others to come throughout the set.

Two more live favourites from the debut album followed: 'Growin' Up', and 'It's Hard to Be a Saint in the City', after which Bruce started telling one of his stories. One of the things that endured Bruce to his followers at the time was his humorous, highly fanciful, but supposedly autobiographical stories, which mostly featured characters from the Jersey Shore or incidents illustrating the scuffling nature of his career thus far.

Bruce doesn't do, or didn't do, routine introductions - he did actual stories, some of which were thematically the same, though changed from night to night, but still illustrated his desire to fully engage with the audience, without the distancing superstar mystique that seems to be *de rigeur* these days.

In that sense I suppose he was rather Dylan-esque, since Bob had a reputation for spinning the odd yarn before he gave up talking to his audiences all together. But it wasn't showmanship for the sake of it: when, in the middle of one of his songs, for dramatic effect Bruce crawled out into the audience across the tables, scattering bottles of beer and wine in his wake, apart from the laughs it was a moment of intimacy that really bonded the performer and audience in a way that most shows don't even attempt. That one good-natured gesture showed a fearless bond with his fans that will doubtless be as permanent a memory to all the others present that night as it is to me.

Then, when the up-tempo rock 'n' roll numbers saw Bruce, without any kind of sense of shame, jumping on the grand piano and belting out the song, it transmitted a strong sense of humanity and joie de to the audience, who lapped it up. As importantly, it drew the audience into an enveloping mutual live experience that ended up being more than the sum of the parts, something transcendental that can only exist, dare I say, when all present really believe. Which, I suppose, explains the undoubted power of gospel choirs.

Woven between the live classics that early Bruce adopters had come to hear, were his exemplary choice of covers, different every night and drawn equally from the Brill Building's original versions and the British Invasion covers: 'And Then He Kissed Me' by

The Crystals, 'Sha La La' by the Shirelles, 'When You Walk In The Room' by Jackie de Shannon (probably learned from The Searchers' version), 'Up On The Roof', 'It's Gonna Work Out Fine' and 'Pretty Flamingo'.

In the middle of the set you got what would now be a well-known story but was new to us then - how Bruce and Miami Steve first met Clarence Clemons (not a strictly true tale but highly entertaining). Evoking perfectly that sense of menace that can envelop seaside towns out of season, Bruce described how he and Steve first encountered a strange and threatening form materialising out of a swirling rainy mist late at night on the Asbury Park boardwalk, which turned out to be Clarence.

The story culminated in Clarence allegedly putting out his hand, which, when it touched Bruce's, provoked the sparks that 'fly on E Street.' Cue the slow version of 'The E Street Shuffle', totally different from the album version, with Miami Steve playing sympathetic and adroit slide guitar. In 1975, Bruce was already 26, and he'd been a working musician for about nine years, so as well as the feeling that he was on the verge of his big break, there was an indefinable sense of nostalgia, a longing for times that were just a bit more simple, fused with the realisation that you can't go home anymore.

It was the intimacy of those slow songs at the Bottom Line that was to suffer the most with the subsequent huge success of *Born to Run*. Bruce is an entertainer, and once he started playing 3,000+ size halls, the spaces weren't intimate enough to carry the familiar troubadour / raconteur role. Having said that, I did see him in 1981 at Wembley Arena (11,000 capacity) and he was still fantastic, but to me there's nothing like seeing a performance where the audience is close enough to feel and see every nuance of the entertainer's mood.

It meant that Bruce could get away with occasionally performing a song in an entirely different style from that on album. Though we didn't know it yet, 'Thunder Road' is a balls-out 'two against the world' anthem on the *Born to Run* album, and somewhat of a Springsteen staple, but in the much more stripped-down Bottom Line version, performed entirely solo by Bruce accompanying himself on piano, it was far more revealing and vulnerable: less bombastic and ultimately more moving.

At the centre of the Springsteen '75 live set was perhaps not 'Born to Run', but 'Kitty's Back', which is in itself a song constructed around light and shade, dynamics and theatrics, prefaced by an archetypal Bruce shaggy dog story, ending with an alleged third party uttering 'Kitty's back' - and into the song.

Already an audience favourite, 'Kitty's Back' showcased rare band keyboard solos over a swinging groove, with guitar/sax set pieces, followed by individual solos: Clarence, Bruce, Steve, followed by more weaving in and out of the album arrangement, a call and response section, and a final wailing finale. Then straight into the classic 'Rosalita' - cue standing ovation, from those not already on their feet, and a more muted encore of the Gary US Bonds classic 'Quarter To Three.'

As we staggered out into the hot Manhattan night, it would have been around 11 o'clock, and, notwithstanding the fact that I'd been queuing since 10 in the morning I was elated, excited and energised. I can't imagine what state Bruce was in after a full two-hour-plus set, having done it six times in the preceding three days, but, however he felt, he had the stamina to promptly go out and do a further 2-hour set straight away to the late show crowd.

Three years later I was back at the Bottom Line for another great series of shows with the Be Stiff tour - but that's another story.

UPTOWN THEATER

2 OCTOBER 1975 MILWAUKEE, WISCONSIN

WAS THERE: CRAIG SCHULTZ

The 1975 show was intimate and amazing; seeing most of *Born to Run* live was life-changing, (*Born to Run* had come out that August, and Springsteen ended up on the covers of both *Time* and *Newsweek* later that month).

To further imprint this night on our psyches, about 40 minutes into the show (right after 'Thunder Road') the WQFM-FM DJ Bob Reitman stepped on stage, Springsteen by his side, telling the 1,800 in attendance that they had to evacuate because of a bomb threat, clearing the theater for nearly three hours.

The crowd waited patiently in the cold (this was October in Wisconsin) while the venue was searched completely. Thankfully no bomb was found. Meanwhile Bruce and his band were waiting and drinking at their hotel bar. When they re-emerged just before midnight they were loose and ready to rock the house, which they did, closing the show well after 2am.

I WAS THERE: DANIEL M ZIERVOGEL

I saw him at the old Uptown Theater, Northside of Milwaukee. Three of four songs in there was a bomb scare. They stopped the show and emptied the place and restarted very late. The show then went on into the morning. An amazing gig. I believe it was before the *Time* magazine cover.

Bruce Springsteen and the E Street Band's first performance in the UK was on 18 November 1975 at Hammersmith Odeon, West London. The mood was one of great expectation. Springsteen arrived surfing a wave of hype from his 1975 album *Born to Run*, a major hit in the USA. His label, Columbia Records, were keen to sell him, the streets plastered with posters advertising the show. One read: 'Finally, London is ready for Bruce Springsteen'.

> I didn't see the Future of Rock'n'Roll, or The New Bob Dylan. I'm told by Springsteen's own standards, this was a bad gig, by the standards of the audience it appeared to be a highly – but not wildly – successful gig. By my standards it was a so-so gig, rich with unfulfilled potential but in no way a classic.

Tony Tyler, NME

HAMMERSMITH ODEON

18 NOVEMBER 1975 LONDON, UK

I WAS THERE: TINA FLEMMING

I was 14, just out of my David Cassidy phase and well into Motown, visiting my sister in London from Brighton when her friend decided he was going to educate me in the art of real music. He took me to Hammersmith Odeon, where he'd heard some guy from the US East Coast was appearing, with big things predicted. As the lights went down and the band came on and they struck the first few chords of

'Thunder Road', I knew I'd never look back. And I haven't. Over 40 years on I love him, the band and his music as much today as I did then. I've seen him 13 times since and every show has been a life-affirming experience.

'Thunder Road' remains my favourite song, while 'Lost in the Flood', 'Rosalita', 'Born to Run' and 'She's the One' were also standouts. I remember being in awe of the sound and energy of the band and was totally smitten by the charisma of the front-man.

I've subsequently seen Bruce twice in Vancouver, three times in London, three times in Sydney and twice in nearby Hunter Valley, as well as in Seattle and Amsterdam.

SETLIST:

01. Thunder Road
02. Tenth Avenue Freeze-Out
03. Spirit in the Night
04. Lost in the Flood
05. She's the One
06. Born to Run
07. The E Street Shuffle / Havin' a Party
08. It's Hard to Be a Saint in the City
09. Backstreets
10. Kitty's Back
11. Jungleland
12. Rosalita (Come Out Tonight)
13. Come a Little Bit Closer
14. 4th of July, Asbury Park (Sandy)
15. Detroit Medley
16. For You
17. Quarter to Three

1976
The Chicken Scratch Tour kicked off late March 1976 and ended in Annapolis, Maryland at the end of May. The name of the tour was given by the band's road crew, due to many of the shows being in secondary markets in the South.

In outtake photos of Bruce Springsteen from the Eric Meola photo session for the *Born to Run* album cover, Bruce proudly displays an Elvis Presley fan club badge.

As with many young musicians of his time, a seven-year old Springsteen was inspired to pick up a guitar after seeing Elvis playing 'Don't Be Cruel', 'Love Me Tender', 'Hound Dog' and 'Ready Teddy' on the *Ed Sullivan Show* in September 1956.

'Everything starts and ends with Elvis', he said in 1978, and Bruce envisioned 'Fire' could be recorded by his idol. It was written after he saw Presley perform at a 28 May 1977 concert at the Spectrum, Philadelphia. He later said, 'I sent Elvis a demo, but he died before it arrived.'

After the April 29 show in Memphis' Ellis Auditorium, Springsteen decided he'd attempt to meet one of his biggest musical heroes and took a taxi to Graceland. Upon arrival (along with E Street Band guitarist Steven Van Zandt) they noticed a light on in a second-floor window. Bruce proceeded to jump the gates and walked to the front door but before he reached it security intervened, Bruce inquiring, 'Is Elvis home?' Presley was in fact in Lake Tahoe. The guards not having any idea who this visitor was, (even after he tried to explain and state that he'd been on the covers of *Time* and *Newsweek*), they politely escorted Bruce to the street. Years later Springsteen would tell the story in concerts and reminisce about what he would have said had Elvis answered the door.

MONMOUTH ARTS CENTER

1 AUGUST 1976 RED BANK, NEW YORK

I WAS THERE: MICHAEL BODAYLE

In August of 1976, I had the pleasure of seeing two Springsteen shows with the E Street Band at the tiny Monmouth Arts Center in Red Bank, NY (now called the Count Basie Theatre). As one would expect, these special concerts between the *Born to Run* and *Darkness on the Edge of Town* records were a hard ticket indeed.

However, I somehow twice managed my way in through the hard work of asking everyone I saw if they had an extra ticket. My thrill of hearing the new song 'Rendezvous' each night wasn't capped off by meeting Bruce, but I did learn something valuable in Red Bank that would help me make my first Springsteen encounter.

The intel I gathered was simply the fact that Bruce had shaved his beard. Recall that back then, without Facebook and Twitter, this kind of news travelled at a snail's pace. Seeing those August shows helped me recognize a clean-shaven Mr Springsteen a few weeks later on the night of September 4, 1976.

It was a Friday night, and a friend and I made the journey down to Asbury Park to see Hot Tuna play at the Casino Arena on the Boardwalk. Getting a late workday start on our drive down to the Shore, we walked in just in time to catch the end of the opening set by David Sancious. During the break, I met an old high school friend who said he heard Bruce was standing back in the crowd listening to the jazzy sounds of his former E-Street Band keyboard player's band. We also caught wind that Southside Johnny & the Asbury Jukes were playing across the street at the Stone Pony.

After a few songs by Hot Tuna, I convinced my friend that we were in the wrong place. Surprisingly, we easily made it into the

Pony as a local band was playing. Eyeing up the room with a bottle
of Heineken in hand, I spotted the 'Beardless Boss' sitting alone
unrecognized on the jukebox. Full of courage from who knows
where, I approached him with the words, 'Bruce, can I buy you a
beer?' He quickly responded to this total stranger of a teenager with
'I'll take a Blackberry on the rocks.'

After securing and delivering said drink, I joined Mr Springsteen
atop said jukebox for the next 15 minutes or so where we chatted
briefly and listened to the band. He pointed out how the lead singer
was in the first band he ever played in. (I believe it was George
Theiss from The Castiles.) Bruce was so kind, friendly and relaxed,
and for some reason, I was on my best non-star-struck behaviour. My
friend later joined us, and as we departed, Bruce bought us a pair of
Heinekens. For almost 40 years to this day, that bottle remains in a
treasured spot on the bookshelf of my study.

This dreamlike evening was capped off by a great set from the
Jukes with Bruce joining them on stage for their usual encore of Sam
Cooke's 'Having a Party.' If only somewhere there was a picture of
us sitting on that jukebox together!

Two weeks later, on September 19, 1976, I went to see The Band
at the Palladium in New York City. Formerly known as the Academy
of Music, this was the same venue where a few years earlier they
recorded their sensational live record, *Rock of Ages*. Although they had
dipped a little in stature since then, they were touring in support of
their strong new LP, *Northern Lights – Southern Cross*.

Whenever I frequented the Academy/Palladium, I made a point to
stand by the backstage door to try and catch band members coming
in and out of the show. While waiting beforehand to try and meet
Robertson, Danko, Manual, Hudson or Helm, I was surprised to see
my (still unrecognizable to most) new friend Bruce. Quite puzzled
to suddenly be within striking distance of him, I said 'Hey Bruce,'
somehow thinking he'd remember his Heineken-drinking friend from
the jukebox at the Pony. This encounter lasted only a minute or so,
but I was able to get a 'We're gonna be playing here!' out of him.
This news was about his bringing what later became known as 'The

Lawsuit Tour' to the Palladium for a six-show run starting at the end of October.

My two other Springsteen encounters were the result of a single event occurring during the 1978 Darkness tour on which I saw 15 shows. On the weekend of August 25-26, I travelled with three friends to see the Friday show in New Haven, Connecticut and the Saturday show in Providence, Rhode Island. One of my friends was a great amateur photographer, and because of his kindness and talent, had befriended Bruce's legendary No.1 Springsteen fan and assistant, the late 'Obie' Dziedzic.

Well, as memory serves, we somehow met up with Obie after the New Haven show and in a joyous mood she gave us all a bunch of confiscated counterfeit Springsteen T-shirts. (Those cheap ones that last about two washes!) She also asked a favour of us to carry a big black garment bag to Providence and deliver it to her the next day at the hotel. If only instead she told us Bruce was about to drop in and play with John Cafferty and Beaver Brown downtown at Toad's Place. That appearance proved to be the launch-pad for this band's eventual national success that started with the hard-core Springsteen fan-base.

Nonetheless, we carried the cargo to Rhode Island, and now that the statute of limitations has expired, I can admit that we of course opened the garment bag. You should have seen our eyes bulge out of our heads when we saw that inside was the black suit that Bruce was wearing nightly on stage. Deciding not to hold it ransom, we took it over to his hotel, and our timing was such that right after our delivery to Obie, the E Street Band bus pulled up in front of the hotel.

Waiting by the lobby door, we saw the band roll out of the bus. This third meeting with the Boss was one that found him scratching his sleepy head and rubbing his bloodshot eyes. My excited and unnecessary news to him about our completed garment bag mission was totally lost on him and produced nothing more than a yawn and a groan.

My final time meeting Bruce Springsteen was that night after the Providence show when Obie graciously invited me and my three friends back stage. Totally in awe and unprepared, to this day I cringe thinking how if I only had a *Born to Run* album for all The E Streeters to sign. However, I did have the notepad I used to write down the nightly set-lists and managed to get that treasured autograph.

I recall a happy, smiling Springsteen, who certainly didn't know me from Adam when I asked for his signature. I did preface my request with the fact that it was my eleventh show on the tour, which he unsuspectedly acknowledged for me in writing. Sadly, back then taking pictures wasn't a common thing, and none were taken while we were backstage. Still, like the three prior meet-ups, it was a moment I'll never forget.

The closing to this tale is my one further attempt at an encounter that just didn't happen. In 1996, I found myself in Salt Lake City for one of the solo Tom Joad tour shows and decided I'd try the backstage door after the show. Out-of-the-way city and small venue, I thought I might have a chance. This time, I also had with me a brand-new camera. I'd give it my best shot to get that much-desired photo with Bruce.

So, after the show, I waited outside backstage with a small group of fans. Those were the days when post-show Bruce would take the time to meet with people who worked at local food banks. While I waited, I saw these folks leaving with smiles on their faces after having met him. After hanging around for who knows how long, I finally gave up and went home since he obviously had left the venue through another exit.

Well, it could have been worse. Had I gotten that photo op, there would have been an even sadder ending to this story. The new camera was broken, didn't work and was returned as defective. But who knows, maybe someday we'll meet again somewhere when I have my camera handy and buy him another drink.

COLLEGE AVENUE GYMNASIUM

12 OCTOBER 1976 NEW BRUNSWICK, CANADA

I WAS THERE: JOHN WOODING

The anticipation, it was palpable. The show was unbelievable. It opened with 'Night,' one of the unsung gems from *Born to Run*. Clarence Clemons came out wailing on the sax, setting the tone for the whole evening.

Bruce told great stories. He told the story of his poor relationship with his father, a theme that ran throughout much of his writing in that time-frame.

THE PALLADIUM

2 NOVEMBER 1976 NEW YORK CITY

I WAS THERE: PAUL REITZ

Like many others in the Seventies, it was the *Born to Run* album that turned me on to Bruce Springsteen. I remember first hearing songs

from that record on our local New York radio station WNEW-FM 102.7.

My first Bruce Springsteen show was on November 2, 1976, at the Palladium (formerly the Academy of Music) on 14th Street, NYC. There were two songs from that performance, which have stayed in my memory to this day.

The first was 'Spirit In The Night.' After hearing it that evening, I remember going to the local record store the next day to find the album it was on. It was on *Greetings From Asbury Park, NJ*, which to this day remains my favourite Bruce album.

The second song that stood out for me was 'It's My Life.' That night was the first time I ever heard it. All I knew was that this was THE song. The emotions Bruce put into his version hit every chord, amped up to 11, with this teenage boy. I was going to grasp that song and make it my anthem too. Little did I know until I searched for a copy, it wasn't a Bruce song at all but one by The Animals.

At this show, Bruce had the 'Miami Horns' join him on a couple of tunes that night, that horn section unrelated to that of the Asbury Jukes. Many years later, I learned that this date was part of what later became known as The Lawsuit Tour.

1977

JAI ALAI FRONTON

MARCH 5 1977 ORLANDO, FLORIDA

I WAS THERE: HUGH GARRY

It was in 1977 at the Jai Alai Fronton. It held about 3,000 people and what I remember most is that the band had to start three times.

Something was wrong with the sound. Instead of becoming angry, Bruce just kept starting over. We hadn't seen the energy this group put out in a long time. A super show. Unfortunately, it was the one and only time we saw him.

1978

❧In all my years in this business he is the only person I've met who cares absolutely nothing about money ❧

John Hammond, Columbia Records'
vice president of talent acquisition; 1978

THE SPECTRUM

26 MAY 1978 PHILADELPHIA, PENNSYLVANIA

I WAS THERE: STEVE DRINGUS

I ventured stealthily up to the third level during the sax solo of 'Spirit in the Night.' When it was time for the vocals to come back in the spotlight came on and Springsteen sang while sitting on some girl's lap. It took him some time to get back down to the stage. When he did, he said, 'Guess I'll never do that again.' Same show during the encore the band left. He stayed still, the band came out with one of those World War II canvas stretchers, he fell back on it and they carried him off, still playing the final chord. Unreal.

MEMORIAL HALL

16 JUNE 1978 KANSAS CITY, MISSOURI

I WAS THERE: TOM BLAKE

There is actually a great recording online. Search 'Springsteen
Memorial Hall '78'. *Darkness on the Edge of Town* was just released.
Funny thing was looking at the cover of *Born to Run* and hearing that
bold deep voice I expected a guy about 6ft 2ins to walk on stage.
Little did I know he was on a stool leaning on Clarence Clemons for
the album cover. Out walks this guy, all of 5ft 9ins. Everyone was
there to see what all the hype was about. We found out. As soon as
'Badlands' was over, everyone in the place looked at the person next
to them, mouthing, 'Whoa!'

BAYFRONT CENTER

29 JULY 1978 ST. PETERSBURG, FLORIDA

I WAS THERE: NORA TUCKER

In the summer of 1978 I worked at The Listening Booth record store
in a mall in Pinellas Park, Florida. Our manager, Marilyn, or 'Chick',
was from the Philadelphia area and all of us who worked there
were Bruce fans. We made friends with a guy from New Jersey who
came in the store and talked music and Bruce. He stood in line and
bought us the first tickets on sale for his show in St. Petersburg for the
Darkness on the Edge of Town tour.

Bruce had to cancel some shows the week before due to illness.
The day of the show, we bought a floral arrangement of roses and
delivered them to the Holiday Inn. It was located across the street
from the Bayfront Center so we figured he was there. We tried but
weren't allowed to deliver them to Bruce's room. Lewis, Chick and
I sat in the hotel lobby from 10.30am until late afternoon. First
Clarence Clemons came down and autographed Lewis' copy of
Darkness on the Edge of Town. Clarence told us Bruce was feeling fine

Bill DeYoung, Donna Reilly and Nora Burns Tucker at The Listening Booth Record Store 1978

and he left for the soundcheck. Roy Bittan came through and said the same.

Two men walked across the small lobby and got to the door. Another couple jumped up to greet them and we realized it was Bruce and an assistant. Bruce was wearing a plain white t-shirt and jeans. He was totally non-descript and we hadn't even recognized him. He then came over to us and we gave him the roses. He sent his assistant back to the room with the arrangement. The rest of us failed to bring any records and had bought copies of a teen magazine in the hotel gift shop, with a black and white photo of Bruce, totally unflattering. As he signed it, he said, 'I look like I'm trying to catch flies.'

I was dumbfounded, I couldn't speak. He asked, 'Where are you guys from?' Lewis answered, 'We're from all over but I'm from New Jersey.' Then Bruce asked, 'What do you guys do?' Again, I couldn't answer that 'I work in a record store and play music.' 'We do different things,' said Lewis. His assistant returned and it was time for him to leave for the soundcheck. Bruce got to the door, I found my voice and called out, 'We're all looking forward to the show tonight.' He turned back around to me and said, 'Thanks.'

When we got to our seats at the Bayfront Center, Lewis said, 'Right here is where Bruce will jump down from the stage.' The first four rows were the comps, but there was an aisle up to our row. Row five went the length of the floor and created another 'front row.' Directly in front of our four chairs was a square of floor.

The show kicked off with 'Oh, Boy!' by Buddy Holly. Bruce looked down at his t-shirt and said, 'I got ink on my shirt.' That was from signing our stuff in the same shirt! The next tune was a roaring version of 'Badlands'. For the third song he put down his guitar, took the mic. and began one I'd always sung, 'Spirit in the Night.' After the second chorus, Bruce jumped off the stage and stretched out across our laps, about four of us! Next, he stood up, put his foot between my knees and the other foot between Lewis' and stood on our chairs. We braced his legs at the calves to hold him steady. He sang the quiet part of the third verse that way. I had been too shy to talk to Bruce, but he found his way into my lap!

The whole night was a wall of sound and emotion. My husband had not been a fan and didn't understand my devotion to Bruce until that night. Our friends, about 10 of us, didn't want to go home and danced through the streets of downtown St. Petersburg in the heat of that July night. It was perfection.

TOWNSHIP AUDITORIUM

31 JULY 1978 COLUMBIA, SOUTH CAROLINA

I WAS THERE: BILL FLETCHER

I was 21 years old and met some friends who were in college at the University of South Carolina at that time. Township is an intimate theatre. It seats about 3,000. It was the Darkness tour and I remember that it was hot as blue blazes in Columbia that night. It can be one of the hottest cities around in the summer. I live about 90 miles away in Spartanburg. I skipped my own band's rehearsal that night to see Bruce. I didn't tell them I wasn't going to be there. That band was a real stickler for being at rehearsal, but there was no way that I was going to miss this show.

I had discovered Bruce like many, via *Born to Run*. To have him play

a smaller venue like this before he became a mega-star was the best. It was north of a three-hour show, with a mix of the songs from new album, *Born to Run* and earlier. He was working the crowd like a tent revival preacher. I've never seen that kind of energy for that long before or since. I even remember he and Clarence climbing into the balcony during 'Rosalita', the place going nuts, Bruce drenched to the bone.

We all left to hit one of the local bars after and were all exhausted and amazed at what we had just seen. To have seen him when he was just starting to become a household name and before MTV was fantastic. You knew when you left that night you'd witnessed true greatness. It's the only time I've seen him live. I'm OK with that. It would have been hard to top.

THE AGORA

9 AUGUST 1978 CLEVELAND, OHIO

I WAS THERE: JIM GIRARD

It was obvious to the lucky thousand or so Clevelanders that they were witnessing a truly historic event. Springsteen in Cleveland was no longer a club act. He could fill at the time the Coliseum, the biggest venue around.

Part of what made the show so legendary was that it was broadcast live on WMMS and eight other FM stations across the Midwest, including St. Louis, Pittsburgh, Chicago, Detroit, and Minneapolis. It would later become one of the most bootlegged concerts in history, only receiving an official release in 2014.

Springsteen had been out of the public eye a couple of years after *Born to Run*, lengthy litigation with his former manager preventing him from working and releasing any music. It was unfortunate after making the *Time* and *Newsweek* covers. His career was on the way and then this. The public wanted more but he couldn't deliver. The label felt they had to reintroduce Bruce to the masses, gain those people he'd already won over and further his career. They decided on a series of club concerts and to regionally broadcast them.

It also helped WMMS, coinciding with their 10th anniversary. And it was something Cleveland could be proud of, in an otherwise bad year.

Bruce and the band poured their hearts and souls into the performance, but what makes a great performer better is the audience. And in 1978 there was no better rock'n'roll audience in America. Play the East and West coast and people sit on their hands. They don't get as excited, they don't sing along, they don't become part of the concert. There's that coolness factor, which isn't very cool. When an act plays Cleveland, the audience get really enthused, get behind the band. That's why it's looked at as part of one of Springsteen's greatest if not his greatest concert. He had 100% connection with the audience, he and the band were firing on all cylinders. It was a perfect storm, an incredible two to three hours of music, reintroducing Bruce Springsteen to the rest of the country.

In Cleveland they never stopped loving Springsteen. The same is true for the Eastern seaboard. For the rest of the country he was this new artist they first heard with 'Born to Run'. Then the momentum was building, he was developing, then - bang - the lawsuit hit. These concerts helped jump-start his career after he had just released *Darkness on the Edge of Town.*

Hearsay led more stations to broadcast the show. Even though Springsteen played San Francisco, the station that originated that broadcast also broadcast the Cleveland show later, and a number of others ended up getting copies and playing it. It was either the first or second most bootlegged concert in history, along with Led Zeppelin at the Coliseum.

It was the single best concert I've ever seen. One of those unique nights where everything came together. The audience was great, Springsteen was at his absolute peak. Pure entertainment, pure energy. I've seen thousands of concerts but compare all of them against this one.

CIVIC CENTER

26 AUGUST 1978 PROVIDENCE, RHODE ISLAND

I WAS THERE: DEBBIE JOHNSON

I'm from Rhode Island and my first time seeing him was in Providence on the Darkness tour, then again in 1980 for The River tour, one of my most memorable, Bruce running and jumping on the piano, the Santa song, and alluding to John Lennon, the night he was killed. This first impression of Bruce, his music and electric energy would mesmerize me. I've been fortunate to see him close to 50 times and no two shows are ever the same.

The Rising tour in 2009 was incredibly powerful. He sang the words that echoed our pain, sadness and anger. Bruce soothed our soul, then lifted us, made us feel empowered, made us feel hopeful.

Every time he plays in Boston he rocks the city, three and a half hours non-stop. At Madison Square Garden in 2016 he made you feel like you were in his living room. When he was with Tom Morello and the Seeger Sessions band at Mansfield Mass in 2006 it was the most fun I've ever had at a Bruce concert. Every night, every show, every tour is different. You can count on three hours of pure entertainment. I've heard him do his songs a half-dozen different ways. It never gets old. The magic of Bruce.

I've been listening to his music since I was 13. That's 42 years. From the moment I heard 'Born to Run', his music has been an intricate part of my life. His words, lyrics, songs, characters, the stories he tells, relevant, fictional, historical, they are complete, whole and empathetic, they fill my soul.

I felt like we were a generation with conflicted feelings, trying to navigate our way through adulthood, questioning our truths. Bruce's music was and is us. It gave us a conscience. It put names and inadvertently faces on people. His characters are all of us. In the darkest hours Bruce's music always shined a light. Herein lies the magic - his unique ability while showing us raw and naked ugly truths, always giving us hope, reminding us to have faith, to believe, to dream and never give up.

In concert, people aren't just exhausted by three-hour plus shows, but that he's provoked such an array of emotions, angst, frustration, sadness, hope, fun, faith. That's part of what's so exhilarating.

And my favourite Bruce song? It's an obscure one, 'The Way.'

THE CAPITOL THEATER

19 SEPTEMBER 1978 PASSAIC, NEW JERSEY

I WAS THERE: ARLEN SCHUMER

Bruce Springsteen and the E Street Band (in its longest-running version) have never been better, on a pure musical level, than they were during the Darkness on the Edge of Town tour. There have been larger shows, 'grander' shows, shows with more spectacle; but for maximum rock'n'roll, those shows can't be beat. And September 19th at the Capitol Theater, Passaic, in Bruce's home state of New Jersey, was arguably his single greatest live performance.

First, it was Bruce's single largest audience up to that point, broadcast up and down the entire East Coast, Bruce's original fan-base. This was therefore not only a thank-you to those loyal fans, but a de facto live LP in the making (with Jimmy Iovine, Bruce's engineer on *Born to Run* and *Darkness*, mixing).

Though the entire tour was brilliant, and the band always played at an impossible level for radio, something about this show put it above and beyond even Bob Dylan at the Royal Albert Hall '66. Perhaps it was that Bruce had something to prove, not to old fans, but the larger rock world listening in, suspect of 'The Boss' since the *Born to Run* hype of 1975, an unknown rocker from (gasp!) New Jersey absurdly making the *Time* and *Newsweek* covers.

When he seemed to fade from view during that subsequent lawsuit, the hype seemed justified. But not to Bruce. When he emerged three years later, he took to the stage with a wild, yet deliberate abandon. These were the demons that drove Bruce to not only write *Darkness* but perform it with hell-for-leather drive and enthusiasm. And this performance was the best.

It sounds tremendous: a booming, thunderous performance played to diamond-hard precision, every instrument mixed and balanced perfectly. It sounds exactly like the show: when Bruce's guitar rips into the 'Prove it All Night' intro, it sounds like a buzzsaw's berserk drone; when Clarence blows the first note of any solo, the crowd roars like when a baseball player hits a home run in the bottom of the ninth. I should know, because I was there. How did I get there? Let me back-track.

The day *Darkness on the Edge of Town* was released (May 28th), the record manager of Korvette's department store (Route 4, Paramus, New Jersey, no longer there) told me there was a fanzine about Bruce Springsteen called *Thunder Road*, and a lightbulb appeared over my head. I knew I had to become its art director. I was familiar with fanzines, due to my love of comic books, with fanzines published about them since the early Sixties; he gave me the name and number of its editor/publisher, Ken Viola, whom I called that night with the intention of at least contributing. We met soon after and became good friends. I did become the art director, at least as much as I could while attending Rhode Island School of Design full-time ('76-'80).

Ken was also head of security for John Scher, the concert promoter and owner of the Capitol Theater (no longer there) in run-down Passaic, North Jersey. He was promoting Bruce's August date in

Rochester, NY, and through Ken's recommendation I illustrated special shirts for the road crew (you can spot a roadie wearing one in *The River* tour book, and me wearing one in the Capitol Theater video, when Bruce comes out to the audience during 'Spirit in The Night'). It was a great break, but nothing compared to what followed.

To celebrate Bruce's 'homecoming' after the triumphant summer of *Darkness* to a three-night stand (the first broadcast up and down the East Coast) Scher wanted a special marquee designed for the Capitol. Thanks again to Ken, I got the job. working on a design built around Bruce's guitar. After completing the artwork, I negotiated my 'fee' - six sixth-row center seats for opening night. It was the third time I saw Bruce live, my first his headlining debut at Madison Square Garden on August 21, my next in Springfield, Mass. On September 13, but this was the closest I'd ever be.

The day came, and five RISD classmates and I climbed into my '74 Plymouth Duster and drove from Providence to Passaic.

Increasing the anticipation was the last thing Ken Viola told me - if we hung out after the show for about an hour, there'd be a good chance we'd get to meet Bruce and the band.

Four hours later, rounding the corner of Jefferson and Monroe streets in Passaic (I grew up in Fair Lawn, a 10-minute drive away), the first thing we saw, like a beacon in the night, was the marquee I illustrated, suspended in the crisp, chill autumn night like the monolith in *2001*, emitting a powerful yellow neon aura: *'We'll meet 'neath that giant Capitol sign that brings this fair city light.'*

We saw the show of our lives. Anyone who heard the radio broadcast or bought the first bootleg, the triple-LP *Piece de Resistance*, the CD bootleg years later, *Passaic Night*, or the VHS bootleg of the first two hours, knows what an awesome, incredible show it was. Though all of the Darkness shows shined, and all their prior radio broadcast concerts for years have been de facto live albums, that Capitol Theater show stands above the rest, with at least seven songs standing out as definitive live versions of not only that tour but Bruce's entire career: 'Streets of Fire,' 'Promised Land,' 'Prove it All Night' (with its amazing, extended, never-played-anymore guitar solo intro), 'Candy's Room,' 'Because the Night,' 'She's the One' (with an equally-definitive prelude/cover of Buddy Holly's 'Not Fade Away'), and the extended 'Backstreets' (with its rare 'Sad Eyes' interlude).

The sound mix by Iovine is crystal-clear, distinguishing each instrument perfectly, yet still creating a live version of Spector's dense Wall of Sound (*Born to Run*) with sacrificing clarity (*Darkness*) - a breakthrough in live rock'n'roll recording, to this day never duplicated or bettered. Listen how full the band sounds when it kicks into the main theme of 'Promised Land' after Bruce's harmonica intro, or how Garry's bass parries Steve's guitar and Clarence's sax in their solos; Max's machine gun drumming at the end of 'Prove it.' Roy's jazzy piano at the beginning; the seamless transition from 'Not Fade Away'- Bruce singing like Elvis on alternate lines- to 'She's the One,' Steve's tasty rhythm guitar licks up front in the mix; Bruce's screaming, wrenching guitar solos - the greatest in a single show of his performing career - on 'Prove it.' 'Streets of Fire,' 'Candy's

Room,' 'Because the Night' and 'Backstreets.'

Ah, 'Backstreets' - the dark horse candidate for *Born to Run*'s best deep cut is known for having more than one 'definitive' live version. Some say March 4, '77 in Jacksonville, Florida, for Bruce's soul-shattering scream of rage, 'You lied!' during the interlude. Some say the stream-of-consciousness, improvised, extended performance later that month at Boston Music Hall. At 18 minutes it's certainly the longest 'Backstreets'.

For my money, it's the Capitol Theater's. In addition to all the aforementioned reasons why everything from the Capitol is pretty much definitive, its version of the 'Sad Eyes' interlude is classic, the most like spoken-word poetry/performance art - you actually hear Bruce's measured breathing syncopating with Roy's music-box piano. The build-up of '*Little girl we've got to stop*' to its crashing crescendo sounds as awesome as it was to behold: the stage going pitch-black (Marc Brickman's hyper-dramatic lighting) on Bruce's final 'Stop!' - the crowd hushed then exploding a moment later, as the band begins to reassemble, individual spotlights fading in until the white light finale of the familiar 'Backstreets' theme, leading to Bruce's aching, wordless howls - some of his best ever - over a most orchestral grandeur. That's the definitive 'Backstreets' live. To this day, I've yet to hear any Darkness show that can hold a candle to it, song for song, note for note. It's perfect.

When the show ended, we met Ken, and sure enough, 45 minutes after, Bruce and most of the E Street Band emerged to mill around in the seats with maybe two dozen fans that had hung around. First I saw Max, telling a friend he was leaving in a minute to visit his Mom. And there was Bruce, still drenched in sweat, entertaining about a dozen fans in a semi-circle, telling old drinking stories. Then I spotted Jon Landau and approached him.

I introduced myself, told him I'd love to meet the man who changed my life; Landau smiled in agreement - 'He changed my life, too.' To my surprise, he went up to Bruce and interrupted his anecdote, telling him there was someone special he wanted him to meet. All eyes turned to me. In one hand I held the original marquee art, the other had the Capitol program book opened to my marquee-inspired illustration, and I was wearing my Rochester roadie shirt. Bruce, without saying a word, looked it all over, sort of nodded in approval, and signed the artwork (as everyone in the band had, except for Clarence, who wasn't there).

Then I said something to Bruce, something I'd been wanting to tell him since I first heard 'Born to Run' over AM radio in Mom's 1966 Valiant the first time in the summer of '75, the song that started it all for me. I had read what rock'n'roll meant to Bruce, how it entered his life and changed it forever. I wanted to communicate with equal sincerity what he meant in my life. We were surprisingly about the same height, so I could look straight in his eyes. Though I must've worn a smile from ear to ear, I didn't want to come across as just another gushing fan, so my words came out evenly and carefully: 'Bruce, I just want to tell you your music means more to me than anything else in the world.'

In the split-second I finished, there was that flash of connection in his eyes, when you can tell the other person knows exactly what you mean, from the heart. Though I knew of Bruce's legendary generosity and sensitivity towards fans after a show, nothing prepared me for his reaction. He didn't say 'thanks;' he didn't say a word, didn't shake my hand, or pat me on my shoulder. He hugged me like a brother!

And all I can recall is hearing some kind of spontaneous, audible reaction from the fans standing around us, a burst of exclamation, as if to say, 'The Fan meets The Idol - and that's the way it should be.' Thanks to Murphy's Law, my friend David, who shot photos during the show ran out of film. Only the memory remains.

True fans get to a point in their lives when the desire to meet the artist, to receive some form of personal acknowledgment, overwhelms even their adulation of the work itself. Most reach that point, lots move through it. Some, like me, are fortunate enough to have that desire fulfilled.

CAPITOL THEATRE

20 SEPTEMBER 1978 PASSAIC, NEW JERSEY

I WAS THERE: CORINNE CLARKE

I've seen Bruce 40 times in concert, the first time at the Capitol Theatre when the concert was filmed and he first performed 'Santa Claus Is Coming to Town.' My boyfriend Fred and I slept in lawn chairs overnight to get the best seats. We got tickets in the seventh row. Bruce came down into our row during 'Spirit in the Night'

Corinne Clarke's hand on Bruce's shoulder

and I had my hand on his shoulder while he was singing. The concert was about four hours long and the best night of my life.

I met Bruce on the street on Madison Avenue when he was with Julianne and he talked to me. I exclaimed that all my friends down the shore loved him and wished they could meet him. Bruce said, 'Tell all you friends, I said 'Hi'.' I fell down on the ground after he was out of sight.

I moved down the shore to Ocean Grove (right next to Asbury Park) and commuted three hours a day to law school so I could be near Bruce and the band in 1980-82. I was the appointed scout for the Stone Pony to let everyone know when there was gossip of a potential appearance. Bruce did show up a couple of times and played with the band. One time, Miami Steve was there at the bar and I sat with him for a while (before he was married) and he walked me out to my car. He was very polite. Another time, I met Clarence at a bar on Ocean Avenue in Little Silver and hung out with him. He bummed a cigarette from me.

My best friend Chantal and I loved this cute little Mexican Restaurant in Long Branch and became friends with the owners. The E Street boys loved it too. We sat next to them several times at the Casa Comida, which has since grown and moved to another location. We didn't bother them when they were there, but it was very cool.

CAPITAL CENTER

2 NOVEMBER 1978 LANDOVER, MARYLAND

I WAS THERE: PHILLIP KRAUSZ

I got a call from a friend of mine tending a bar on Cross Street in Baltimore in the Eighties asking if I wanted to see Springsteen that night. One of his regulars couldn't go and gave him four tickets to the Capital Center in Largo, Maryland. It was a great high-energy show and Clarence Clemons was on top form on the sax.

SETLIST:

01. Badlands
02. Streets of Fire
03. Spirit in the Night
04. The Ties That Bind
05. Darkness on the Edge of Town
06. Independence Day
07. The Promised Land
08. Prove It All Night
09. Racing in the Street
10. Thunder Road
11. Jungleland
12. Fire
13. Candy's Room
14. Because the Night

15. Point Blank
16. Mona / She's The One
17. Backstreets
18. Rosalita (Come Out Tonight)
19. Born to Run
20. Detroit Medley
21. Quarter to Three

PATRICK GYM

4 NOVEMBER 1978 UNIVERSITY OF VERMONT, BURLINGTON

I WAS THERE: JEFREY MESERVE

I was 17-years-old and we had a pre-Springsteen party the night before he played UVM (we did the night before because we wanted to be sober for the show). Someone started a rumour that Bruce was going to show, so we had a pretty big turnout. It was a progressive drinking party - the drinks got stronger on each floor.

We were on the third; you had to do a shot of Jack Daniel's to get in the door!

All of *Born to Run* really spoke to me due to similar relationships in my life. In Bruce's version of 'Because the Night', the line *'What I've got I have earned, what I'm not I have learned'* is one of the most profound of all time! 'Land of Hope and Dreams' and 'The Ghost of Tom Joad' with Tom Morello are also hard to beat, and 'The Wall' and 'Terry's Song' are extremely moving.

I've seen him in Lewiston ME,

Augusta ME, and Burlington VT where I was enrolled in school at UVM. I was a National Caliber Cross-Country Skier and a good friend/teammate with whom I trained came home after his first few weeks of college (I was a senior in High School) and during a training session told me if I did nothing else the rest of the day I needed to get a copy of *Born to Run* and give it a listen. I was immediately blown away by the opening harmonica of 'Thunder Road' and preceded to wear the grooves of the record out.

REILLY CENTER

10 NOVEMBER 1978 OLEAN, NEW YORK

I WAS THERE: JOANNE HAGEMAN

I travelled an hour for his show from the college town of Alfred to Olean NY after I heard his music on our college radio station.

At 21 years, and in my second cover band, I recall the full-bodied sound The E Street put out. Clarence Clemmons was the stand out for me. His commanding presence, and how he could shape the crescendo of each song. Their sound was unlike any concert band I had heard.

Bruce had such an aggressive delivery. His face was pained and jaw so tight as he sang. As a lead vocalist, it was a delivery that intrigued me. Inspiring me to reach deeper in my future performances. As a lyricist, I remember wishing I was from the places his songs portrayed. Lots of grit - similar to my native Chicago. One show and I was hooked.

MAPLE LEAF GARDENS

16 NOVEMBER 1978 TORONTO, CANADA

I WAS THERE: EARLE BROX

The first show I saw with Bruce and the E Street Band was at Maple Leaf Gardens in Toronto. In those days he'd take a break and play a second half. The show was so long, the subway system had to be kept open longer. That first show hooked me forever and I've been a fan since, having seen The Boss upwards of 20 times. When you go to a Springsteen show, you get 'Brucified.'

SPECIAL EVENTS CENTER

7 DECEMBER 1978 AUSTIN, TEXAS

I WAS THERE: GARY MCKEE

After the intermission, the auditorium went inky black, Christmas lights came on, framing the stage, sleigh bells began ringing a familiar tune, and an extremely deep bass voice filled the darkness. 'Ho, Ho, Ho, Ho, Ho, Ho', sleigh bells chimed in, then Springsteen's voice warned in the darkness that: 'You Better Watch Out, You Better Not Cry, I'm Telling You Why….' The next line exploded as a single white spotlight penetrated the darkness revealing Clarence Clemens, Springsteen's legendary saxophonist, all six foot five inches of a man dressed in a Santa suit with his huge bass saxophone blasting out 'Santa Claus Is Coming To Town' and the E Street Band kicking in, full blast. It was a Merry Christmas, indeed. The only recorded version of this classic was on a *Sesame Street* album; Bruce wanting to make sure his fans would buy it and support the noble institution that *Sesame Street* is.

For decades after, this particular show was rated in the top 10 of the best live shows in Austin. Bruce crowd-surfed as the stage guys fed out the microphone cord and reeled it back in. All 9,000 plus folks were in ecstasy the whole show. Bruce was climbing all over the speakers, and it seemed like Roy Bittan's piano was on a riser above the band on the side of the stage. I remember everyone having this big grin on their faces after, exhausted from the intensity.

THE SUMMIT

8 DECEMBER 1978 HOUSTON, TEXAS

I WAS THERE: ED GRAY

Almost 40 years ago, I saw Bruce Springsteen for the first time. Both
the stub and *Houston Post* review were published in *Backstreets Magazine*
in 2010. I knew that night in '78 changed me, but it took a couple
of weeks thinking through it to understood how. I confess I'm a little
nervous about playing the Houston '78 Bootleg: House Cut DVD. I
was a 17-year-old high school senior in Sugar Land and had an older
cousin in Houston who had been preaching Bruce to me and to be
sure to see him any chance I could. For the most part, my concert-
going buddies had never heard of him and didn't care to pay $8
just to go see him play 'Born to Run.' Then KLOL (101FM), who
had 'The Fever' on regular rotation, began

playing cuts from
the new *Darkness
on the Edge of Town*
record. I instantly
liked the title track.
It was a completely
different, raw, angry,
and tough sound for
a guy whose eight-
track vinyl tape case
was packed with the
mainstream suspects
of the day. The
*Darkness on the Edge of
Town* eight-track was
added - enough ammo
for me to justify a
couple of $8.35
concert tickets.

A heart on fire for rock 'n' roll
— *Post photo by Jerry Click*

A few weeks before the show, KLOL simulcast the Fox Theater Atlanta show. I was able to record a handful of songs with a portable cassette recorder and microphone held up to the speaker in my room. Now I knew something special and unique was rolling towards Houston. I also remember a concert billboard on I-59 just outside the Summit. Within a couple of days of the show, build-up on the radio stated that it was the first time Bruce had sold out a full arena (17,000+) away from the East and West coasts.

My date that night was Kim. We had dinner at Luther's BBQ then headed to the Summit. Her crash course on Bruce took place between her house, Luther's, and the venue. Once inside, I saw the *Darkness* t-shirts for sale. I wanted one, but knew I'd have to buy one for Kim and didn't have enough money. We picked up a couple of beers and headed to our seats. As we waited for the lights to go down, I remember feeling a different type of electricity in the air to other concerts I had seen. People telling first-timers like me they were not going to believe what they were about to experience.

Just after 8.30pm, the house lights dropped and the place went nuts. They opened with 'Badlands' and 'Streets of Fire.' I remember telling myself after just the first four or five songs the band could leave now and this place would give them an encore. I'd seen Led Zeppelin, Aerosmith, Bad Company, Eagles, Journey and remember thinking those bands' entire shows didn't pack the energy and passion I'd just seen, heard, just from that opening.

> **❛If anybody came here to throw firecrackers or bottles, you can get the fuck out, OK?❜**

Bruce Springsteen

I remember Bruce and Clarence going into the crowd during 'Spirit In The Night.' I remember 'Thunder Road', 'Santa Claus' (I swear it snowed on Clarence – maybe the beer was kicking in), 'Fire', 'The Fever' and 'Because the Night.' I remember the sound being 10 times better than any concert I'd heard. Bruce's guitar solos and vocals were crystal-clear. I remember thinking Bruce's vocals alone were a musical instrument. I also remember Kim had a curfew and we had to leave after the 'Tenth Avenue' encore.

The next morning, I bolted out of bed for the newspaper to find the review, which I have saved. It was the perfect review, truly capturing the performance and the crowd's ecstatic energy. I returned to Dulles High on Monday and tried to explain to concert-going pals what I had discovered and what they'd missed. My most often-used phrase became, 'Yeah, but you have to see him live.' I did my best to get the word out, writing 'Springsteen Live' on my book covers and on every high school desk I sat at for the rest of the year. Each morning I'd pull into the high school parking lot in my '74 Gran Torino blasting *Darkness* songs from my 6x9 Jensens.

Unquestionably, that night would recalibrate my appreciation of music and live music for the rest of my life. It was the finest musical experience of my life. It made me a Bruce fan to this day. But the most valuable lesson I learned that night in Houston was the 'power of discovery' and that the best live music and songwriters are not always mainstream. I soon left most 'arena acts' behind in search of other 'discoveries.' I stumbled across the Joe Ely Band one night in 1981 at Nick's Uptown in Dallas. His intense energy and stage presence was the closest I'd seen to Bruce, his high-energy shows perfect at filling the 'void' between Bruce tours. It's these discoveries for me – Joe, the late Stephen Bruton, Alejandro Escovedo, Dave Alvin, Tom Russell, Terry Allen, Robert Earl Keen, and others, that allowed me to escape a few hours a night on countless nights the last 32 years to truly appreciate live music and a well-written song. It's these discoveries that are a piece of my core and have shaped my musical fabric. It is these discoveries that are the direct result and ultimate reward of that Friday night with Bruce Springsteen at the Houston Summit.

> ❮ At every date he goes out
> and sits in every section of the hall
> to listen to the sound. And if it
> isn't right, even in the last row, I hear
> about it and we make changes ❯

Bruce Jackson, sound engineer; 1978

SEATTLE CENTER ARENA

20 DECEMBER 1978 SEATTLE, WASHINGTON

I WAS THERE: DAN EVANS JR

I first started listening to
Bruce Springsteen and
the E Street Band in high
school around 1977, and
in 1978 I saw my first
two shows. They came
through Seattle in June
and played the Paramount
Theater (capacity 3,000)
- a great introduction to a
Springsteen concert, three
hours long with lots of new
material from *Darkness on the
Edge of Town*, released earlier
that month. However, it was
a show six months later that
has stayed with me.

On December 20th, they

were back in Seattle at the Center Arena (capacity 5,000), their last show before a Christmas break. A few days earlier they played San Francisco Winterland, broadcast in its entirety over many FM stations – including one in Seattle. I listened to and taped it, so had a good idea what they might play.

I distinctly remember that after the encore we were slowly making our way out hoping they might come back. After about 20 minutes the band did, with all the roadies and the house lights on, to collectively play and sing 'Rave On!' and 'Twist and Shout' to about 200–300 fans. They had been touring non-stop since May and you could tell everyone was excited for the Christmas break.

I've been fortunate to see him many times in venues big and small over the years, from that first show in 1978 to Springsteen on Broadway in January 2018. Over the years, his words and music have helped guide me, energize me, remind me, and undoubtedly delivered its share of happiness and sadness to many life events.

Looking back, some shows were better than others. As I sit here today I know what really mattered as a fan, is that he emptied the tank for us each and every time. As I walked away from each show selfishly longing for more, I never felt empty. I remember some shows better than others and for as long as I am here I'll never forget that night in 1978, standing on a rickety folding chair, watching the band and crew have so much fun playing those two covers to a small group of fans who wanted 'just one more.'

COLISEUM AT RICHFIELD

31 DECEMBER 1978 RICHFIELD, OHIO

I WAS THERE: DAVID MILES

I first heard Bruce on WMMS in Cleveland when *Born to Run* was released. I bought the album and it remains one of my all-time favourites. I have all his albums now - some vinyl, some CD. I used to have an eight-track too.

I first saw Bruce and the E Street Band on New Year's Eve '78,

when I was 19, at the Richfield Coliseum. This was also the home venue for the Cleveland Cavaliers. I lived in Akron, Ohio, so the drive was short. I vividly remember the band played 'Santa Claus Is Coming to Town', with Clarence on sax.

I saw the band again on August 7, 1985 at Cleveland Municipal Stadium, home to the Cleveland Indians and Cleveland Browns at the time. This was the Born in the U.S.A. tour and the band played three hours, the stadium packed. I remember how buff Bruce looked compared to 1978.

1979

THE FAST LANE

14 MARCH 1979 ASBURY PARK, NEW JERSEY

I WAS THERE: PAUL REITZ

My other favourite Bruce performance was not a scheduled show. It was March 14, 1979 with Robert Gordon headlining at an Asbury Park club called The Fast Lane. Since Robert had a hit with 'Fire' and a show in Asbury Park, a 'Bruce Alert' went out. Bruce Alerts were passed among music friends when there was a strong possibility that Bruce would make a surprise appearance at a show.

Sure enough the alert rang true and Bruce joined Robert on stage for 'Fire' and 'Heartbreak Hotel.' One would think this would be the highlight of the evening, but no; there was one more thing that topped his live performance - Bruce stepping up to the bar next to my friends and I. He spent some time talking and having a shot of

Jack Daniel's with us. I thought this was my chance, grabbing a Fast Lane flyer, which I asked him to sign. I have it to this day.

Next time I saw Bruce was at his first headline show at Madison Square Garden, New York City on August 21, 1978. At that point, he was well on his way to becoming the force in music he is today.

MADISON SQUARE GARDEN

23 SEPTEMBER 1979 NEW YORK CITY

I WAS THERE: BARBARA QUINN

The first time I saw Bruce in concert was at the No Nukes Concert in 1979 at Madison Square Garden. What a thrilling night. He leaped and also crouched on the floor along with Clarence, still playing. He also sang with Jackson Browne and Tom Petty.

The energy rush is incomparable. You become a disciple in the church of rock'n'roll. I also saw him at Boston Garden and Meadowlands and at the Paramount in Asbury Park.

His music and those concerts moved me to write my latest novel; *The Summer Springsteen's Songs Saved Me*, a tribute to the healing power of Bruce's music. Each chapter is titled with a Springsteen song, that song woven into the fabric of the chapter. It takes place in Bradley Beach and Asbury Park, Springsteen country, and follows the journey of a woman learning to accept the past and embrace the future.

Bruce singing 'Devil with a Blue Dress On' and having Jackson Browne join him on 'Stay' at No Nukes were memorable. There was also a point where Bruce then Clarence climbed on the speakers behind Max on the drums.

I was 29 when I attended that concert - about the same age as Springsteen, who went into a patter about having a 30-year-old heart that wouldn't allow him to continue. But of course, he did.

I became a Springsteen fan in 1973 when we were living in the San Francisco area. A law school buddy of my husband's, a part-time DJ and from Jersey, brought over Bruce's first album. We were blown away and continue to be awed. We went to Springsteen on Broadway recently and were touched and amazed at his ability to constantly push the envelope of entertainment, taking his talent into new areas.

I WAS THERE: MARILYN BABCOCK

I saw him at the Muse Concert, Madison Square Garden, New York City. It was his birthday and someone gave him a cake on stage, which he threw into the crowd.

1980 The River Tour opened at the Crisler Arena, Ann Arbor, Michigan, on October 3, 1980 and saw Springsteen playing 140 shows in support of fifth studio album *The River*. For the only time in his career, he opened some concerts with his signature song, 'Born to Run.' At the very first Ann Arbor show, he was famously struck dumb, forgetting the words.

A couple of Springsteen concert traditions began during this tour. Near the end of 'Sherry Darling', Springsteen pulled a young female out of the front rows and danced with her on stage; this practice becoming famous when he did it on the Born in the U.S.A. tour during 'Dancing in the Dark.'

The most famous of the dates on the tour was probably the New Year's Eve 1980 show at Nassau Coliseum on Long Island, New York. With a set-list of 38 songs, it's one of the longest Springsteen shows of all time.

KIEL OPERA HOUSE

17 OCTOBER 1980 ST. LOUIS, MISSOURI

I WAS THERE: JANE SCHAPIRO

The February 1981 issue of *Musician* magazine has Bruce Springsteen on the cover and carries a 12-page interview, the rock star discussing his music, concerts, and experience with fame. I keep a page of this interview in my desk drawer so I can take it out every so often. It's the page where the interviewer asks Bruce, his popularity rapidly growing, if he can still walk down the street without being recognized. Springsteen responds with a story:

'The other night I went out. Went to the movies by myself, walked in, got my popcorn. This guy comes up to me, real nice guy. He says, 'Listen, you want to sit with me and my sister?' I say, 'All right.' So we watch the movie [laughs]. It was great, too, because it was that Woody Allen movie *Stardust Memories*, about a famous director who's beleaguered by his fans and this poor kid says, 'Jesus, I don't know what to say to ya. Is that the way it is? Is that how you feel?' I say, 'No, I don't feel like that so much.' And he had the amazing courage to come up to me at the end of the movie and ask if I'd go home and meet his mother and father. I said, 'What time is it?' It was eleven o'clock, so I said, 'Well, OK.''

Steve with his house guest Bruce Springsteen

So I go home with him; he lives out in some suburb. So we get over to the house, and here's his mother and father, laying out on the couch, watching TV and reading the paper. He brings me in, and he says, 'Hey, I got Bruce Springsteen here.' And they don't believe him. So he pulls me over, and he says, 'This is Bruce Springsteen.' 'Aw, g'wan,' they say. So he runs in his room and brings out an album, and he holds it up to my face. And his mother says [breathlessly], 'Oh yeah!' She starts yelling, 'Yeah!' She starts screaming.'

And for two hours I was in this kid's house, talking with these people. They were really nice. They cooked me up all this food, watermelon, and the guy gave me a ride back to my hotel a few hours later.'

Springsteen got most of the details right, except for the city: he thought it was Denver, Colorado, but it was St. Louis, Missouri. And though it's true that the mother didn't believe he was Bruce Springsteen, it wasn't the album cover that convinced her. Only after she'd examined Springsteen's American Express card did she finally accept his identity. But all the rest is true; especially regarding the 'real nice guy' who invited Springsteen to sit with him and his sister then took him home and served him watermelon. That guy was my friend Steve.

Steve and I were both raised in the heavily Jewish, upper-middle-class suburb of Ladue. We went to the same elementary school, but we weren't friends then. Steve was popular and known for his jokes. I was a shy girl who had only one close friend. In the spring of our sixth-grade year, Steve was absent for several weeks. Rumour had it that he was in the hospital. Finally, a teacher reported that Steve had diabetes. None of us really knew what this meant, but we passed the word diabetes back and forth like a medicine ball. When Steve returned, he looked the same as he had before, so we stopped talking about it.

In ninth grade Steve and I had adjacent lockers. Whenever I went to deposit my books, I'd see him holding court with a group of people, going on and on in mock seriousness about, say, the difference between a Steak 'n Shake Steakburger and a Dairy

Queen Brazier Burger. For Steve, daily existence consisted of a series of absurdities, and his role was to expose them. He poked fun at everyone and everything, including himself. His disarming and self-effacing humour transcended the social divisions in high school, and everyone from the jocks to the debate-clubbers stopped by his locker for a bit of banter.

Of all the subjects Steve liked to expound on, music was his favourite. His father owned a music store in north St. Louis, and Steve knew every band, singer, and song on the rock scene. I, on the other hand, listened to only the top ten on KXOK. I even had a poster of teen idol David Cassidy on the door of my locker. Every time Steve passed me in the hall, he'd belt out Cassidy's Partridge Family hit 'I Think I Love You' with exaggerated emotion.

I was drawn into Steve's inner circle and soon began spending time with him after school and on weekends. We played in pickup softball and soccer games, cruised around in his red Bonneville convertible listening to music on his eight-track-tape player, and in the winter went sledding on Mrs Cave's hill. Nobody had ever set eyes on Mrs Cave, and rumours circulated about her: Widow? Spinster? Witch? One night, standing at the bottom of her hill, we noticed a lamp burning in her third-floor window. 'Go on,' Steve dared me. 'Knock.'

It was there, with Mrs Cave's mansion looming behind us, that we first kissed. From that moment on, Steve and I were a couple. I never did knock on Mrs Cave's door.

In 1973 Bruce Springsteen released his first album, *Greetings from Asbury Park, N.J.*, and Steve bought a copy. 'You've got to hear this guy,' he would tell anyone who stopped by his locker. Most of us didn't get it. Springsteen was not singing typical pop or rock songs. He was narrating long, rambling stories about growing up on mean streets that could not have been more different from our manicured cul-de-sacs. Granted, his stories were packed with colourful characters, but his music was a far cry from the fluff that The Carpenters and others were offering on the radio. 'Blinded by the Light' came the closest to something we could snap our fingers to, and still we'd get lost in its winding lyric. Except for

Steve. He memorized every word to every Springsteen song. I can still see him driving and singing 'For You,' his face pinched and red. Springsteen's restless yearning spoke to him. Perhaps this should have been my first clue that Steve had his own restlessness brewing beneath the surface.

After high-school graduation Steve and I headed in different directions, but we remained close. I went to a small school in Colorado. Steve enrolled in Macalester College in St. Paul, Minnesota. We talked often that first year, and in the Spring he hitchhiked to Colorado and surprised me with a visit. We never defined the rules of our relationship while living apart, but it was obvious that neither of us was ready to call it quits. When we returned to St. Louis that first summer, we resumed our usual pastimes, which included my listening to Steve sing along to Springsteen albums. *Born to Run* had just come out, so he had a whole new repertoire. As Springsteen's fame grew, the singer gave no sign of selling out. 'He's really a nice guy,' Steve told me again and again. This fact was important to him.

In the spring of my sophomore year in college, I squeezed into the phone booth at the end of the dormitory hall and listened as Steve spoke to me from Israel, where he'd gone over spring break. Between the bad connection and the noise in my dorm, I could hear only bits and pieces. The gist of it was that he was not returning to school after spring break. He wanted to stay and study under the auspices of a program called Aish HaTorah (Fire of the Torah). Founded in 1974 by the American rabbi Noah Weinberg, Aish HaTorah began as a learning center whose activities included reaching out to wandering Jewish souls and delivering them back to their roots via study and observance of ritual.

I had never considered Steve a wandering soul, and the idea of him wanting to immerse himself in religious study seemed absurd. Surely his cynicism would prevent him from committing wholeheartedly to the irrational demands of religion. Then again, I realized, it can be difficult to live a life in which one's only sacred belief is that nothing is sacred.

In our correspondence Steve began referring to God as 'G-d' and 'Hashem,' and Israel as the 'Promised Land.' His letters were sprinkled with Hebrew and signed with his new name: Shlomo Zalmon. Most disturbing to me was the absence of any words of affection. I got a queasy feeling that I was losing him to a competitor far more daunting than any college coed.

Steve - or Shlomo - finally returned after finishing his studies in the yeshiva. Bearded and wearing a hat and a tallit with the traditional fringes (tzitziot) hanging at his sides, he backed away when I stepped forward to hug him. (Orthodox Jewish men are forbidden to touch any woman but their wife.) That single gesture marked the end of our relationship, as I had known it.

At first, I tried arguing Steve out of his new-found faith, but he was unshakable, and the distance between us grew. Then I adopted a different approach: Perhaps if I found my own faith, the two of us could stay together. If nothing else, I might understand Steve's transformation better. And maybe an Orthodox life would provide me with the same answers he had found. I spent a year walking to an Orthodox synagogue every Sabbath, learning Hebrew and the prayers, and practicing the daily rituals. I even studied Torah with a Rabbi. But invariably I'd come up against a rule that I just did not get. (Why couldn't I tear toilet paper on the Sabbath?) It wasn't that I didn't understand Orthodox Judaism; it was that I couldn't accept it. In order to observe the 613 mitzvot, or commandments, one has to have faith that every word of the Torah is God-given. It was I, and not Steve, who was too cynical.

Still green in his devotion, Steve tried to convince me this was the right way for every Jew to live. He pushed, I pulled, and we finally came to an unspoken acceptance of each other's choices. We would still be friends. We just wouldn't touch.

Steve made many other changes in his life: He kept kosher. (Because his family wasn't observant, this meant eating all his meals on disposable Styrofoam plates.) On Friday nights he slept at Orthodox families' homes. And since listening to female singers was prohibited, his musical tastes narrowed. But Springsteen, with his all-male E Street Band, remained OK.

In October 1980 Springsteen was scheduled to perform two nights at the Kiel Opera House in St. Louis. Steve got tickets to the sold-out Saturday show from a connection through the family's music store. The Thursday before the concert Steve called to ask if I wanted to accompany his sister and him to see *Stardust Memories*. I don't remember why I said no. I think I just didn't feel like going to a Woody Allen movie. This, of course, was the movie where Steve saw Bruce Springsteen standing at the concession counter with a rolled newspaper under his arm.

Steve told me later that, when he realized Springsteen had come alone to the theater, he thought, maybe he wants company. What do I have to lose? I will never get this chance again. So he approached him, and they ended up sitting together. While watching the movie, Steve began to feel guilty: Was he the sort of obnoxious fan the film depicted? Springsteen assured him that it wasn't the case; in fact, he was enjoying himself. Steve relaxed, and when the movie was over, he offered to drive Springsteen back to the hotel. First, though, he wanted to introduce him to his parents.

What Springsteen did not mention in that *Musician* interview is that while they were in the car, Steve, with his felt hat and his tzitziot dangling down the sides of his jeans, slipped a bootleg tape of one of Springsteen's concerts into his eight-track player and began to sing. At one point he turned to Springsteen in the passenger seat and asked him to help out with the chorus. For those of us who had spent countless hours in Steve's front seat, listening to him sing Springsteen songs, this is the best part of the story.

When Steve and his sister walked into their parents' house with Bruce Springsteen in tow, they found their father sprawled on the couch in a sleeveless undershirt and slippers, watching television. Their mother was sitting at the kitchen table in a housedress. In high school Steve's mother had been known as 'the short mom with the big mouth.' She was funny and generous, but she was not afraid to speak her mind, and she refused to believe that this man standing in her living room was Bruce Springsteen. So she made him pull out his wallet and show her his credit cards. After that, they talked, and she served him watermelon. 'You seem like a nice boy,' she told him, and she asked if he was a good son. He told her about his family and, as he was leaving, asked if she wouldn't mind calling his mom in California and telling her that he was doing fine. (Because this request sounds so un-celebrity-like, I called Steve's mother recently to confirm it. It's true: she did call Springsteen's mother, and for the next couple of years they corresponded through cards).

Steve invited Springsteen to Sabbath dinner the following night and told him to bring his band mates - especially his Jewish drummer, Max Weinberg. But they had to play their first concert at the Kiel Opera House that Friday night. Springsteen did, however, give Steve a dozen tickets and backstage passes to his Saturday-night performance.

In the *Musician* interview, Springsteen concludes the story this way: 'And I went back to that hotel and felt really good because I thought, 'Wow (almost whispering), what a thing to be able to do. What an experience to be able to have, to be able to step into some stranger's life.' '

Steve invited me, and a group of his friends to accompany him to the concert. We were sceptical of his story at first. It's not that we didn't trust Steve. Maybe we just couldn't believe that, every once in a while, life could actually meet our expectations: a fan can meet his favourite singer, and that singer can turn out to be a really nice guy.

Sitting in the center of the concert floor, we sang and clapped, but, as much fun as we were having, we were still waiting for proof of Steve's story. As it turned out, we didn't have to wait long. Midway through the concert, Springsteen leaned into the microphone and dedicated the next song to his new friend Steve.

When the concert was over, we all hurried backstage, and I shook Springsteen's hand and mumbled something about enjoying the show. The rest is a blur. I remember sticking my hand in a jar of M&M's on the way out.

After that Steve's life resumed its inevitable uneven course. His father died the following year, and not too much later Steve began to struggle with his diabetes. In and out of the hospital, he underwent dialysis, a kidney transplant, a heart bypass, and eye surgery. On October 11, 2003, Steve died. The last time I saw him, he was completely worn down, but he never wavered in his religious faith.

I still think of that night when Springsteen dedicated a number to Steve in front of thousands of concertgoers. The song was 'The Promised Land.' Sometimes even worldly moments can be holy.

MEMORIAL COLISEUM

25 OCTOBER 1980 PORTLAND, OREGON

I WAS THERE: ROBBIE OSBOURN

It was October 1980, about six months after the Mount St. Helens eruption. He talked to the crowd, saying something like 'I heard that mountain has been throwing some ash down on you.' He then went into a rousing rendition of 'On Top of Old Smoky.' There is audio of him on YouTube.

I was a 21-year old senior at the University of Oregon. It was about a 110-mile journey from Eugene to the Memorial Coliseum in Portland. We had rented a room in what then was the Holiday Inn, just across from the venue. We staged a party there, going all out. We had 1 keg of Heineken, and a keg of Lowenbrau. The cost was substantial, but we felt worth the effort.

This was pretty epic. The Boss had been on an upward arc, thanks to the covers of *Time* and *Newsweek*. In addition, his past three releases were widening his fan base. This concert was in support of *The River*, and this was early into that tour. It was a great show, and 'Jungleland' was transcendental. That song ranks among my top three live performances (with Bob Seger's 'Turn the Page' and Hall & Oates' 'Man Eater'). I'd see him again in 2000, with my two sisters, the only concert we attended together.

SPORTS ARENA

3 NOVEMBER 1980 LOS ANGELES, CALIFORNIA

I WAS THERE: TOM TICE

In 1980 I'd been a huge fan of Springsteen for a couple of years. I'd heard the legendary Roxy show on KMET while driving around with a date on a Friday night. Impressed with the radio show, on a whim we drove to San Diego and saw him that following Sunday, tickets at the door $5.75.

So, when he returned to L.A. on The River tour, I was thrilled to grab a floor seat for the fourth of the shows at the Sports Arena.

Before, I went to the backstage entrance and began chatting with the guard there, just general stuff. It was just curtained off and I could see the buzz of activity going on. So, I hung out hoping to catch of glimpse of the band. As we chatted, I stressed how excited I was about the show and how I'd been looking forward to it for weeks. Finally, I asked, 'Any chance of getting back there?' He said he couldn't make any promises, but to come back at the break and he'd let me know.

The show was one of the legendary ones of an artist and band in their full prime. Even years later thinking about the story he told about his Dad (which was personal and universal at the same time), and then the musical transition from 'Independence Day' into 'Factory,' brings a lump to my throat. Finally, he stopped for a break at the point many bands would have been finished.

I went over to see my new friend, and as I approached he gave me a nod and a smile, then made a great show of turning his back and looking off into the distance. In a flash I'd snuck backstage, for the first and only time.

Now, what does one do when they are backstage? I had no idea, so I milled about, tried to look like I belonged there and generally hung to the side. After a bit, the band came out of their dressing rooms and headed toward the stage, walking right past me. I edged over near the wings and watched them begin to play from my unique vantage point. There is a bit of stirring to my left and Flo and Eddie (of the Turtles) rushed past and were introduced as the band played 'Hungry Heart' (they'd sung back up on the album).

Then things go from amazing right into the realm of surreal.

I'm listening, keeping my head down and trying not to attract attention and I notice a pair of really fancy boots on the fellow standing beside me. They are tapping along to 'Hungry Heart' and whoever owns them seems to be digging the show as much as I am.

I raise my gaze and look to my right directly at Bob Dylan, now standing a foot away from me and who had apparently stepped closer as I was watching Flo and Eddie hit the stage to my left. I smile and try not to act like a complete idiot but I'm thinking 'Yeah right, I'm watching Springsteen and standing next to Bob Dylan. OK, when do I wake up?'

As the song ended, I step over to a nearby table and pick up a Wolf & Rissmiller meal voucher and quickly ask, 'Mr Dylan, might I have your autograph?' He graciously scribbles on to the back of the ticket then we both turn back to watch the show. After a while I edge away, pretty much in a daze, stop and thank my new best friend (a security guard whose name I never learned), then head back to my seat for the rest of a 30-song, three-or-so hour show.

I've seen Springsteen about 20 times, but nothing can match seeing the 'New Dylan' performing for the real Dylan at that show on the legendary River Tour.

MADISON SQUARE GARDEN

27 NOVEMBER 1980 NEW YORK CITY

I WAS THERE: MARY MACRIDES

I remember my first Bruce show like it was yesterday. December 1980, Madison Square Garden, Christmas. I have been a fan since the first time I heard Bruce and the E Street Band circa 1973. It was Christmas in New York; the night was full of magic. My boss gave me two tickets as a gift, and I was over the moon.

Bruce hit the stage on the shoulders of The Big Man, both in Santa hats. He played for almost four hours and I lost my voice singing along to every song. I have never experienced a live concert like this one and continued to see Bruce every time he toured for the next 40 years. I have never been disappointed. Bruce and the band touch my soul like no other. I laughed, cried and fell more in love than ever. I've been fortunate enough to see many great artists over the years. Not one has ever made me feel the way Bruce did and still does. Long live The Boss!

THE SPECTRUM

6, 8 & 9 DECEMBER 1980 PHILADELPHIA, PENNSYLVANIA

I WAS THERE: LEE DOYLE

I've been a fan since right before *Born to Run* was released. They were playing the song on the radio in Philly months before the album came out. I couldn't wait. Saw my first show in 1976. The Chicken Scratch Tour or Lawsuit Tour, depending who you talk to.

Many memorable shows over the years. One standout that I'll never be able to forget. I saw him at the Spectrum in 1980 during The River tour. I was with five friends. Wonderful show, high energy right to the very end as usual. After the show, we all piled into my Mercury Cougar to drive home. We turned on the radio and there was Beatles music playing. We bounced around the dial looking for a station playing some Bruce. Every station we turned to was playing Beatles. We wondered what the heck was going on. We settled on WMMR, our usual go to station. The next song was a John Lennon song. I'd like to say it was 'Imagine' but I'm pretty certain it wasn't. One of my friends in the back seat immediately gasped. She knew then that something bad had happened without hearing anything but songs. Right after that song the announcer came on and told us that John Lennon had died. It was December 8, 1980. We sat in silence, six of us packed into the car, until we got home. After dropping everyone off, the tears finally started rolling down my face.

One of the most amazing aspects of the show wasn't apparent until well after. This was in the days before cell phones, texting, social media, etc. Years later I read that Bruce learned about John Lennon's death during the break. He wasn't sure what to do. He knew that announcing it would devastate everyone in the building, so chose to go out and do his second set like nothing happened. Maybe he even worked a little harder, which is pretty difficult for a guy like Bruce, who puts so much into every show. But he got it done. Given there was very little chance that anyone in the arena would get the news until after the show was over, I believe he did the right thing. He played his heart out.

CIVIC CENTER

11 DECEMBER 1980 PROVIDENCE, RI

I WAS THERE: PAULA WHITNEY

I first became entranced with Bruce and his music when I was 13. I was sick with hepatitis and later developed GI diseases. The song 'Growin' Up' just grabbed me and pulled me into the character and story. This is true of all his music today. His music helped me deal with being in the hospital

Paula Whitney and husband Lew

a lot (almost 40 surgeries) and escape some of the pain (as well as pain
med). My favourite Bruce songs (so many) are 'Badlands', Ain't No Sin
to be Glad You're Alive', 'Janey Don't You Lose Heart', 'Born to Run',
'Thunder Road', 'Land of Hope and Dreams', 'Darkness on the Edge
of Town', 'Growin' Up'. Favourite Bruce album? Tough call – *Born to
Run, Live in New York City* and *Wrecking Ball.* Best concert? I've been to a
few so I'll tell you just three stories.

I was a teenager dating someone and my parents went away for the
weekend - yeah, I had a party! Anyway, I could not find my boyfriend
anywhere only to find him talking with some other chick.

He ended up taking her to the Bruce concert in Providence, RI,
where we lived at the time. At first, I was pissed, but then said, 'The
heck with it'. Those were the days you could still get a ticket the
same week. I told my Mom (sorry Mom) I was going with a group of
people. I drove down and got a ticket - I had the best time! I was 17.
Another couple I met who were 18 bought me a few beers that night
and I bought my first concert T-shirt, baseball style, with Clarence
and Bruce on the front.

Years later when I was married (I had been to a bunch of concerts
in between) my husband Lew and I bought tickets for his World
Acoustic Tour, which we saw at the Providence Performing Arts
Center. As luck would have it, I had my ears pierced for the second
time about a week before and my right ear became infected. The oral
antibiotics were not working. My right ear was huge, red, infected
and inflamed. I begged my husband to go and promised I would
go to the hospital the following morning. Cellulitis was running
down my neck by this point! I spent a month in the hospital on IV
antibiotics and pain meds - totally worth it.

I always told my husband he needed to see Bruce with the E Street
Band. We were living in Denver in 2009 when my sister generously
bought four tickets for my birthday that March and we saw him in
April during his Working on A Dream tour. I invited a friend and her
husband whom had never seen him. That day my poor husband Lew
had flu, 102' temperature, throwing up, GI symptoms. He sucked
it up and went. He's like the British gentleman in *Springsteen and I* -

wishes his concerts were shorter. He does like some of his music but gets more of a kick out of me going to concerts, seeing me go nuts.

We got to meet Jake Clemons in April 2014 in this total dive bar, pretty dark. My hubby and I are both disabled (it was standing only) so we asked for chairs. Sat three feet from Jake and the band. I had him sign my first Bruce concert shirt, but like an idiot didn't have him sign his CD & T-shirt. My dream one day is to be in the pit and be able to get up on stage and maybe somehow have the band sign my original T-shirt. That would be cool.

Paula Whitney meets Jake Clemons

BOSTON GARDEN

15 DECEMBER 1980 BOSTON, MASSACHUSETTS

I WAS THERE: DAVID ROCHE

The first time I saw Bruce was at Boston Garden, a week after John Lennon was shot and killed. You could hear a pin drop during 'Point Blank.' He also did 'I Fought the Law' at that show, and of course 'Santa Claus Is Coming to Town.' Magical night, with snow falling as we left.

I WAS THERE: CHIP TUTTLE

This was my first real show. I was 17 and a junior in high school with a couple of my friends. The band came on, 1-2-3-4, and ripped into 'Born to Run.' The old building shook. When the lights went up during the song, you could see what you already felt, 16,000 people packed together sharing the communal exuberance of the music. Three hours later, exhausted and wet, we shuffled out of the Garden amazed and appreciative of what we'd just experienced.

That was my first of about 20 shows. I've brought my wife, my kids and several others through the years so they could share the same infectious joy.

1981

MARKET SQUARE ARENA

5 MARCH 1981 INDIANAPOLIS, INDIANA

I WAS THERE: PAUL CHURCH

At the time Queen, Blondie, Air Supply, and Christopher Cross dominated the airwaves. Disco was dying and The Clash was becoming the only band that mattered.

Central Indiana liked rock'n'roll, gravitating to REO Speedwagon, Bob Seger and Johnny Cougar. I first heard 'Hungry Heart' and took a gamble, dropping $12 on a double disc ($40 today). It owned me. We had to see this guy who only existed in *Circus*, *Rolling Stone*, and *Crawdaddy* to me.

The original show for February 9 was moved back to March 5. This was fine because it went from a Monday to a Thursday, the first

day of the weekend at Ball State. Market Square was 30 miles south of Muncie. Typically, the air was smoke-filled.

The second song, 'Out in The Street' blew my mind. He crowd-surfed. In the crowd I feel at home. Sax and harmonica on 'Promised Land' brought you to your knees.

After the intermission it was 'Cadillac Ranch.' Big cowboy hats and the guitars at center stage, rocking in unison. 'Ramrod' was a ball, I believe he ran across the stage and slid through Clarence' legs.

Our hands were throbbing and swollen, our voices were gone.

As long as 'Born to Run' was still on the shelf, we knew he wasn't done.

Encore 'Jungleland' provided an opportunity to pee during the extended solo. 'Born to Run', voices back, hands still sore, brilliant performance with 1981 technology, flashing house lights. 'I can't do anymore' he said after lying on the floor. 'OK, one more' – 'Detroit Medley.'

We stumbled out of that smoke-filled room completely numb but thrilled that we had seen this skinny dude give US his all until we couldn't take anymore.

I saw him twice in '84 and '85, once at Market Square Arena and once at Hoosier Dome. He was big time then, bulked up and with high expectations. Of course, he met them. But as glad as I am that there's no video to diminish my memory of 1981, I'd love to see THAT guy again.

FRANKFURT FESTHALLE

14 APRIL 1981 FRANKFURT, WEST GERMANY

I WAS THERE: DAN FRENCH

When Bruce Springsteen and the E Street Band toured Europe in
the spring of 1981 to support *The River*, I was living in London, out
of work, with only a home-made fanzine *Point Blank* to my name. I
had time on my hands but was broke. I hitch-hiked most places and
slept on friends' floors and sofas. Selling a few fanzines meant I could
buy basic necessities to live on, or occasionally stretch to the luxury
of a train ticket, and in a few months had already bought me some
good friends and many pen-pals I'd never met. When the UK tour
was postponed by a couple of months, so the European leg started
on the Continent rather than in Britain, I thought I'd have to wait for
my first Springsteen concert. I was wrong.

After spending from December 1980 to March 1981 collecting
tickets for his UK shows and the postponement news, I got a letter
from German pen-pal Rena with a note saying, 'See you at the
Canadian Pacific Hotel, Frankfurt, 13 April'. Enclosed was a side
balcony ticket for Frankfurt Festhalle the next day.

My friend John H had been promised a ticket for a Paris show and
was going to stay with a

friend there. I arranged to meet him there at Easter and get tickets for various friends. Tipped off as to the expected date and place of sale, I hitched there but found no trace of tickets at the box office or supposed venue.

The only indication that Bruce was coming to Europe at all was a window display of singles and posters in a Metro subway: 'Bruce Springsteen en France'. But I was told the tickets had all sold before I even arrived. Disheartened at disappointing my friends, I splashed out on a train to Frankfurt, giving up hitching after hours wasted, arriving late on the 13th. Tired and bleary, I was overjoyed to see a huge red sign outside the Festhalle - 'Bruce Springsteen and the E Street Band, 14th April.' At last.

Across the street was the Canadian Pacific hotel: huge, modern and expensive. A self-conscious tramp, I asked at the reception for Rena. A phone call to her room showed she was out, so I left a note: gone to sleep in the park (I couldn't afford a room). However, just around the corner from the lobby, Rena was waiting in the bar, copies of my fanzine *Point Blank* displayed. And who should then wander in but the E Street Band, staying in the same luxury hotel, buying Max a drink for his birthday. Clarence saw Rena and being a gent, sat with her, put his arm around her and boomed, 'Hey, little girl, are you married?' So there's Rena, sat between Clarence and Bruce, surrounded by the band, celebrating. And there's yours truly huddled in a sleeping bag under a tree near an ornamental lake.

Several drinks later, Rena finds my note, saying to Clarence: 'Hey, we've got to go find Dan in the park.' They rush round the park, looking for me, shouting 'Dan French, come out tonight!' Guess who slept through it all.

At nine the next morning, even more dazed and bleary, I call Rena again and go up to her room and meet her for the first time. 'Dan! Come on, we have to go and wake Clarence.' Uh-huh. Clarence? Clarence! Can it be? Are they here? Another door. She knocks, and eventually a deep, sleepy voice answers. It's dark inside. There's a huge guy gripping my hand warmly. It's him. I'm speechless, knees shaking. Clarence has a terrible hangover and can't face the daylight.

'I had such a bad dream, baby' he moans, 'Thanks for waking me.'
More handshakes, and he flops on the bed. We have breakfast in the
hotel, spotting Max and various crew. I begin to wake up and realise
what's happening.

After a leisurely morning we go back to CC's room to wake
him again at midday, first knocking on a door marked 'Do Not
Disturb' which Rena calls at: 'Bruce. Bruce?' No reply. Clarence is
as glad to see us as if we'd been long-departed friends, but still not
fully awake. About 2 o'clock, he finally gets up on our third visit,
slowly gets washed and dressed. Larger than life, twice as natural.
What a start to the day.

Around four or five, leaving Clarence with Glen, his personal
manager, to sort his stage clothes, we wait in the lobby with some
US roadies. A girl from CBS Germany checks details on a clipboard.
Rena introduces me to Barbara Carr, Jon Landau's assistant.

Gradually, the whole band filters in with various girlfriends, wives
and crew. 'There he is,' says Rena, pointing. Who? That guy with
dark glasses and a leather jacket over his shoulder? It's Bruce. I had
to look twice to make sure. They stand near the exit, waiting for
the King. Clarence makes his grand entrance at last, and they're
ready to soundcheck. Rena and I walk out with CC and the band
to a minibus. Let's walk, they say. It's just over the road. I'm within
a couple of feet of Bruce as we climb security fencing near the
entrance. Bruce jumps over and drops his jacket, which I pick up and
pass to him, saying: 'Able to leap tall buildings at a single bound.'
'Right,' he mutters, pre-occupied. We come to the security limit and
Clarence takes us in with him and the band.

The Festhalle seems huge. Only 4,000 seats? Two balconies, a
figure-eight shape. Glen tells us, 'You better have these. Stop you
getting questioned.' Two backstage passes. 'You got tickets? Have
these instead.' Row 14, stalls. Thanks, Glen! 'You're welcome. Keep
off the stage now.' As Bruce walks around the hall, the band's on
stage. Roy's crystal-clear intro to 'Hungry Heart' sounds perfect.
Rena takes photos, despite being told not to. I sit front-row centre in
the empty seats, hardly believing what's happening.

An awkward moment when a merchandise guy tells me to stop
giving away magazines, fearing it might affect programme sales. I'm
too happy to argue. They're all playing now apart from Bruce, who's
circling the balconies with Bruce Jackson. 'Prove It All Night', and
Bruce joins on guitar then vocals – serious-faced but magnificent,
effortless, in his element. After one and a half to two hours he's
satisfied and it's back to the dressing rooms. The kids are building
up outside, the armed police look alarming. Harry Sandler, road
manager, gives the band Dutch editions of *The River*. 'Fainter blue
sleeve,' I say to Roy. Yes, he nods.

We're in Clarence's room with him and Glen when Bruce, tense
with hunched shoulders, wanders in. I offer him the seat, Glen waves
us out: Bruce wants to talk to the Big Man. Time to find our seats.
Hey, there's Mike H, over on the Mead Gould coach trip, and other
familiar faces. Lots of American GIs (a base nearby). The excitement
is electric. From a hum to a buzz then a roar as the lights go down.
Talk about adrenaline rush – we're up and on our chairs before we
know it. Out of the noise drones the organ whine of 'Factory'. This
is it. It's really happening, living a dream. I don't know if the show
was good or not – I didn't care – nothing could go wrong. I scribbled
the initials of the songs down, yelled myself hoarse and dry.

After, Rena and I went backstage: I took a couple of
programmes and a badge. Exhausted, elated and parched, we
waited at least an hour in a room outside the dressing room. No
drink or food to be had. Various people were waiting for Bruce,
including a German reporter who interviewed Jon Landau, who
stressed, 'no tape interviews'. After an age Bruce wandered out,
leather-jacketed, hair slicked back, grinning and fresher than
before the show. He greeted friends and well-wishers, spoke to a
reporter briefly. At last he turned, about to go, and walked to us.
He looked at Rena and me, his eyes dark but somehow glazed.
I grabbed my moment, stuck out my hand: 'Hi, Bruce!' Rena
said: 'This is the guy who does the magazine.' 'Oh yeah? Where
are you from?' London, I said, feeling dumb. I remembered
the souvenirs, and asked: 'Could you sign these for a couple of

friends? They have to catch a bus home.' 'Sure.' He signs the poster centrefolds. I gave him a Point Blank leaflet – all the paper I had on me. 'This is for me'. He wrote: 'To Dan – thanks for your support. Say hello to everyone for me, Bruce.' I gave him the badge: 'Some girl wanted you to have this.' He shook hands again and waved goodbye with a smile. 'I'll see you in Britain, if not before!' I called. Bruce nodded and was gone, hungry but willing to sign more autographs for fans outside. Rena and I left him to it after I returned the programmes to Mike and Kev and said goodbye, and we went back to the hotel.

Next morning, we had a late breakfast, took photos outside, and left – but not before I encountered Roy and asked for a scribble. 'Sure,' he smiled. 'Take it easy.' No one else was there. We took a train back to Rena's in Mannheim, I met her neighbours, Hubert and Ilona, and the next day went into town to eat and visit her friend's hi-fi shop. In the afternoon she called some hotels in Munich until she found Clarence in the Hilton, asking if she and three friends could come to the show tonight. Sure, said the Big Man, ask Glen for tickets when you come. Hubert drove Ilona, Rena and I 200km to Munich, reaching the Olympiahalle just before eight, found Glen.

There was a different feel from Frankfurt – moody. Early into the show the crowd surged into a space near the front and Bruce had to stop before introducing 'Independence Day', asking people to go back to their seats. Rena and I moved from the guest rows on the side down into the stalls where there was room to stand and dance.

As it was the last night in Germany, there was a big reception backstage, and we took the chance to eat and spot Roy, Max, Danny, Garry and Clarence mingling. Bruce and Steve didn't show. We spent a while hunting for dressing-rooms backstage, but no luck. So we drove to CC's hotel, went to his room, and he welcomed us with champagne. We sat and listened to his latest recordings on 'Dedication': 'That's me!' he'd say, on a sax solo. His other cassettes included the Fabulous Thunderbirds and Stevie Wonder. Rena took photos and got Ilona and Hubert to take some.

We stayed a couple of hours. Clarence offered us rooms at the

Hilton, but the others had to go to work the next day, so we drove back in the wee hours and left CC to travel to Paris the next day. It was light when we got back to Mannheim, and I slept until the afternoon. We ate, played records and watched videos. Rena couldn't go to Paris, so I tried to hitch from the outskirts of town, giving up after a long wait, cold and restless. I took a train again and slept rough once more. Good Friday, I think it was.

I found the address where John H was staying before the show that night, and once again felt like a tramp at the posh block of apartments. It was a relief to speak English to a familiar face, sitting on a sunny balcony having coffee. We agreed - although I didn't have a ticket to wander to the Palais de Sports on the northside of town, have a look around. We walked from the Metro over the bridge of the river to the odd-shaped sports hall rising on the far banks.

No sign of any posters or ads for the show, but we walked up the drive as far as we could, found a small box-office. Inside, a little old lady was opening envelopes containing tickets for both shows! I borrowed money from John (it took me six months to repay) and we bought tickets. We couldn't believe our luck. I was going to see Bruce twice more. We waited for our friends, a queue building up in the late afternoon, trickling in from town across the bridge.

We queued as the sun went down. Around five, a couple of vans came up the drive past us, greeted by cheers and waving. They had to drive slowly up the narrow road we were partly blocking, and I had a good view of a smiling Clarence and Bruce. They waved, and I'm sure Bruce's face showed recognition. Soon we heard the familiar booming echo of 'Hungry Heart' and 'Prove It All Night.' Around seven they opened the gates and we filed in, looking at the hall, trying the outrageously-priced drinks and snacks. To the right and back of the stalls were steps, like an amphitheatre, and large windows to the right. To the left was a raised section of guest seats, filled with familiar people, a roped-off enclosure.

We went back to our seats, near the back of the stalls. We agreed to sit where we were for the first half, then go down the aisle near the front for the second set. When the lights went down, we rushed as far forward as we could, as did a lot of others. Before long the crowd was crushing together, people wedged against the loose, folding chairs, which were snapping like matches and being passed out over the sea of fans to the roadies at the side of the stage. Geoff and I were stuck in the middle. After what seemed like ages, there was the hum of the intro to 'Factory', and it was show time.

After both nights I hitched back to a small hotel with Geoff and Kristina; one night we got as far as the band's hotel with a couple of crew, then went on to our hotel. We sneaked out in the mornings since they'd only booked for two. The worst thing about each night was the crush, before and during the show. The second night they wisely took the remaining chairs out, but it seemed fuller. I recall the familiar organ intro turning not into 'Factory' but a strange new song about dreams. And both nights we were treated to the first plays of 'Can't Help Falling In Love', which I recognised from the Stylistics' version and fell in love with, especially the

Breath-taking way it faded to the kick-start of 'Born to Run.'

During 'Hungry Heart', the crowd sang *'Everybody's got a hungry heart'* for all four lines of the chorus, and in 'Thunder Road', there was a faint response to Bruce's invitation to sing *'You ain't a beauty but hey you're alright'* – the language barrier wasn't so obvious in Germany. 'You gotta practice,' joked Bruce the first time, and 'Close!' the second night! I thought I'd take off with delight when the medley ground to its usual halt only to be followed with '*Do you like good music?' Yeah! Yeah!'* Still a favourite. And in the medley on the second night we got 'High School Confidential'. What a thrill. Despite a nasty scene outside when three American girls and other fans waiting to talk to Bruce after the show only to be warned off by armed guards and guard dogs, those were my favourite two shows of the four. I told a 'little gorilla' roadie, 'The French guys don't seem to understand – we always get allowed to wait for Bruce after a show.' He said, 'You don't seem to understand – this is a foreign country, and while we're here we have to follow the local rules.' The three girls were close to tears. But we all had to leave.

On Easter Sunday I hitched back to London, wishing I could have gone on to Barcelona, Lyon, Brussels, Rotterdam, but extremely happy I'd seen three more shows than I expected, and all of Britain to come. I wanted to go with John H to Brussels or Rotterdam, but they clashed with signing on. I didn't want to risk being late a second time. Mats E sent me a ticket for Gothenburg, but the boat would have cost £60. I had to pay my rent. I still have the ticket.

More magic in the night followed during the rescheduled UK dates, including meeting Clarence again at Newcastle airport as they arrived to start that leg of the tour. At Brighton Centre, I was up against the stage, having abandoned my front row centre seat the moment the lights went down, part of the crush, bruised and battered. I could pat Bruce's boot as he walked by, he was so close. Then there was the sight of staff sweeping out after an agricultural show at Stafford's Bingley Hall before the fans could get in. By chance, some friends

BINGLEY HALL,
County Showground, Stafford
EXIT 14,
M6 MOTORWAY
Harvey Goldsmith Entertainments presents—

**Bruce Springsteen
& The E Street Band**
Wednesday, 20th May 1981
Evening 7-30
STALLS
£6.50
ROW
12   SEAT
32
To be retained.

and I bumped into Bruce on the street in London, on my birthday, between two Wembley Arena shows. Mary said she spotted him 'by the backs of his boots.'

By the time of those shows, we were worn out and sick with a bad cold, some kind-hearted soul giving us towels, saying, 'Go take a shower.' We had showers backstage at Wembley Arena, and I found two used plectrums in the shower stall. All absolutely true.

I finally make it to Gothenburg to see Bruce 22 years later, no longer hitchhiking alone but travelling with some of the best friends made along the road. And the magic continues.

OLYMPIAHALLE

16 APRIL 1981 MUNICH, WEST GERMANY

I WAS THERE: DON SHEPARD

A group of us went by train from Geiblestadt Air Base. The Olympiahalle was packed, with probably a third of the crowd military members. So excited to see The Boss. The opening music stopped and you could see the E Street Band come out on stage. I noticed Clarence Clemens first and remember telling my buddy how big he was. 'Little Steven' Van Zandt was waving his arms to the crowd, giving us a big hello.

It went silent when Bruce walked up center stage with an

American flag bandana in his hand. The spot light came on him, the crowd went crazy and he was waving that bandana. His first words were, 'I know there are a lot of American soldiers in the crowd, this is for you'. Clarence started playing 'God Bless America' and the crowd went crazy. They then went into their regular set starting with 'Factory'. Towards the end, he again acknowledged the US military when he sang 'This Land is Your Land'. Great show.

FOREST NATIONAL

26 APRIL 1981 BRUSSELS, BELGIUM

I WAS THERE: PHILIP VAN DE VELDE

It was Bruce's first concert in Belgium. I was not sure what I was to see. At that moment I listened almost only to hard rock. But he surprised me so much. From that moment I said to myself, this guy I will follow.

It was 13 years later that I went to my second Bruce concert. Why so long? I suppose my life at that moment in time. From that I went to more shows, and now I've seen Bruce 12 times.

It was the album *The River* that for the first time my Dad liked my choice of music. I know that now, and that he listened to the other albums, especially *Nebraska*.

In Antwerp in 2006 for the Seeger Sessions Band, I sat up high and with the song, 'Further On' I had tears in my eyes, thinking how it would be great if I was here with Dad (he passed away in 1995).

He would like that kind of music. The man beside me asked if I am ok, and I told him why. For the rest of the song he held his arm around me, with a smile of the woman with

Philip Van De Velde meets with fellow Tramps fans

him, I never forget that Dutch Man.

Also, being with my best friend on a Bruce concert gives me a special feeling, watching him and see him smiling, singing, it gives me such a good feeling. Thank you, Bruce, for giving me that feeling, and all the Tramps in the world.

NEWCASTLE AIRPORT

10 MAY 1981 NEWCASTLE-UPON-TYNE, UK

I WAS THERE: GREG TURNBULL

I got to meet Bruce at Newcastle Airport on his arrival into the UK for The River tour; the first time the band had been to the UK since *Born to Run* in 1975. I think I was the first to greet Bruce as he rushed for the bus outside. I caught him in its headlights, asked him to sign my *Born to Run* LP and welcomed him to the UK and wished him well for the show the next night.

CITY HALL

11 MAY 1981 NEWCASTLE-UPON-TYNE, UK

I WAS THERE: KEVAN HUNTER

This was one of the first gigs Bruce played on English soil since the infamous Hammersmith Odeon shows of 1975. The concert did not take place on March 31st as stated on the ticket, but May 11th because Bruce was exhausted, after the long American, Canadian and European legs, so the tour was postponed, allowing him to recover. Bruce walked on stage and performed an acoustic 'Follow That Dream.' You could hear a pin drop. Then the band came on and exploded into 'Prove It All Night' and continued to blow the roof off the City Hall.

A few years ago, the City Hall had an open day, organised by the manager. After being showed around the hallowed hall he opened the floor to questions and was asked what the best concert he'd seen in his 40-year tenure. Without hesitation he named this one, and after hundreds of gigs I've seen, I must agree.

THE APOLLO

13 MAY 1981 MANCHESTER, UK

I WAS THERE: KAREN BARTON

CITY HALL, Newcastle-upon-Tyne

Harvey Goldsmith Ent. presents—
**BRUCE SPRINGSTEEN &
THE E STREET BAND**
IN CONCERT

Tuesday, 31st March 1981
Evening 7-30

STALLS

A. B. Cooper (Printers) Ltd. MANCHESTER

J   25

Retain this portion

I have been a fan of Bruce Springsteen for 39 years now, my journey starting via Patti Smith's album *Easter* and 'Because the Night.' Back in the old days of vinyl we got to read the sleeve and learn about the artists, lyrics, etc. Intrigued, I started to explore who Bruce was, and got hooked.

I had older friends who'd been to the Hammersmith Odeon concert in '75. I listened to their stories of this amazing performer. Having just left school and only 16, there was no way I was going to get to that show. My parents would never have allowed me.

But once The River tour was announced, myself and a few friends lined up outside Manchester Apollo in cold mid-February for tickets for two days. Luckily, the garage opposite had hot running water and we were able to fill hot water bottles to keep warm, get food and stay suitably nourished.

So my first Bruce live show was that May, that leg of the tour re-scheduled after he got sick. The anticipation had built and by the time of the show I'd bought the back-catalogue and was now well and truly a fan. With ticket in hand (row C) my friends and I left our hometown Blackpool with much excitement. The tour had been in full swing across the US and Europe, with the music papers full of reviews, detailing the energy, power, force and rock'n'roll that is Bruce Springsteen and the E Street Band.

Manchester Apollo came alive that night. Were we really prepared for what we witnessed? I'm not sure we were. Bruce commended the stage, the band, the music and us, the fans, the minute he stepped on stage, leading us through stories of his childhood, his adolescence, relationships (good and bad), difficult times and happier times; we sang along, screamed, shouted, clapped, fist-punched the air, cried, laughed, danced and hung off every word, every chord, every riff, every 1-2-3-4.

It was without doubt the best thing I'd ever witnessed, not just the music but the honesty, the generosity of their time, their engagement and connection with us, the songs, the sentiments, the stories. We have lived those lives of difficult relationships, hard work, disadvantage, segregation, love and loss. We relate, connect, understand. There were sparks out on the streets of Manchester that night.

I've been to many shows since, and those feelings ring true for every consequent show. Bruce will be remembered as one of the greatest live artists of all time. I know so many people; myself included who walk away from one of his gigs feeling like they'll never experience anything quite like it again … until his next show.

I WAS THERE: TONY MICHAELIDES

I have a few Bruce stories but like many will always remember the first time, the first time 'proper' he'd toured the UK. He played one other show at Hammersmith Palais in November 1975, but it had soured him a little. I saw him on consecutive nights with my ex-wife Marie. I was working as a promotions rep for Island Records but still knew a lot of the local record storeowners from my days as a sales rep. I had many friends and colleagues at Granada TV so when it was obvious a lot wanted to go I saw my friend Barry, who owned a store in Manchester. He was the local ticket agent, and I bought the two front rows in the circle for the first of Bruce's two nights. Everyone was thrilled. So was I until I realised I lost £32 because I forgot to charge them all the booking fee. Fortunately, I wasn't aware of that until after the show. I'd have hated to have sat through the show thinking mine cost more than theirs.

I saw every show I could those next few years, up and down the country, but the first will always hold the fondest memories. He's an artist who sets his own standards; once you've seen him you expect the very best. He's one of a rare breed, cares about his fans just as much now as he ever did. Bruce will always be 'The Boss'.

THE PLAYHOUSE

17 MAY 1981 EDINBURGH, UK

I WAS THERE: PETER HOFFMANN

These were the pre-internet days, so no live footage of him was available and he didn't get much airplay. He was still something of a hidden secret amongst the cognoscenti. Prior to him coming to Edinburgh I'd been loaned *The River* from a girl I was friendly with on my course. It was never off the turntable; one of the tracks was 'Little Girl I Wanna Marry You.' Shortly after we started going out together. Alison, out of loyalty to her previous boyfriend gave him her two tickets for the first night (the gig had been cancelled from the end of March).

We were lucky to get to the second night. Walking past the Playhouse thinking we might hear something - the crowd were all in and the concert had just started. Then Harvey Goldsmith appeared at the door with two spare tickets, waving them at us. Despite being poor students, we had the money on us. Our seats were only half a dozen rows back, but everyone was up dancing. The gig was a revelation and remains the best concert I've been to. Since then I've always enjoyed watching others see Springsteen for the first time. And to paraphrase Charlotte Bronte, Dear reader, I married her…

According to my eldest son I've been to 60 concerts. He's the real fan. I suspect he's the most knowledgeable person in Scotland on The Boss, following him throughout Europe.

I WAS THERE: ALLAN CROW

The concerts were actually planned for March, then rescheduled. My ticket stub shows the original date. Tickets cost £5.50 or £6. If only charges were as minimal today.

My Dad stayed in one of the row of houses right opposite the stage door at the time, and occasionally got complimentary tickets to compensate for the disruption caused as bands such as the Stones sucked up so much power the residents struggling to get a decent TV reception, not to mention the dull thud of the bass and drums pounding through their brick walls.

So, I got two Springsteen tickets for free. I mentioned to my music teacher at Wester Hailes Education Centre I was off to see the gig. He told me Springsteen would change my life. When I go back, I still pick out my seat in the stalls - Row Z, Seat 49, about one third back to the left of the stage. Perfect view.

Outside, I was offered £100 for my ticket - an astronomical sum to a skinny kid who lived seven floors up in the flats at Cobbinshaw House, Sighthill. I figured this guy had to be worth seeing. The memories of the gig are little more than fragments; vivid snapshots from an evening which sparked a lifelong love affair with Bruce's music that will probably be played as I'm carried out the door in my coffin.

Pre-gig, we stood in the foyer waiting for him to finish his soundcheck, which legend has it took some three hours - effectively a show before the show as he drilled his band one last time.

I recall peering through the square glass windows that led to the stalls, watching as the final checks were done. I can still recall the sonic boom of Clarence Clemons' sax solo in 'Independence Day', which hit me square in the chest and knocked me back into my seat, and the thrill of watching him and Springsteen sliding on their knees across the Playhouse stage.

There's a memory of Springsteen on top of the piano conducting the crowd, a mass rendition of the first verse of 'Hungry Heart' and a rollicking 'Sherry Darling', and while much of his music was new to me, the sheer power of the performance was captivating, exhilarating and utterly joyous.

I've seen Springsteen play across the UK, at Hyde Park and the Olympic Stadium. I watched him transform Wembley Arena into a village hall to celebrate the music of Pete Seeger and sat on the banks of a stream outside the Millennium Stadium, Cardiff listening to him soundcheck 'Racing In The Streets' inside an empty stadium. It was a glorious summer's evening, and it felt like a private performance for an audience of one.

But that very first Playhouse gig stands out among them to this day. To paraphrase Jon Landau, this was my rock'n'roll future - mine and 3,000 others packed into the Playhouse that night. To me, 'The River' had a carefree swagger and joyfulness that pretty much stands the test of time three decades on.

After the gig we headed round to my Dads, opened the garage which was opposite the stage door, and got much, much closer than the fans who were behind cordons either side of the lane.

The cars were lined up, and, one by one the band departed. I can still recall standing - and waiting, and waiting - until I saw Springsteen depart, a rolled-up white towel around his neck.

That gig had a postscript too. When Clemons died in 2011, I penned a piece in the Fife Free Press on what The Boss, the big man and E Street meant to me. A reader shared his memories, and we got chatting about those Playhouse gigs. I remarked it was a shame no footage of the gig existed, as my memory was of him signing off with a blistering rendition of 'Rocking All Over the World.' A day or so later he emailed an mp3 file of the entire gig mixed from the sound-desk, including that Fogerty/Quo classic.

It would have been perfect symmetry had he booked the band back into the Playhouse for a residency with the 2016 River tour, but such days are long gone. Theatres have long since been swapped for the biggest stadia in the country. The 6,000 of us who saw him

back then would be lost in the circa 60,000 audiences at Hampden, Wembley, The Etihad, and even Coventry.

But the chance to hear *The River* played live once more - in full or even in part - marks this tour out as something special. I may even do something I haven't done in decades and buy another programme, to sit with the original 1981 edition.

WEMBLEY ARENA

29 MAY – 5 JUNE 1981 LONDON, UK

I WAS THERE: JEAN STEVENSON

This was my first ever gig - a surprise present for my 19th birthday from my then-boyfriend. Sheer joy. I'd liked Springsteen but not heard anything except the singles. My overwhelming memory was the entire audience spontaneously breaking into the first verse of 'Hungry Heart' and Bruce grinning on stage. I've been to hundreds of gigs since then, but seldom have I seen a gig where the artist was there for his own enjoyment as much as ours.

I WAS THERE: PAUL BEARD

My journey started in April 1976, aged 23, when I first heard and fell in love with the music of Bruce Springsteen. From that day forward, he's been the soundtrack to my life and as each year passes his music gains another layer and sinks deeper into my soul.

I had to wait until 1981 for my first Springsteen concert experience, at Wembley Arena on the original River tour. Since that evening I've attended 62 more nights of pure joy and raw emotion, around the world, where I was lost in the stars for that brief moment in time. I know that's not as many shows as hard-core fans and perhaps some even class me a lightweight in comparison, but it's probably many more than the average fan. I'd have loved to see more but unfortunately was restricted by time and money, and am truly thankful, treasuring every single moment of the ones I've been a part of, all now a memory etched in my mind forever and revisited many times due to the magic of bootlegging and the gift of official downloads – the wonder of modern technology!

I WAS THERE: DAVE EDMUNDS, MUSICIAN

I wasn't on the guest list or anything, but with my good friend, Capital Radio DJ Roger Scott, we parked up at Wembley Stadium. Taking a deep breath, we surfed through the over-sold throng on Roger's

all-access pass to witness Bruce
Springsteen and his E Street Band
play their entire, exhilarating, three-
hour-plus set to above expectations.

Shuffling our way towards
the exits among the herds of
thousands of exhausted Bruce-
worshipers, I felt a firm grip
on my shoulder: 'Bruce wants
to see you!' The firm grip
belonged to a massive, heavily-
tattooed security guy with an
intense New Jersey accent
who was yelling into his CB
radio, 'I've found him!'

I'd never met Bruce Springsteen before and had no
idea what he knew about me, except perhaps 'I Hear You Knocking.'
How had he known I was at the gig? The security guy led me
through the backstage area to Bruce's dressing room, where he
was sitting alone. Being careful not to blurt out, 'Great show, man!'
(you don't do that) and before either of us could say anything a
noisy E Street Band stormed through making their way towards the
hospitality area: 'Hi Dave, love your records!' And, 'Hi Dave, you're
terrific, man!' – and so on. And off they went.

We talked – about what I don't recall. He asked if I'd been
recording lately and I said, 'No' – 'Got anything…?' He strapped
on his Fender Esquire and explained, 'This is like a Chuck Berry
thing that tells a story without repeating any of the lyrics, like The
Promised Land.' And he played 'From Small Things Mama, Good
Things One Day Come' (not the snappiest of titles) – from beginning
to end. It was perfect for me! 'It's yours, man!'

He hadn't recorded the song but promised he'd lay down a rough
cassette with just guitar and vocal – for me! 'Gimme a couple of
weeks…' and I could pick it up at his manager's office, in New York.
In such encounters, promises can evaporate before you leave the

room. The way things worked out, I needed to be in New York a few weeks later, and that's the truth. I went to his manager's office and, sure enough, there was a cassette of Bruce's song, with my name on it, awaiting me. That's class.

Six months later, midway through a US tour with my band, I was playing at the Peppermint Lounge in Manhattan. Bruce turned up - unannounced and alone but for his Fender Esquire. It was good to see him. He waited patiently in the dressing room until the end of my set, then – although the audience knew something was cooking – he sauntered onstage. You can imagine. We played a load of Chuck Berry songs and ended with 'Small Things.' So, good things one day come.

I WAS THERE: NIALL BRANNIGAN

I was 19 years old when Bruce Springsteen burst into my life in 1975. He was still only 25. I had spotted my ex-girlfriend on the arm of her new beau, whilst walking through town. But it wasn't what was on his arm that attracted me. It was what was under his other one. *Born to Run* had been out just a few weeks but there was already a buzz around it from the *Melody Maker* and *NME*, the weekly music papers I pored over, avidly. The cover poked out from behind my successor's arm, Bruce's tousled hair and guitar head-stock visible on the stark, white background. I bought the album the next day and fell head over heels in love - with Bruce's World.

It was to be nearly six years before I was able to catch Bruce live. By then *Darkness On The Edge of Town* and *The River* had also been released and added to the rest of my collection which, having gone back to buy the first two, was now five albums strong. The reputation of Bruce and the E Street Band as a live music force of nature was well cemented and, when The River Tour came to Wembley Arena in May 1981, I would have killed for a ticket. I got two, seated on the floor of the arena, for Friday 29 May. My then-wife came with me, more out of curiosity than anything else. For most of the gig, I wasn't even aware she was there. To be honest, I wasn't even aware anyone else was there until much later.

What's Springsteen's most famous song? 'Born to Run', right?

Lights down, audience roars, everyone on their feet and 'Mighty'
Max Weinberg belts that roll around the drum-kit that heralds the
start of one of the best rock'n'roll songs ever written, right at the
start of the set. Fourteen songs later they took a break. 'Badlands'
had blasted around the old arena and, as the applause still rained
down, Bruce and Roy Bittan played the opening bars of 'Thunder
Road'. Everyone sat back down. Except one. I stood on my seat and,
as Bruce started into the lyric of my favourite song of all time (still is,
I'm having it at my funeral, thanks,) I belted out the words with him,
oblivious to the steward at the end of our row, waving at me to sit
down. Bruce and I got to the most important lines in the song':

> *'Show a little faith, there's magic in the night,*
> *You ain't a beauty but, hey, you're alright,*
> *Oh, and that's alright with me.'*

And, as the band wound up to that crescendo,

> *'Except roll down the window and let the wind blow back your hair.'*

Everyone else was on their feet anyway. The thrill was
visceral. My heart was bursting out of my chest, tears stinging
the back of my eyes, my throat straining to be contained in my
body as I stretched it to its very limit. It was the most exciting
thing I had ever seen or heard in my life.

The rest of the gig was a blur of sound, lights and
adrenaline. Songs 16 to 24 were almost wall-to-wall *The River*,
the mood easing during stunning, back-to-back versions of
'Stolen Car' and 'Point Blank' before the roof came off during
'Candy's Room' (from 'Darkness') and 'Ramrod'. An epic
version of 'Rosalita (Come Out Tonight)', with Bruce dancing
on Roy's piano, jumping off the drum-riser and knee-sliding
into Clarence Clemons, ended the main set, and they were
gone.

The place went nuts. I had never heard a noise like it at a

gig. I had witnessed something that gripped me by the throat, lifted me off my feet and screamed into my ear,

*'Just take my hand, give yourself to me and I
will give you the best time you will ever have.'*

When they came back out for the encore and the intro to 'Jungleland' started up, nobody sat down. I sang every word of Bruce's opus, sang about The Rangers, The Magic Rat and those *'backstreet girls dancing to the records that the DJ plays.'* Then the song broke down and Clarence's wondrous sax solo wound its way into the night. Bruce waved for the lights to come on and even he looked surprised to find every single person on their feet, on their seat, roaring and dancing with delight, lost in the magic of the music. A spot-light bounced off a glitter ball and the audience were covered in a parade of shards of light, frozen in a glorious picture of shared pleasure, shared joy and shared exultation. I wept.

Three more songs, including a never-ending 'Detroit Medley', and it was all over. My shirt and jeans were plastered to my body, the sweat running down my back, my socks soaked inside my shoes.

Three weeks later, three weeks of floating on air, reliving the joy of that night, my Dad died.

On 29 May I had no idea he was ill, my Mum had kept it from her six children, wanting to protect them from what was to come. Standing on that seat, singing to my hero, I had no clue that the biggest hero of my life was so wracked with cancer that he would last just 23 more days.

I have never been able to separate the two events.

NATIONAL EXHIBITION CENTRE

7 JUNE 1981 BIRMINGHAM, UK

I WAS THERE: JIM WILKINSON

It was a Roxy Music concert in Preston in 1975 which kindled my thus far 43-year obsession with The Boss and came within an ace of putting me in the Hammersmith Odeon that November. But a sixth-form dispute meant I had to wait another six years to see Bruce and the E Street Band.

Outside the Guild Hall at the Roxy Music gig, local record shop Ames put up a display of recent releases and I was transfixed by the *Born To Run* cover, which I took it upon myself to liberate on the way home. I'd read about this 'New Dylan' hairy folkie type in the *NME* but this looked authentically glamorous, edgy and rock'n'roll to appeal to 16-year-old me.

Studying the lyric sheet, I knew I had to hear this album and on a pocket money budget the cheapest way possible was to borrow it off the one sixth-form pal ahead of me in the game who already owned it.

In time-honoured fashion, it was recorded on one side of something like a Boots C90 cassette tape (I wish I remembered what was on the other) and as it re-configured my DNA, endorsements from Nick Kent, Charlie Shaar Murray, and later Julie Burchill and Tony Parsons in the *NME* - who led me to Bowie, Iggy and the Velvets and later approved the best of punk - served to ratify the feeling I had that this was the very stuff my soul needed.

Jim Wilkinson (far left) and friends

There were only two lads at school with cars that winter, and with a recent influx of those exotic creatures, girls, to our Boys' Grammar, a plan to attend a London gig carried with it the prospect of not only spending time in their company but perhaps getting off with one.

Alas, after much lobbying for the historic Hammersmith shows from myself and Zeb, owner of the Bruce vinyl, it was decided Paul McCartney and Wings at Wembley would be more of a sure-fire romance catalyst for Macca-adoring lovelies than some bloke in a woolly bob-hat nobody had really heard of. Zeb went to Wembley. I sulked.

Roll forward six years and I'm a regular gig-going man about town with an office job at the Gas Board. I'd given up university after a year, but with a little brass in pocket was in my mate Graham's Triumph Dolomite with the aforementioned Zeb, heading down the M6 from Lancashire to the NEC.

We are in effect the three of the school friendship bunch stuck in our hometowns in the East of the county, mundane jobs but with the means to go out at weekends, go to the football and most liberating of all, see the acts who make the 7-inch and 12-inch pieces of plastic which truly exorcise the plodding mundanity of our day-to-day existence. We are almost the subjects of early Springsteen material, young people hemmed in by our circumstances and surroundings with an aching feeling of somehow missing out.

I was no gig virgin at 22: I'd seen Bowie several times since my debut gig in 1973, Mick Ronson, Queen, Mott The Hoople, Sparks, Judas Priest, Dr Feelgood, Buzzcocks, The Jam, The Clash, Blondie, Elvis Costello, Nico, Ian Dury and the Blockheads, The Specials, Magazine, John Cooper-Clarke, John Cale, The Modern Lovers, and The Fall. And that's off the top of my head.

But nobody had captured that sense of almost spiritual yearning to rise above it all, the frustrations of youth, the indomitability of the human spirit to deal with surprises, sensations, setbacks and failure than the man we were holding tickets to see that night. Still living comfortably with my parents, I was perhaps oblivious to the domestic stresses and strains of just living day-to-day which current album *The River* documented. I knew little about marriage, divorce, parenthood, joblessness, and depression. My hermetically-sealed home life hadn't exposed me to much of that. It wasn't until I was capable of my own brand of fuck-ups that I'd finally hear those songs resonate.

Although that night in Birmingham lifted my rock'n'roll heart to the stratosphere, it was some years before I understood Bruce's point about the 'redemptive power of rock'n'roll'. I had nothing yet to be redeemed from.

But there would be Springsteen gigs in high times and low times to come and the power and glory communicated in that June '81 performance stood me in good stead for a lifetime of failures and disappointments yet to come.

However despondent I ever felt (and many times I did), I always knew one artist could almost empty me of the heartbreak and low self-esteem and make me resolve to get back on my feet. As someone wrote, 'When you come out of a Springsteen gig, you come out determined to be the very best version of yourself you can be.'

We were side-on to the stage in the NEC that Sunday night and actual details I recall are sketchy after seeing the band so many times since. I certainly remember Pete Townshend on stage for the encores. The thrill of seeing The Boss and The Big Man interact for the first time. The band possibly still dressed a little 'like pimps', in 1975 causing otherwise-adored BBC DJ John Peel to harbour an irrational dislike of Springsteen for decades. When *The River* was out, he was playing Dire Straits.

The sheer length of the gig and diversity of the music blew us away. There was even that sense that's almost unique to Bruce's gigs – coming out singing a song you never heard before. 'Jole Blon' remained a mystery to me as far as its origin was concerned for several years.

Did this guy just pull songs out of the ether? Make them up on stage? The E Street Band's powers seemed so all-ranging that you could have believed it. Listening back to bootleg tapes and CDs and eventually, miracle of miracle, official releases of recordings from the time, it's clear that 1978's fiery, impassioned concerts tightened the band up from their jazzy, improv-orientated incarnation of earlier years.

The 1980-81 gigs took it a step further. This band was now mighty, unequalled. Cool and confident with its growing legend and right to be mentioned in the same breath as behemoth rockers such as the Stones and The Who. Townshend's presence that night told you the old guard were as happy to be reflected in Springsteen's stark light of brilliance as he was to be mentioned in the same breath as his forbears and contemporary giants.

It was the last but one date of the tour's European leg. And while 1975's Hammersmith audience found the look or sound of the band alien or foreign, if London wasn't quite ready for Bruce, a triumphant 'River' continental jaunt followed by UK dates proved he could work a European or British audience as well as he could hold a Bryn Mawr or Philly crowd in his hand.

We stayed the night at another school pal's halls of residence in Edgbaston. None of us could sleep and after emptying a few cans, relating the splendour and magnificence we'd just seen, we went outside to have a hit in the night darkness in the college cricket nets. A planned trip to a one-dayer at Headingley was aborted due to lack of sleep.

No spectacle could have compared to what we'd seen, so three tired boys made their way home to find careers, loves, homes, marriages and children which the music of Bruce would forever be the epic soundtrack to. Cheap flights to far-off places were a thing of the future, like the Internet, so after that it was scouring the news pages of the music press for
four years.

MEADOWLANDS ARENA

2 JULY 1981 EAST RUTHERFORD, NEW JERSEY

I WAS THERE: STAN GOLDSTEIN

New Jersey hits the big time with its own arena and who better to open it then Mr. New Jersey himself, Bruce Springsteen. To many, this arena was the house that Bruce Springsteen and the E Street Band built.

I was there for the arena's opening night for Bruce Springsteen and the E Street Band, Bruce having now headlined there 56 times.

Tickets were available through a mail-order lottery and got seats for the opening night, up near the last row in the upper deck on the side of the stage. I really don't have great memories of this show, Bruce seemed a big tight and it was not as great as some of the other River tour shows I had seen at the end of 1980.

I was excited about New Jersey having its own big-time arena. I remember being disappointed that the roof was so generic-looking compared to the cool inside roof of Madison Square Garden. But it was nice not having to cross over the river.

This was the first show Bruce ever performed Tom Waits' 'Jersey Girl.' It was also the last show he opened with 'Born to Run.' He opened many River tour shows with it.

There was the opening six-night stand on The River tour. Followed by an incredibly-powerful 10-night stand when Bruce was on top of the world during August of 1984 on the Born in the U.S.A. tour. We had an 11-night stand in the summer of 1992 with the 'other band' on the Human Touch/Lucky Town tour. To top that off, there were 15 dates on the Reunion tour with the E Street Band during July/ August 1999 that fans are still buzzing about almost 16 years later.

Since then there have only been 13 Springsteen shows at the arena, including two open-to-the-public rehearsal shows, three solo shows on 2005's Devils & Dust tour and a headlining gig on 2004's Vote For Change tour.

Bruce did also play next door at Giants Stadium six times in 1985, 10 nights in the summer of 2003, three times in 2008, five times in 2009 and three times at MetLife Stadium in September 2012.

RICHFIELD COLISEUM

29 JULY 1981 RICHFIELD, OHIO

I WAS THERE: ANDREW MIKULA

I saw Bruce and the E Street Band in, I think the year was

1981, at the old Richfield Coliseum near Akron and it was the tour supporting *The River*. No opening act, just Bruce and The E Streeters rockin' the place off its foundation. Special treat was when Southside Johnny came out to sing 'I Don't Want to Go Home' with him part-way through the set. The band covered Creedence Clearwater Revival's 'Who'll Stop the Rain' and did almost all of *The River*, along with all of the great stuff off his first four LPs. Had great seats - dead center about 15 rows back from the stage. Not that I, or anyone else did much sitting. An amazing night.

1984

The Born in the U.S.A. tour was the supporting tour of Springsteen's seventh album *Born in the U.S.A.*, which was recorded during sessions at The Power Station and The Hit Factory in New York between January 1982 – March 1984. It was his longest and most successful tour to date and also the first tour to feature Springsteen's future wife, Patti Scialfa.

The first show on June 29, at Saint Paul, Minnesota included the filming of the iconic 'Dancing in the Dark' music video with then-unknown actress Courteney Cox. With 156 dates and a total attendance of 3.9 million, the tour grossed $80–90 million overall.

SUMMER 1984

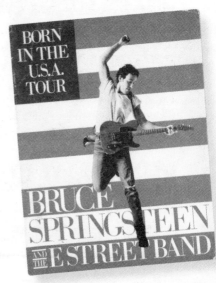

I WAS THERE: NILS LOFGREN

We were both at an audition in 1970. He played there with Steel Mill and I played with my band

Grin. I was aware of Bruce and had kind of kept tabs on him, buying tickets to see the E Street Band play in '74 and '75 and again in 1980. I was on the road a lot doing my own thing, but whenever I could, I'd buy a ticket and go see them play, because they're an amazing band and I love Bruce's song-writing.

In the early Eighties I was living in L.A. and Bruce was there working. One morning I saw him, and he said, 'Hey! I just finished this double album called *The River*. Want to hear it? I jumped in the car, we went over the studio late morning, he put me in a chair in this little room and I listened to both albums. It sounded like the first big step in recording for that group, where they got the sizzle and electricity of the live show into the record, every track.

When Steven Van Zandt left the E Street Band, Bruce needed a guitar player and because of our friendship through the years, he gave me a call and I jammed with the band for a couple of days. I don't know if they played with other guitar players or what the thought process was. I just know that he asked me to join the band and I said yes.

ST. PAUL CIVIC CENTER

29 JUNE 1984 ST. PAUL, MINNESOTA

I WAS THERE: COURTENEY COX

I moved to New York by myself when I was 17. I modelled for the Ford Modelling Agency, but I'm not 5-foot-10 so couldn't do any of the beautiful print ads or anything. I'd done two days on a soap opera and a New York telephone advert. I went to this commercial audition for the Bruce Springsteen video to 'Dancing in the Dark'. Brian De Palma was directing it and I walked into this big casting room and all these dancers were there stretching and I thought I'm not really in the right place, I was really nervous. I then met with Brian, who asked me to dance. I said OK, but I'm not really a dancer. I started moving a little bit, I was so nervous and embarrassed, but got the job.

It was a bigger story than just what you saw in the video. It was me and two other girls and they filmed us buying t-shirts, then we were putting our make-up on in the bathroom, it was this whole thing about being exited and going to see a concert - we can't wait to get there and then one of us gets picked out of the audience to dance on stage. They filmed all this stuff but didn't show all that. We were told Bruce was going to pick one of us out of the audience and I was like, 'Not me, no!' I did not want to be the one who danced in front of 30,000 people. But he picked me.

When I saw the world premiere of the video on MTV I waited and waited for my spots - I thought maybe they cut my scenes. Then, when I finally appeared, I thought, 'That's it? Oh, well.' But it got me through the door in so many places.

After, there were tons of offers for me to be in other rock videos, but I didn't want to do them. I know how easy it is to get pegged into a stereotype and want to be very careful with my career.

I WAS THERE: SHAWN CONNER

I was 18 and seeing Bruce for the first time. The show was in St. Paul, Minnesota. In Winnipeg, where I was living, a company ran bus tours down to the Twin Cities for concert and sporting events, but after utilizing the service for The Who and U2, I was flying down, unable to get time off work to spend two days on a bus.

The show was June 29 and the first of the Born in the U.S.A. tour. for the album would 'break' Springsteen into superstardom and become the biggest-selling record that year in the US. By the end of the tour, Springsteen and the E Street Band would be playing stadia to upwards of 60,000 people. He'd never play to audiences that big again, unless you count his Super Bowl half-time show a few years back.

But at the beginning of the tour, Springsteen's stardom was still manageable, the crowds still no bigger than arena-size (granted, he actually played three shows at the Civic Center). Three things stand out about that show. First, waiting outside the Civic Center by the loading dock and hoping for a glimpse of Springsteen. Instead we got Clarence Clemons getting out of a tour bus and waving to

Springsteen graces the cover of Newsweek on 27 October 1975

Another City, another show - Springsteen on stage in the Eighties.

Audrey Hunn's denim jacket signed by Springsteen, see page 260

*Arlen Schumer and friends out side the Capitol Theater
New Jersey 19 September 1978. See page 80. Photo David Reiss*

Darren Aherne's signed River album, see page 234

Dan French backstage with Springsteen 1981.
See page 115. Photo from Point Blank Archives

Clarence Clemons has a beer at the Munich Hotel,
Munich, Germany, 16 April 1981, see page 115.
Photo from Point Blank Archives.

The single 'Cover Me' gave Springsteen a number seven US hit (which he originally wrote for Donna Summer)

'Badlands' released in 1978 peaked at number 42 on the US singles chart

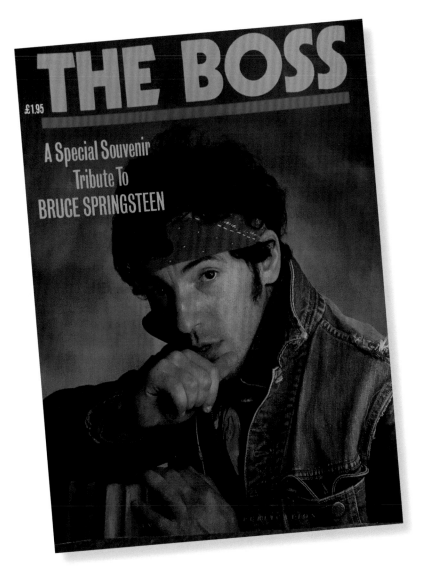

*A special 36-page souvenir magazine
published for the Springsteen1985 UK tour*

us hardcore Springsteen-o-philes silly enough to waste a summer afternoon outside the venue.

The second thing I remember is, more than halfway through the show, Springsteen inviting a woman from the front rows to dance with him during *Born in The U.S.A.'s* first single, 'Dancing in the Dark.' Brian DePalma was filming the song for a video and the band ran through it twice, each time with the same dancer, actress, Courteney Cox.

The third thing I remember is Elvis Presley singing 'Can't Help Falling in Love' as, two-and-a-half hours after the show began, the house lights came up.

Since that show, I've seen Bruce Springsteen in Anaheim, Tacoma and Vancouver. Each show has been great, but nothing quite compared to the thrill of the house lights dimming and seeing him on stage that first time. In fact, until just a couple of days ago I thought I'd had my fill, that I don't need to see him play for over three hours with a 17-piece band while touring an album that I like but don't love. That said, I don't think I'd be able to live with myself if I miss another one.

I WAS THERE: KARYN PURDY

I had a front and center ticket to the St. Paul show where he filmed 'Dancing in the Dark.' At the last minute, I chose not to go. Turns out I'd have been in the video. When Courteney Cox went onstage, the seat was a couple down from there, the person with the other ticket is in the video. I'm glad now I didn't go!

I WAS THERE: SANDY TAPP

I'm 19 years old, with two girlfriends, and our seats are literally as far up as they go, our backs to the wall of the arena. My friend Deeds has been into The Boss for four years - a passionate fan.

He opens with 'Thunder Road', followed by 'Prove It All Night.' I'm mesmerized. The energy, the crowd interaction, the E Street Band. I keep looking at Deeds, speechless. I'm hooked. He recorded the video for 'Dancing in the Dark' that night and had to play the song twice due to a recording error. Courteney Cox's career officially kicks off, and my complete fascination with Bruce.

MEADOWLANDS ARENA

20 AUGUST 1984 EAST RUTHERFORD, NEW JERSEY

I WAS THERE: STAN GOLDSTEIN

If I was listing my favorite shows at the arena, this would be No.1, and in my top-five Bruce shows of all time. What an incredible night, cementing the legend of Bruce and the E Street Band. I recall this show ending at 12.40 am and even though it was a Monday night, I don't think one person left early. It was the final night of the 10-night stand. Bruce and the band were on top of their game and so were the fans. One word to describe it - powerful. I still have my ticket stub.

Steve Van Zandt, who left the E Street Band prior to this tour, was a special guest during the encores. The Miami Horns - Richie 'La Bamba' Rosenberg (trombone), Mark Pender (trumpet), Stan

Harrison (tenor saxophone) and Eddie Manion (baritone saxophone) - guested on several songs.

Before 'Born to Run,' Bruce addressed the crowd: 'I'd like to just take a second and thank all you guys for coming down tonight, I know a lot of you guys been here more than one night, almost everybody. If you can, when you go home, thank your friends for making this stay here such a great time for us.'

TACOMA DOME

17 OCTOBER 1984 TACOMA, WASHINGTON

I WAS THERE: SCOTT TAPPIN

I saw him on the Born in the U.S.A. tour, back-to-back nights in Tacoma, with my girlfriend. Bruce threw his bandana into the audience and as I was trying to catch it I hit the girl behind me in the boobs and got punched in the face. Good times.

COUNTY COLISEUM

22 OCTOBER 1984 OAKLAND, CALIFORNIA

I WAS THERE: BARRY RAWLINS

A friend of mine got tickets and took me because the girl he invited didn't want to go. I was a month past shoulder surgery for a recurring dislocation and still had my arm in a sling, couldn't clap my hands very well. Did I mention we were inside 20 rows at the Oakland Coliseum? Effing amazing. It was my first Bruce show, saw the

stadium show too the following year. Too bad rock music is in the shitter now. He wouldn't stand a chance today.

KEMPER ARENA

19 NOVEMBER 1984 KANSAS CITY, MISSOURI

I WAS THERE: TOM MUETZEL

I first started listening to Bruce in my freshman year in high school in the fall of '75. A girl I really liked, Jerri Allen, turned me on to *Born to Run*. She was insistent I give the record a listen and bought me a copy. After that, I bought *Darkness on the Edge of Town, The River, Nebraska,* The Wild, *the Innocent and the E-Street Shuffle* and *Greetings From Asbury Park,*

NJ, in that order. Still have all of them plus more after. I am, and will always be, a vinyl collector.

I had to work three jobs at the same time to pay my way through college in Springfield, Missouri in 1984. I worked for the university (Southwest Missouri State University) in the Art Department, as a doorman at Lindberg's bar and at Spin-It Records on South Glenstone. Spin-It was owned by a guy named Joel Grey, who had a few record stores in the Chicago area (Oak Park). His son came down to MSU (then SMSU) and Joel set him up with his own business. The son, Alan, tired of it and wanted out. Joel hired myself and a few other guys to run it. Although we were pretty far away from the parent company, Joel took good care of us and periodically made concert tickets available for the big tours. He called down a couple of weeks before Thanksgiving and told us he had arranged for two tickets - I got them.

When *Born in The U.S.A.* came out, it was such a departure from *The River* and *Nebraska*. It was more pumped up (kind of like Bruce, himself) and energetic. Though it was still serious subject matter, instead of you feeling kind of melancholy and introspective, listening to this record, you felt like those times in your life where you got beat but gave as good as you got. We could not keep the record on the shelf. I remember *Born in The U.S.A.*, *Material Girl*, and *Purple Rain* dominated our sales over the course of a year but *Born in The U.S.A.* resonated in a big way to the kids in this Midwest town. It was easily our biggest selling record of that period.

The drive up from Springfield to KC was only about three hours. We ate at The Golden Ox, a classic old steak place with bright orange leather chairs down in the stockyards near Kemper Area. As we came up to the building, there was a huge radio promotion going on. The station was giving away a pink '59 Cadillac Eldorado convertible to support the flip side of 'Dancing In the Dark.' The vehicle was not in mint condition and had clearly been thrown together for the event; the car's body was seriously loaded with Bondo. But who cared? It was stupid-cool and we wanted it badly. Next to the doors, were mountains of food that were brought by concertgoers as part of a Thanksgiving promotion. At our door alone, there had to been somewhere around 6-8 tons. I keep thinking that there was a deal that if you brought food donations, you got tickets for hot dogs at the concession stands.

The concert lasted about four hours and had an intermission at the half way-point. He played the entire album plus songs from his previous records. The first half was primarily his earlier stuff, 'Tenth Avenue Freeze-Out', 'Rosalita' and such. At one point, as he started to play songs from *Nebraska*, I remember he remarked that it was 'probably not Ronald Reagan's favourite record.' When they played 'Dancing In The Dark', he grabbed some girl out of the audience, just like the video later released on MTV, and danced with her. At the encore, he played 'Santa Claus is Coming to Town' (the first time I ever heard that song done by him). The familiarity and affection between him and the band, but particularly Clarence Clemons on that song felt very genuine. When they got around to 'Born to Run', the lights came up suddenly and it brought down the house with all the fire and power they could deliver. I was blown away by that moment.

While the concert was, and still is, a strong memory for me, what stuck with me most was the sense of family and camaraderie with other fans as we left. Sharing a beer and conversation with strangers in the parking lot, lots of people milling around in a great mood, not really ready to leave. I have been to 40 or 50 concerts in my life, seen many of the greats, and it may have been a bi-product of the upcoming holiday, but the way Bruce and the band connected with the audience that night stayed with me for some time and was something I have never experienced since.

I WAS THERE: PAUL OMSTEAD

On the Born in the U.S.A. tour, at Kemper Arena, the crowd danced all night. More than 30 songs and four and a half hours of pure awesomeness. By the end, I was doing the throat-slash gesture every time they went into another song. In jest, of course. I walked in a casual fan and left thinking the man and the band were gods. Still the best concert I've ever been to, by a long shot.

1985

GREENSBORO COLISEUM

18 JANUARY 1985 GREENSBORO, NORTH CAROLINA

I WAS THERE: SKIP WEISMAN

With 84 shows in 38 years I could write a book myself just on my experiences with live Bruce concerts. But two stand out more than others that are life-affirming and unique enough that other fans would enjoy hearing about them.

In Greensboro, North Carolina, on the Born in the U.S.A. tour, Bruce and the E Street Band played back-to-back nights at the Coliseum. Because of demand, me and my buddy Ric could only get tickets for the first show. We were determined to get in the following night so the morning after driving up to see if there were any returns. It was about mid-morning and the ticket office was not yet opened. But I bumped into a ticket scalper, looking to sell. They were in the third row behind the stage. I grabbed them and don't recall the price.

Walking around the arena to head back home I ran into a friend who worked part-time as an arena security guard. I knew him from my job as assistant general manager of minor baseball team, the Greensboro Hornets. Jerry told me he was assigned to the stage door and would be there later in the afternoon. He said, 'If you want to get a message to Bruce, I can see what I can do.'

I rushed back to write a letter, put it on team letterhead and poured my heart out to him, telling my story of growing up in Central Jersey, 30 minutes from Freehold, and my fanaticism for his music and what it meant to me. I also asked a favour, including a team baseball cap. I asked if he'd tell his Glory Days baseball story.

Later I got back to see Jerry and knock on the door. I show him my package and he said he'd be right back. Five minutes later a roadie came to see me, and I explain. He promises to deliver the package.

That night, me, Ric, and two other friends are sitting in our third row behind the stage seats. I didn't have the courage to tell anyone what I did. I never thought Bruce would get the package and read my letter before the show so didn't want anyone disappointed.

About five or six songs in, during 'Out in the Street', I glance over to Max and see a small 'green and gold' reflection on the plexiglass surrounding the drums. I took my binoculars out and zoomed in to see my team's baseball cap on the stage. I start jumping up and down, yelling to my buddies, 'He's got the cap.' They had no idea what I was talking about and it was too loud to really explain.

The very next song is 'Glory Days' and Bruce goes back to get the cap. He carries it to the front of the stage, says, 'I'm kind of in a professional mood tonight', and as he puts on the cap, adds, 'I was sitting backstage and got a letter from the assistant manager of the Greensboro Hornets, and it reminded me of when I was a young kid playing little league baseball...' He then went into the 'Glory Days' story intro. I got a couple of photos with an SLR camera I smuggled in.

My only regrets are that I didn't copy my original letter, so have no memento of the request, and I didn't put my seat location in the letter. If I had, there would have been a good chance that roadies may have been sent to find me. Even though I wore my green and gold team jacket it wasn't enough to get past security. But it wouldn't have changed my love for Bruce and his music, and it certainly raised my level of respect and belief in his commitment to his fans. A few months later I found a bootleg recording of the show, one I'll cherish forever.

SYDNEY ENTERTAINMENT CENTRE

21 MARCH 1985 SYDNEY, AUSTRALIA

I WAS THERE: CLIFF REEVE

I first heard 'Born to Run' in late '75 or early '76 and immediately started telling anyone who would listen that one day, Bruce would rule the word. Laughter and mocking, lots of it. I had to wait until the Born in the U.S.A. tour in the mid-Eighties for the first chance to see him live. And I will never forget the sheer exhilaration of finally being in the same room as my idol.

I boarded a Greyhound bus in Kalgoorlie, Western Australia, with a five-months pregnant wife who didn't even have a ticket and travelled nearly three days to Sydney for one show. Afterwards I hung around and got Patti Scialfa to sign my programme. The next day we got back on the bus to come home. Every gruelling moment was worth it.

Fast forward to 2013 and after missing several tours because Bruce didn't play in Perth, we flew to Melbourne for one show. At least No.2 wife had a ticket this time.

Shortly after we started hearing rumours of a 2014 return, and while dismissing them as fanciful there was a glimmer of hope that maybe, just maybe, he might tour with the new album.

This time Perth would be included. I told my wife if he was doing 10 shows in Perth I was going to 10. I had to settle for three. The most important aspect of the night was that I was able to take my son to his first Springsteen show, and it was a killer.

After, we waited at the stage door, hopeful of a hello. Little did I realise we were in the wrong damned place. Cars and people came and went and then a figure in boots, jacket and sunglasses emerged from the back of the stadium. I made a motion to go through the gate, to absolutely no avail and yelled out a hello to the shadowy figure. I got a wave as he got into the van and thought, 'Oh well, at least there was that to take away'. The security guard only then informed us where the van would exit. I'm afraid my son was left behind as I bolted to the rear with such gusto that big Tony, Bruce's security guard, asked me to, 'Slow down, take it easy Sir.'

There, sitting in the front of a black van, surrounded by a small group of maybe 20 people was Bruce Springsteen. Earlier in the night my phone died, so I couldn't get a photo. All I had to be signed was my ticket. When he handed it back I asked if I could shake his hand. 'Sure', and there it was. I went back stage after the next two shows and got a signature on *The Wild, the Innocent* and then *Asbury Park* the third night. The shows were amazing too.

Jump to 2017 and three more shows for Perth in late January. And I was there again. A friend gifted me a GA ticket for the opening night, so I could be at the front, closest I'd been for any show and despite the grind of the roll call it was once again, astounding.

I hung around with a small group after each show but Bruce high-tailed it each night. Being a long-time radio journo, I managed to pull a spot for the press conference on the afternoon of the opening show though. We were told the ins and outs - Bruce and the band will play a song or two for final soundcheck, the band would leave then Bruce would take our questions.

They ran through 'Land of Hope and Dreams' and 'New York City Serenade' before Bruce summoned us 'come forward.' I got one question towards the end, after queries about Trump and his newly-released autobiography. I asked, 'Bruce, in 'Better Days' you sang about being a poor man in a rich man's shirt. How hard is it to be Bruce Springsteen these days?' 'You know what, it's pretty easy' My God, Bruce Springsteen is talking to me! Shortly after, I heard time was up, but said 'Bruce, one more thing …' I took my shot in front of everyone. 'May I shake your hand?' 'Here it is, sir.'

The shows were of course amazing and after four decades I finally saw 'Jungleland', as the start of the encore on Wednesday, 25 January 2017. Yes, I wept.

MELBOURNE SHOWGROUNDS

3 APRIL 1985 MELBOURNE, AUSTRALIA

I WAS THERE: NEIL WYATT

I'm from Drouin, Victoria, 100km from Melbourne. I've been an avid fan from about 12, when 'Born to Run' blasted on to our hand-held transistor radios. That song will be my funeral song and the thing that still blows me away is the start, with its exploding drum solo. The sax and chant that follows still excites. I remember all my friends at high school wondering

who this guy was that I was so infatuated with. As time goes by a lot realized I was onto something. *The River* album was the one that got a lot more mainstream followers, and by the time *Born in the U.S.A.* there were many more converts.

When Bruce announced his first Australian tour I couldn't get tickets quick enough for Melbourne Showgrounds. The show was dominated by *Born in the U.S.A.* but the special songs were 'Racing in the Street' and concert regular

'Badlands.' I remember staring at the crowd during 'Born to Run'. The whole arena seemed to be bouncing up and down, like on a wave. I was blown away.

I've seen Bruce at least once on every tour to Australia since, including his acoustic set at the Palais, a very up close and personal show, with many anecdotes. Recent trips included an awesome show at Rod Laver Arena (24 March, 2013), the inclusion of Tom Morello on guitar adding an even greater dimension to the amazing E Street Band, The transformation of the *The Ghost of Tom Joad* unbelievable. 'Land of Hope and Dreams' was emerging as a massive concert song. I even got to grab Bruce by the arm as he came through the crowd. One of my also-fanatical Bruce fans (Bruce Tucker) spied this from across the arena and was fucking jealous as all hell.

The next two shows at AAMI Stadium proved Bruce gets better with age. The first I introduced my son Jordan to The Boss and he at 21 proved there is no generation gap. He loved it as well. I remember standing with him near the front sharing some cold beers, Bruce's acoustic 'Thunder Road' taking us to another place. He even played 'Factory'.

The last show I attended (I went both nights in Melbourne) were again inspirational and I got into the front row of the pit. It was over 30 degrees and sweat was pouring off him but at 67 he still gave all he had. Standouts were 'Trapped', 'Born to Run' and 'Dancing in the Dark', a showpiece for the incredible sax solo Jake Clemons has made his own, slotting into the huge shoes of the Big Man with ease. This night was also my wedding anniversary and unfortunately my wife had to miss out. It would be wrong to not pay tribute the greatest support band in the world, the E Street Band. Beside all these life-changing memories, I still crave to see 'Jungleland' live, hoping this can come true one day.

I have relatives in New Jersey, have been there twice and visited the Stone Pony, E Street and 10th Avenue. My life has been enriched by having Bruce take me through the journey, and his love and support of Australia is profound.

I WAS THERE: DEB MONOTTI

I've seen Bruce eight times, the first in 1985 in Melbourne for the Born in the U.S.A. tour. I've been hooked since. Most recently I travelled to see him and the E Street Band in Barcelona for the start of The River tour in Europe in 2016, then went to four of the Summer '17 concerts in Australia. Hanging Rock was the standout - a fabulous setting, Bruce was happy, the crowd was great. I was transported to a different place. I just hope we haven't seen the last of him on tour. I would be devastated.

SLANE CASTLE

1 JUNE 1985 DUBLIN, IRELAND

I WAS THERE: ANNE COX HAYDEN

It was my first concert, and what a brilliant concert it was. It was the most gorgeous sunny day. Not that we get many in Ireland. The bus companies organised buses from our city centre to Slaine, County Meath, taking about two hours. I was 18 and went with my then-boyfriend. I became a fan when he gave me a copy of 'The River' on single.

The song that stood out was 'Born in the U.S.A.' I remember getting squashed, as we were right up the front, with Bruce concerned for his fans. My two favourite songs were 'The River' and 'Trapped'. I kept the ticket and brochure as mementos of that special day, one of those days that'll always stick in my mind. I've attended every Springsteen show in Dublin since.

BRUCE SPRINGSTEEN AND THE E.STREET BAND
SLANE CASTLE Saturday 1st June 1985
Gates open 3-00pm   Concert from 5-00pm
TICKETS £15.00 No Refunds, No Exchanges
No Bottles, Cans, Tape Recorders, Cameras,
Folding Chairs, or Umbrellas. CONCERT RAIN OR S
ANYONE SEEKING TO GAIN ADMISSION USING A COUNTERFEIT TICK
WILL BE PROSECUTED

BRUCE SPRINGSTEEN
AND THE E STREET BAND
IN CONCERT
AT SLANE CASTLE
SATURDAY 1th. JUNE 1985
GATES OPEN
AT 3.00.P.M.
CONTENTS OF
PROGRAMME ON PAGE 2.
OFFICIAL PRICE £1.00

I WAS THERE: FRANK MCNALLY

It was 1985, and money was scarce. Some of us were so strapped for cash that we heroically ignored the hype preceding his appearance at Slane. Until the afternoon itself, that is; whereupon our resistance collapsed.

It was a beautiful day and I remember listening to the wireless - as we called it – in a house in deepest south Dublin, when the station went live to Slane for a report on the start of the concert. Sure enough, Springsteen was already on stage – I could hear him in the background. And the effect was electrifying.

It was a bit like St Patrick – a much earlier headline act in Slane – lighting the paschal fire. Bruce was calling me to Meath, and I had to go. I dropped everything and went, catching a No.15 bus into the city, then a 19A out to Finglas. From there, I started hitching.

They were days then when you got one lift all the way to your destination, without even trying. This was one of the other days - when friendly farmers driving beat-up Ford Anglia's and in no hurry to get anywhere would bring you from here up to the next turn-off, at which point you had to get your thumb out again. But I reached the outskirts of Slane in four or five instalments and walked the last mile-and-a-half into the village, which was now shrouded in silence.

Was the concert over? Hell, no. It was just the half-time break. During which, I found a forlorn tout who, having a clearance sale, offloaded his last ticket to me for a fiver – 66 per cent off the recommended retail price.

Thus, having heard the start of Springsteen's Slane concert on a radio in Templeogue, and having made at least six separate vehicular trips in the meantime, I attended the second half of the concert, which lasted the guts of two hours. And the great thing was, I still had money left for food. Tell young people that now, and they won't believe you.

I WAS THERE: JOHN KENNEDY

I was working in the VIP lounge at Dublin airport, I made sure I was there because I'm a big Bruce fan and he was leaving for the US, so there I am working away in the corridor and in walks my hero. And what do I do? Nothing, I freeze, he walks up to me, says, 'Excuse me, buddy' and walks by. I stand there with my mouth open. I didn't even say 'hello'. We named our big golden retriever dog Bruce. He had a very hungry heart.

ST. JAMES PARK

4 JUNE 1985 NEWCASTLE-UPON-TYNE, UK

I WAS THERE: ALAN ROBSON, MBE

I hosted Bruce's two shows at St. James Park, and was lucky enough to grab a chat, discussing his all-time favourite acts - all rock'n'rollers. He paid a lovely tribute to Eddie Cochran, Chuck Berry, Roy Orbison and many of the Fifties greats, all pointing at him to just get up there and do it. If the song and voice is good enough it will work. I mentioned that an audience loves an act that will sweat for them. Bruce laughed and said, 'Well they'll get plenty of that!'

The band were kind enough to sign a guitar, and this show was one of the greatest ever at any stadium in Britain. It lasted close on three hours, most people travelling on public transport stayed behind, missing trains, buses, lifts etc. and there is not one who will regret it. The city was at a standstill when the crowds piled out, getting in their cars just in time to hear my chat with the boss on Night Owls, Metro Radio & TFM, and enjoy a few classics they had just heard live.

Lovely genuine and sincere guy, lovely genuine band all feet on the ground. Clarence Clemons, suited and booted, and giving as good a show as he ever did. Bruce in a black leather jacket and biker boots delivering a clean gorgeous sound, not easy in stadia. Later I was back staying at the Gosforth Park Hotel, now a Marriott, then serving 24-hour room service, eating fish, chips and mushy peas, the exact same meal Bruce had after he got back from the gig.

He announced he had given £16,000 to sacked miners following the strike. My abiding memory of a true gentleman of the road and travelling troubadour was when I left him. He shook my hand with both of his, and said 'That was so great, I hope it was good enough for you.' Yes mate, it was.

Alan Robson warms up the crowd at St. James Park

ULLEVI STADIUM

9 JUNE 1985 GOTHENBURG, SWEDEN

I WAS THERE: EVA GARDHEDEN

I was born in Sweden but lived in Canada for a few years. The first time I saw Bruce Springsteen was on TV. It must have been 1979 or 1980. I think it was broadcast from New York. After watching that I was hooked. I was 30 then.

After I moved back to Sweden I went to a Born in the U.S.A. concert at Ullevi, Gothenburg. The song that stood out was 'Dancing in the Dark.' Fantastic concert.

I drove my car with my 8-year old daughter Charlotte from Stockholm. On our way, we met an old friend from Canada. There was no time for more than a hug. We had our seats high in the stand, among over 64,000 people; Springsteen set a record with that performance. He knew how to fill a giant arena and we all felt like a single big rock'n'roll family. The audience jumped up and down so much that the arena, built on clay, was giving way. A couple of days later, those responsible for building the stadium discovered how close to a disaster we

Eva Gardheden and daughter Charlotte

were. After that, Ullevi was reinforced with concrete pillars, extended down to the bedrock.

I then saw Bruce at Stockholm Stadion in 1988 and 1992 in Globen. My most recent was at Ullevi in 2016. Absolutely amazing.

WALDSTADION

15 JUNE 1985 FRANKFURT, WEST GERMANY

I WAS THERE: MARK BARTOVICK

It was a gorgeous summer day and there were probably more American military members in the crowd than locals. It was the longest show I've ever been to, about four hours as I recall. The sound was deafening when 'Born in the U.S.A.' was played and the crowd joined in. The East Germans and Soviets across the border 90 miles away must have heard everything in those moments. I think the last song was 'Twist and Shout', a real jam session that went on for so long you first wondered if it would ever end, and then you hoped it never would. An awesome experience that we'll never forget.

I was a 22-year-old American airman stationed at Ramstein Air Base and travelled the roughly 90 miles to Frankfurt with my girlfriend and my best friend, both of whom were also airmen stationed in Germany, him at Sembach and her at Bitburg. We had been fans for years and were very excited about seeing The Boss on

15. Juni '85 · Einl.: 15 Uhr · Beg.: 18 Uhr
FRANKFURT · WALDSTADION
MAMA CONCERTS PRESENTS

BRUCE
SPRINGSTEEN
& THE E STREET BAND

Wichtiger Hinweis für Veranstaltungsbesucher!
Das Mitbringen von Dosen und Flaschen ist nicht erlaubt, ebenso wie Lebensmittel in Dosen oder Glasbehältern. Camping innerhalb des Stadions ist nicht zugelassen.

Nº 3438

Ton-, Film- und Videoaufnahmen sind generell untersagt. Pyrotechnische Gegenstände und Waffen dürfen nicht auf das Veranstaltungsgelände gebracht werden. Bei Nichtbeachtung kann der Besucher aus dem Veranstaltungsgelände verwiesen werden. Bei Einlaß findet eine Sicherheitskontrolle statt.
Keine Haftung für Sach- und Körperschäden! Rückerstattung des Kaufpreises erfolgt nur bei genereller Absage des Konzertes. Verschiebung über die Vorverkaufsstelle, bei der die Eintrittskarte erworben wurde. Verschiebung des Konzerttermins möglich. Beim Verlassen des Geländes verliert die Eintrittskarte ihre Gültigkeit. Das Konzert wird bei

this tour. A lot of people hadn't yet realized the lyrics for 'Born in the U.S.A.' were more critical in nature than patriotic, but military members overseas loved the chorus and you could hear the song being blasted out of countless speakers in barracks everywhere. Frankfurt had a large US military community in 1985, and there were well over 150,000 US troops stationed within a 150-mile radius of the city, so the proportion of US attendees compared to locals was huge.

They only played a couple tracks from *Born in the U.S.A.*, plus a good mix of older tracks, of which 'Hungry Heart' and 'Ramrod' were among my personal favourites. Most memorable besides those were 'Born in the U.S.A.' and 'Dancing in the Dark', where Bruce pulls a female out of the crowd onstage, like in the video. She turned out to be a military member. Then there was the seemingly- endless 'Twist and Shout' jam near the end. The length and quality of the concert were worth many times the ticket price.

WEMBLEY STADIUM

4 JULY 1985 LONDON, UK

I WAS THERE: SUE BRIGHTON

I've seen Bruce twice; the first time in 1985 at Wembley. At the time I wasn't sure what I had let myself in for, I was going through a messy time, had just got out of a violent marriage and my friend decided I needed to do something different, paying all my expenses. During that concert I'm sure I became a different person. I came away feeling much stronger. That was the day I began to get my confidence back and my life back on track.

I didn't get to see Bruce again until 2017 in Christchurch, New Zealand. I was thrilled when my second husband bought tickets to see him for my birthday. I wasn't disappointed. His performance was as good as 30 years ago. I didn't get up on stage either time, but if the opportunity to see him again arises I will be there.

I WAS THERE: MARK COLLINS

We're an odd bunch, us Bruce Buds. Yes, we're tribal in our love of
The Boss but you'd never know if one of us moved in next door to
you or started dating your son or daughter. We have no 'uniform' so

Very exited Bruce fan Mark Collins

to speak to distinguish us
from other fans of bands
or artists. We're both blue
and white-collar workers,
we're the Hedge Fund
manager, the middle
manager, the nurse and
the barrister. We're male
and female, we're young
and old, we're father, son
and daughter and in some
cases whole families. We're
everywhere but you can't
see us… except when
Bruce Springsteen comes
to town.

I suppose I got into
Springsteen relatively late
compared to the diehards.

It was 1980 when I bought *The River*. I'd heard tracks from *Born to
Run* played on the radio (and loved them) but my informative teenage
years were taken up with the Ramones, Sex Pistols, The Jam, and
later ska music. I'd moved to London and started listening to Capital
Radio, especially Roger Scott, not only a huge Springsteen fan but
also a huge influence on me getting into radio, as I eventually did.
He'd play tracks from *The River* and later the *Live 1975-1985* album
and *Born in the U.S.A.*

I loved his enthusiasm and passion for Bruce. You heard it in his
voice and wanted to emulate him and his taste in music. That's when
I first saw Springsteen live; the summer of '85 at Wembley. I was

hooked. Like the dealer giving an unsuspecting junkie his first hit for free, I now had to go to every live date I could afford and live the religious-like experience of seeing him live.

Like a disciple, I've seen him perform 23 times live in various UK cities and flown with friends to New York City to experience the feeling in his own backyard. That's not many times compared to other Bruce Buds I've met. A Dutch guy in Dublin told me he was on concert No.56. I asked whether his wife minded him going off and leaving her and their son (Bruce) as he criss-crossed Europe. His answer was that he wasn't married and had told his girlfriend he'd only marry her if Springsteen would be Best Man. This is the extent of our blind faith.

But what's it like when you're there in his presence? It doesn't matter which city or festival you're at. You're going to get it all. Bruce can rock you with soul, jazz, folk and crashing guitars but can make you weep at the same time and has even been known to wind up his waist with some reggae at times. Everyone always mentions the three plus hours he usually plays for with the E Street Band backing him all the way, sometimes carrying him too; and it doesn't matter if you don't know every song. You're transfixed by this man who soaks up so much love from his fans that he has to give some back before he becomes saturated and explodes. It's like a religious experience and if the man himself had any political ambitions we certainly would be welcoming President Springsteen on a state visit to this country.

I'm not a follower, I'm a leader; but don't know what it is about this man that makes me a follower. If you've never seen Bruce Springsteen and the E Street Band play live.....well....

ROUNDHAY PARK

7 JULY 1985 LEEDS, UK

I WAS THERE: GILL HOWELL

My first experience of Bruce and the E Street Band. I was hooked. I love listening to the bootleg from that day and it was brilliant to hear Bruce reference that gig when he played Leeds in 2013 (Leeds Arena). That was an incredible experience as is was a much smaller indoor venue than he typically plays.

I WAS THERE: IAN DE-WHYTELL

An incredible event in a wonderful location on a perfect summer day. It was the Born in the U.S.A. tour so that album featured prominently in the set list, but with Bruce you always get value for money, which meant he was on stage for about four hours. I managed to get a great spot just to the left of the pavilion, and a perfect view. The Boss of course had the crowd eating out of his hands from the moment he walked onto the stage at 4pm.

I WAS THERE: BURTON-ON-TRENT BANKER

I was a bank manager in Burton-on-Trent, Staffordshire. Normally the bank would entertain their customers to lunch or similar. I took some of mine 90 miles up the M1 to see Bruce live at Roundhay Park in Leeds. He was great, the weather was good and so was the music. Doubt that would happen these days.

I WAS THERE: MARTIN CASEY

First time I saw Bruce was on the big screen was 1979's No Nukes concert. By the time I walked out of the cinema I was hooked. The only thing I could think about was to see this man live. I started listening to his music nightly and it became an obsession. Little did I realise it would last a lifetime. A year later I managed, along with good friends to get tickets for The River tour. I've been fortunate and managed to see Bruce on every UK and Irish tour since, and also the

Amnesty tour in 1988 and Glastonbury Festival.

Watching Bruce and the E Street Band over the years has given me some of the greatest times I could possibly wish for - every concert has stayed with me for different reasons. And the one that always brings a smile to my face was the Born in the U.S.A. tour.

Martin Casey meets Bruce in London during his book tour

By the time tickets went on sale Bruce was more popular than ever, never off the radio. His fan-base in the UK had gone through the roof. We applied for tickets for Roundhay Park. Some of us were lucky, some didn't but decided they'd go anyway. The day arrived and we set off in convoy for the two-hour drive over the Pennines.

It was a warm humid day and everyone was looking forward to seeing The Boss. When we arrived in Leeds the atmosphere on the streets was electric. The pubs were full, the streets were fuller. Locals sat at the end of their gardens selling ice-cold beer. Merchandise sellers had the best day ever.

After a good few beers we arrived. The sight of that crowd will stay with me forever. Everyone seemed to know they were about to witness something very special. Bruce and the band came on and broke into 'Born in the U.S.A.' The crowd went mad. The first thing

I noticed was the E Street Band had changed and Bruce had muscled up. Nils had joined and the red-headed woman had joined. Patti's voice brought something else and you could see straight away this wasn't going to be a short-term edition. Nils looked like he'd played with them for years. They fitted in. Bruce knew it, the band knew it. They went through the show with an energy I'd never seen before. Every single person on that stage looked like they were having the time of their lives. Bruce's laugh and the Big Man's smile are etched on my memory. They summed the whole day up between the two of them. The songs were fantastic. The stories Bruce told were both funny and poignant.

Personal highlights for me were 'Trapped', 'Thunder Road', and 'Racing in the Street'. Towards the end, Little Steven joined Bruce and the band for the last few songs and you just knew by the way they looked at each other it wouldn't be the last time. Bruce ended with 'Rocking all Over the World', 80,000 happy people singing along - a fitting end to a glorious summer's day.

My wife and I often talk about that day. Memories last forever. Thank you, Bruce and the E Street Band - it's been emotional.

SOLDIER FIELD

9 AUGUST 1985 CHICAGO, ILLINOIS

I WAS THERE: KAREN LANGE

In August 1985, I was a 21-year old in desperate need of help. For a year and one half I'd been under the spell of an emotionally-abusive psychiatrist. I wasn't allowed to make any decisions without his consent and he rarely gave it, claiming I was too fragile. Could I apply for this part time job? Can I go to community college? Can I hang out with my friends? Nope. Nope. Nope.

One subject I didn't talk a lot about with him was my growing fascination with Bruce Springsteen and his music. He was coming to Soldier Field as part of the Born in the U.S.A. tour. My brother Chuck surprised me by getting tickets for the show. I was elated. But first I had to check with my doctor. He laughed in my face, then told me Soldier Field held about 68,000 people and that alone would send me into panic attacks - the kind of which I've never known. He went on to tell me if I went, my panic and anxiety would become so great I'd end up in a psych ward.

But this was a Springsteen concert! Those mythical three and a half hour events I've heard so much about. I took a huge leap of faith and went. And had 0 panic attacks. It was the most incredible concert I've ever been to. I've been to a lot of concerts, but none compared to the party that went on at Soldier Field that night.

In August 1985, I was a 21-year-old in desperate need of help. And I found it at a Bruce Springsteen concert. It shook me out from under my psychiatrist's spell and set me free to live a normal life with friends, family, and Springsteen concerts.

VETERANS STADIUM

14 AUGUST 1985 PHILADELPHIA, PENNSYLVANIA

I WAS THERE: JOYCE ORONZIO

I was still in nursing school in August 1985. The concert was in Philly and because I had to attend classes that day I kept my boys (12 and 15 at the time) out of school and dropped them off at the local mall to stand in line and get tickets for me, my friend and our kids, with my two boys and her two girls the same ages.

We dropped them off at 7am and they stood all day till about 3.30pm when they finally were able to buy the tickets. Bad Mom. I had been a fan of Bruce since the early Seventies but missed him when he came to

Joyce Oronzio (second from left front row)

Widener University around that time here in Delaware County. He did many of his biggest songs that night, but the ones that stand out in my mind are 'Tenth Avenue Freeze-Out', 'Born to Run' and 'Jersey Girl.' I absolutely love 'Jersey Girl', even though he didn't write it. It's the quintessential Philly, South Jersey story of young love here in the working-class towns.

CNE STADIUM

26 AUGUST 1985 TORONTO, CANADA

I WAS THERE: MARLENE ARPE

I knew this concert was going to be great. I'd already seen the band pass through Toronto a year earlier, just after the release of *Born in the U.S.A.* What I didn't expect was how much Springsteen's stock had risen in the intervening 12 months. His popularity had dimmed in the new decade, partly due to *Nebraska*. Hardcore fans like me still loved him, but the hits-laden *Born in the U.S.A.* vaulted him into a mainstream phenomenon to rival Michael Jackson and Madonna, amid heavy radio play.

That CNE show, the first of two sell-outs, was proof positive. I watched with amazement as the family sitting in front of me, a well-to-do middle-aged couple and three kids aged about 10 to 18, all started to put on the pricey Springsteen T-shirts they'd just bought at the merch stand.

Standing before a giant US flag, he and The E Streeters wailed through a nearly three-hour show, including Clarence Clemons, the 'Big Man,' on sax, as though they wished the starry night would never end. 'Let's rip this town apart!' Springsteen said.

It was the most magical night and seemed even then like the end of an era. This was the last summer before the first of the Baby Boomers turned 40, and the Rock Generation really responded to the farewell-to-youth tone of the songs on *Born in the U.S.A.*

It was also close to the last hurrah for CNE Stadium, which closed a few years later. Concert promoters packed the two shows with nearly 140,000 fans; way past official capacity. Furious fire officials had a lot to say about that afterwards.

Rocking by the lake in Toronto never seemed more like a collective pleasure - or mass nose-thumbing to authority - than it did on those two hot nights with Bruce Springsteen in August 1985.

01. Born in the U.S.A.
02. Badlands
03. Out in the Street
04. Johnny 99
05. Seeds
06. Atlantic City
07. The River
08. I'm Goin' Down
09. Working on the Highway
10. Trapped (Jimmy Cliff cover)
11. Glory Days
12. The Promised Land
13. My Hometown
14. Thunder Road
15. Cover Me
16. Dancing in the Dark
17. Hungry Heart
18. Cadillac Ranch
19. Downbound Train
20. I'm on Fire
21. Pink Cadillac
22. Bobby Jean
23. Can't Help Falling in Love
24. Born to Run
25. Ramrod
26. Twist and Shout / Do You Love Me
27. Sherry Darling

HOOSIER DOME

6 SEPTEMBER 1985 INDIANAPOLIS, INDIANA

I WAS THERE: JAMES DUNLAP

On the Born in the U.S.A. tour in my hometown, Bruce told a
story about his life growing up and issues with his father. I was
tearing up and started looking around at the crowd. I swear
80,000 people were on the edge of their seats, balling their
eyes out. I've seen every rock show imaginable, from 1977 Led
Zeppelin to the Grateful Dead in the Nineties, and never saw
anything close to this kind of entertainment. Bruce and the
E Street Band were hands-down the best live show you could
imagine. Not to mention 'Born to Run'.

1986

ASGIRIYA STADIUM

KANDY, SRI LANKA

I WAS THERE: MARK NICHOLAS

On tour in Sri Lanka in 1986, I walked to the wicket as Captain
of an England 'A' team battling to save an unofficial Test
match in Kandy. Mike Selvey, the former England bowler and
lifelong Bruce Springsteen fan, fixed it for 'Hungry Heart' and
'No Surrender' to be played on the PA during the tea interval.
Inspired, I made a few runs and we saved the match.

1988

THE CENTRUM

25 FEBRUARY 1988 WORCESTER, MASSACHUSETTS

I WAS THERE: BRENDAN MELICAN

I just remember they were great seats from an 11-year-old's perspective. Somewhere stage right. My father was a huge Springsteen fan, and a fan of music in general and this was the first time I really saw him get excited about being at a show. I still have his record collection and it's amazing to realize as an adult how your parents sort of shape a soundtrack to your life via the music they listen to. Clemons was a larger than life musician for me as a kid. I remember being floored by his sax in the 'Dancing in the Dark' video. That was like the high-water mark for cool by Eighties standards. But the additional horn section was just crazy to see and hear. It's also probably where my tinnitus originated, even if it's more fun to blame that on late nights at the Lucky Dog in my 20's.

But my biggest memory overall is of the tour t-shirt. I was so excited to wear it to school the next day, but it wasn't the most masculine shirt ever designed and I was a small kid, so it was basically a flowered dress featuring Bruce holding a bouquet, of more flowers. I got picked on a lot for that shirt, not an easy look to pull off in Worcester, circa '88, but I wore the shit out of it.

THE CENTRUM

28 FEBRUARY 1988 WORCESTER, MASSACHUSETTS

I WAS THERE: MARK SENIOR

Why start a tour in Worcester? People were shocked. We couldn't believe it. You would have thought he would've started the tour in the Meadowlands. They didn't have a big production stage with curtains and videos like they do at concerts now. It was just the band. You could see everything.

One of the few things I remember from the show was a girl sitting in the front row with a t-shirt on that said, 'Tramps Like Us.' Springsteen opened with 'Tunnel of Love' singing to Patti Scialfa, the stage set up like an amusement park on the Jersey Shore boardwalk, acting like a kid going on a first date. The show kicked off from there. It was crazy, over in three hours, going by real fast.

THE CENTRUM

29 FEBRUARY 1988 WORCESTER, MASSACHUSETTS

I WAS THERE: NICK D'ANDREA

The night of the show I met with two more recipients at WXLO, at that time located in the former Worcester Center Galleria. We took a tour of the station then walked over with a couple of representatives from the station. I remember the energy of the crowd. It was pretty electric. I specifically recall, as the concert was coming to an end, Bruce acknowledging the crowd and city of Worcester for being a great place to open his world tour. He said, 'We are now going to rock the rest of the world for you.' I am a big fan of 'Born to Run' I still have it on my running playlist, so I was amped to hear that song. Bruce took a different approach with it this time. He played it acoustically during one of the encores - the first one, I think.

He also played 'Dancing in the Dark', in the way of the song's music video. He brought a woman on to the stage to dance, just like in the video. It was little too staged, but cool to see. The song I thought he knocked out of the park was a cover of the Edwin Starr hit, 'War.'

I WAS THERE: TIM GARVIN

When you're a Springsteen fan, you love him almost without critique, but this was a very different show. The Born in the U.S.A. show was a stadium show. Springsteen would tell funny stories in between songs and they went on forever.

This show was orchestrated more than any other show I'd seen. There was a lot of new stuff, which I thought was good, but I wasn't used to it as much as I was the old stuff. I was really a traditionalist. But it was an excellent show because I hadn't seen him in three years. I was dating a woman, Theresa, who is now my wife. I'm not a huge fan of 'Brilliant Disguise.' I've never been a fan of 'Hungry Heart.' I think it's the worst song he's ever performed and that's his biggest hit ever. And I think this show was the first time I've ever seen Springsteen play 'Born to Run' acoustically, which I thought was interesting.

VILLA PARK

21 JUNE 1988 BIRMINGHAM, UK

I WAS THERE: NICK CUNNINGHAM

I saw my hero in the flesh for the first time, around 7.45 that night. That's the detail I remember. A 13-year-old boy at his first gig, almost 30 years later.

I was introduced to The Boss by my Mum from a very early age, probably too young to go to the Born in the U.S.A. tour, so Tunnel of Love Express it was.

The band came on one by one, started to play. I didn't work out it was layering the intro to the title track of the album, probably too excited. My memory tells me he played all the classics, including my favourite, 'Bobby Jean' (seen him twice more since and he hasn't played it). 'Brilliant Disguise' and 'One Step Up' also showed themselves and were epic. I was slightly disappointed with the acoustic 'Born

Nick Cunningham (centre-back) Trinity School photo 1988

To Run', but now look back at that as something special which he'll probably never do again.

Those three-plus hours will never be forgotten. I don't think my eyes moved away from him for the whole time, like watching a magician performing. Epic. The next day I wore my tour t-shirt to school, hands hurting from clapping, voice shot from shouting and singing. This is rock'n'roll, I thought then … and still do.

Almost 20 years to the day later, I took my mum to see him at Old Trafford, Manchester, 2008. I remember saying, 'Wow, 20 years on and his energy is no different.' A guy in his late 50s, charging around like a man in his 30s. Everyone should experience the magic of a Springsteen gig. No support act and three to four hours of hit after hit. Proud to call him my Boss.

VILLA PARK

22 JUNE 1988 BIRMINGHAM, UK

I WAS THERE: MATT BOURNE

I was always a bit jealous of my sister. She got to see Springsteen in Newcastle on the Born in the U.S.A. tour in 1985. I was too young and it was too far from the badlands of Worcestershire for me to go. So by the time the 'Tunnel of Love' tour hit Birmingham three years later, I was beyond excited. Not only was he playing 20 miles up the road, he was playing Villa Park. I was an Aston Villa season-ticketholder - he was playing on my manor.

The only trouble was: where *Born in the U.S.A.* was the rock'n'roll blockbuster, with songs resonating with an enthusiastic teenager, while *Tunnel of Love* was about mid-life crises and divorces, stuff I didn't need to worry about for at least another 20 years. I hadn't yet connected with the songs. By the time I left Villa Park that was to change though.

I remember rolling down the freeway (okay, Walsall Road) with local radio stations celebrating the fact that Springsteen was playing such a parochial date. 'Tougher than the Rest' was the current single and as it crackled from the radio, for the first time I realised the resonance of the new record. Big bold Telecaster lines, what's not to like?

I'm sure Springsteen started every gig on that tour with the album's title track and 'Hello (insert city name), wanna take a ride?', and am sure everyone who attended one of the shows on that tour were along for the ride. One by one the E Street Band rose up from a tunnel on the centre of the stage, eventually Springsteen. The new album's title track seemed the obvious place to start but following it with 'Boom Boom' by John Lee Hooker was a masterstroke. More than anything this signified to me that despite being the biggest rock star on the planet does not necessarily mean you have to play the game. Some may follow a greatest hits formula, and to a certain extent what followed was, but a nod to the great American lineage was bookended by three more cover versions.

The gig featured on the local TV news the following night, a two-minute clip I watched a thousand times, and despite the somewhat expected jibes from my friends that Villa Park 'hadn't been so full for years', it was a powerful evening. Romantic tales of the 'last of the Duke Street Kings' beneath the shadow of an Ansell's Mild advertisement. Good old Ansell's.

CAMP LEJEUNE

4 JULY 1988 JACKSONVILLE, NORTH CAROLINA

I WAS THERE: RICHARD P. SCAROLA

I got a chance to play a July 4th concert as a bassist in the Marine Band with Clarence Clemons at Camp Lejeune in 1988. He was the brother of my band officer, William Clemons. Fantastic. Subsequently, Clarence got us VIP seats for the Tunnel of Love concert in Charlotte. Bruce acknowledged a few servicemen in the crowd that had played with Clarence. It was a great experience.

On September 2, 1988, Bruce Springsteen, Sting and Peter Gabriel kicked off the Human Rights Now! tour at London's Wembley Stadium.

The 20-date tour took place over six weeks as a benefit for Amnesty International in honour of the 40th anniversary of the United Nations' adoption of the Universal Declaration of Human Rights.

The shows featured Bruce Springsteen and the E Street Band, Sting, Peter Gabriel, Tracy Chapman, and Youssou N'Dour, plus guest artists from each of the countries where concerts were held. At each location, the artists and Amnesty leaders held a press conference to discuss human rights.

BRAMALL LANE

10 JULY 1988 SHEFFIELD, UK

I WAS THERE: DEREK BREEZE

At the time I was living in the tower blocks at the bottom of Cemetery Road, which isn't that far from the ground. When the concert started I had to open the windows to stop them breaking from the vibration of the sound. The crowd obviously enjoyed it because the applause after each song was deafening. The atmosphere around the ground was amazing, Even the police were smiling.

WALDSTADION

12 JULY 1988 FRANKFURT, WEST GERMANY

I WAS THERE: NILS LINNECKEN

Like so many others, I became a fan when the *Born in the U.S.A.* hype hit Europe in the mid-Eighties. It must have been 1986. The tour was already over and I started exploring Bruce's music, listening to his older records. The *1975-1985* collection was constantly playing in my room and I was dreaming of seeing the man live one day. Others who saw him in concert raved about how great and intense his shows had been.

I remember how there were three or four of us regularly meeting on Friday and Saturday evenings to listen to Bruce's records together, drinking beer and eating pizza. His songs ignited those little motion pictures in my head when I listened to them, and still do. Through 'The River', 'My Hometown' and 'Darlington County', Bruce spoke to me in a literary way that deeply touched my soul. His music was 'cinematic' on so many different levels and I could indulge in it so many different ways, be it dancing wildly at teenage parties with half a dozen bottles of beer in my belly or lying on my bed alone listening to 'State Trooper'.

Those were the days when I fell in love with Bruce's voice and those little movies he put into my head every time I listened to his songs. I was craving to see Springsteen and the E Street Band live at least once.

In those pre-Internet days we had no clue about what was going on in the studios or what his plans were. Was he ever going to come back on tour?

In the spring of 1988 I finished high school and it was the summer of my life. School was over, the future was wide open, the days were never-ending and sunny, I had a girlfriend, and Bruce was coming back to Europe.

My first show was in the mid-summer of '88 at the Waldstadion, and that night Bruce Springsteen and the E Street Band gave me something that got me hooked for the rest of my life.

I've seen Bruce 80 times since that first night in Frankfurt, in many different cities and countries, but every time the band comes on, each one taking their position on stage, and when Bruce finally steps up to the mic. hollering 'Good evening!' under the cheers of the crowd, I get catapulted back in time and space to my high school years and that steaming summer night in a football stadium in Frankfurt in 1988.

NEPSTADION

6 SEPTEMBER 1988 BUDAPEST, HUNGARY

I WAS THERE: DAVID MACKU

Before I begin let me describe a bit how the world looked 30 years ago. Europe was divided until 1989 into East and West. The West was part of the free world (under the influence of the USA), the East was the Soviet Union's zone of interest. Most of the Eastern bloc

countries were also members of
the Warsaw Pact, in opposition
to NATO. Each sector of Europe
had its own market, way of life,
living standards, propaganda and
world- view. The East knew very
little about real human rights,
although that issue was mentioned
in the constitution. Human rights
had been something like taboo in the
Czechoslovakian press, radio and
television for many reasons.

I still live in a country now called
the Czech Republic. Back then,
as Czechoslovakia, travelling into
the West was very complicated,
not banned as such, but not a
lot of people were able to get
out. Simply put, our leaders
didn't want its citizens to see the
grass was greener behind the
fence. But music and radio can
cross any borders, and we've
known partly what was going
on behind the barbed wire.
Western records weren't on sale
the way fans would expect, but
some albums were available
from time to time, in limited
amounts. So you can imagine how hungry
for Western rock the young people were. There used to be a black
market in those things. A lot were also brought in (partly illegally) by
those who travelled to the West, a big issue at the time.

Regarding The Boss, sometime in 1985 Czech music stores had
a very special offer. For some unknown reason, about five different

Western albums were suddenly on sale, and one of them was *Born in the U.S.A.* Big time. Those albums were imported from Holland and it was our introduction of Springsteen. He wasn't unknown here but Czech radio hardly played him. I remember only one programme about *The River* but knew more of his songs from Radio Luxembourg and Austria Ö3. I had no idea how he looked.

The very first Bruce Springsteen show in the Eastern Bloc took place in East Berlin, and almost everybody who was able to go was there. East Germany was one of very few countries where we were able to travel without visa and police permission, but I wasn't a real Bruce fan. Besides, there were no adverts, music press or anything similar to the way information reaches around the globe today. But news spread in the summer of 1988 that some kind of big concert was going to be held in Budapest, Hungary, featuring Springsteen, Sting and Peter Gabriel.

Budapest and Hungary were quite revolutionary then. While still under a Communist regime, the country started giving its people something they desired - Western music. Dire Straits and others had played there, Queen who were the very first act of their league to play a stadium show in Eastern Europe in 1986, and then Genesis and Peter Gabriel visited. Iron Maiden were the first open- air act to play in the East, in 1984, but played on a car park close to a stadium. I was there as well.

In 1988 we knew something was going to happen in Budapest again, but there was no place to check it. Our press ignored it. But I got an idea and wrote a letter or phoned from the post office to Slovakian capital Bratislava, where there was an office of a Hungarian travel agency, asking about it and if they could send me tickets. They were very kind, sent me a ticket by post, and it cost me very little money. The same happened with my return train ticket from Brno to Budapest. I was ready, I was a student – aged 25 - with plenty of time, ready to go anywhere the music I love plays.

The train, Amicus, left Brno shortly after midnight on Tuesday, September 6 and was packed by the same young people I remembered a year before, when we went to see Peter Gabriel. We arrived in Budapest in the morning (after border control on the Slovak/Hungarian border). I met an English friend (whose name I've forgotten but he looked like Sylvester Stallone, having met him shortly before in Czechoslovakia, where he was with a group of Swedish students) and late in the afternoon we entered a packed Népstadion, full of people from all around Eastern Europe - East Germans, Czechoslovakians, Polish, perhaps some Bulgarians, plus others from neighbouring Austria or West Germany. I didn't speak to them - I just remember listening to their languages.

The human rights issue wasn't important as such, but Hungary's regime was suddenly allowing us to talk about it - the first East European country to allow something so very Western into our closed world. Quite a special event and feeling. I said to myself that must mean something. I didn't know what. Nobody was able to imagine that Communism could ever end.

Bruce and the E Street Band closed the show, kicking off with 'Born in The U.S.A.' It was magic, amazing, wonderful. I was finally listening to those songs I knew from the radio and from my LP of the same name. I remember Sting joined Bruce for one song (or was it vice versa?). The audience went crazy. We all felt like we were somewhere else - music can give you special feelings and imagination, especially when your first language is not English. I remember saying Communism cannot last that long when there is a concert for human rights and somebody shouts that he was 'Born in the U.S.A.'.

All in all, a special event - not just a concert with different artists playing for some special reasons. Communists had opened the gates to this, and I believe it was the beginning of something that continued the next year with the fall of the Berlin Wall, and the Velvet revolution in Czechoslovakia.

Although it was September, it was a cold evening. I wore a raincoat over my T-shirt, and shorts, I was really cold. Bruce closed the show before midnight and I knew my train back home was gone. I was running around the stadium, begging any Czechs to take me behind the border. Four young women in a Skoda invited me in and let me sit on their laps for the next hour, leaving me on the Slovak side of the border, then continued to Pilsen. There I was, alone in the dark, not far from customs, which at first pointed at me by light but then let me pass. I was really cold, hitchhiking in trucks. Suddenly a small van stopped and a very kind man took me across Slovakia and home, talking all the time. Very funny he was, but I was very tired … and happy at the same time. I still owe him something for that journey.

Bruce Springsteen played for the first time ever in the Czech Republic in 1995, performing in Prague in a smaller acoustic show in Palac Kultury. I wasn't there but a man with whom I used to work accompanied him to the theater on Don Giovanni, and they spent an evening together.

OLYMPIC STADIUM

3 OCTOBER 1988 ATHENS, GREECE

I WAS THERE: GOGO THEOPHANOPOULOU

I was 28 when I saw The Boss perform live, having first heard him on the radio in the late Seventies. There was an excellent afternoon show on national radio playing foreign music, especially rock. Later in the Eighties, I would watch video clips on TV. Very few famous musicians came to my country, so the concert I describe was almost unbelievable.

In July 1988 during a trip to Frankfurt, I bought the five-LP set of *Bruce Springsteen and the E Street Band Live/1975-85*, which I have treasured. I listened to it countless times and wished I could see him live. My wish became true a few months later. A colleague at work was also a big fan and told me Athens was one of the cities for the Human Rights Now! Amnesty International concert, with Springsteen among the performers.

The concert was going to take place 500m away from my house, with tickets costing 2.000 drachmas - not very expensive. Along with Bruce, there was Peter Gabriel, Sting, Tracy Chapman and Youssou N'Dour. That day at 4.30pm, my husband, eight work colleagues and I were sat in the upper tier of the Olympic Stadium when the concert begun, among 35,000 people. Two hours later there were 70,000, and most came for The Boss.

The weather was good, but where we were sat it was a bit cold later in the evening. But we didn't mind. Jackets on and dancing. At the start, all the musicians on stage sang 'Get Up, Stand Up.' Later, Bruce duetted with Sting on 'Every Breath You Take.' By the time it was Bruce's turn to take the stage, it was dark. I remember every moment of his performance. All lights off, the first notes of 'I'm on Fire' blasted from the speakers, a spotlight on him, '*Hey little girl is your daddy home...*'' and hundreds of raised hands with lighters. Every time I recall this memory, I feel joy.

Fans in front of the stage raised American flags while he sang 'Born in the U.S.A.' He also sang 'The River', 'Raise Your Hand' and a hot 'Twist & Shout' and 'La Bamba' medley.

Wearing a sleeveless black vest, he shouted, 'I love you crazy Greeks' and we were all singing and dancing. Such a night. At the end, all the musicians returned for a 'Chimes of Freedom' finale. It was a fantastic night I will remember until the end of my life. I am very sad he's never returned, despite visiting other European countries.

1992

Bruce Springsteen's 1992–1993 World Tour kicked off in Stockholm, Sweden on 15 June 1992. The three legs saw Springsteen and his new backing band play 107 shows.

The tour followed the simultaneous release of his albums *Human Touch* and *Lucky Town* earlier in 1992 and was his first of four non-E

Street Band tours, Keyboardist Roy Bittan was the only E Street
Band member retained.

On May 9 1992 Bruce Springsteen was the special guest on *Saturday Night Live* presented by Tom Hanks. Bruce performed three numbers; 'Lucky Town', '57 Channels (And Nothin' On)', and 'Living Proof'.

> Your success story is a bigger story than whatever you're trying to say on stage... Success makes life easier. It doesn't make living easier

Bruce Springsteen 1992

RICHFIELD COLISEUM

22 AUGUST 1992 RICHFIELD, OHIO

I WAS THERE: MICHAEL TELESCA

I learned of the power of Bruce live in the mid-Seventies when I awoke from my progressive rock phase. Any dedicated fan will tell you about the unmatched energy of the live shows, but it has been the unique experiences that have sent me traveling to see him as often as I can. I have heard songs live that were never performed before or since, witnessed the power go out mid-set, experienced star-fuelled guest appearances, and seen Bruce attacked by insects of biblical proportion. I opened my eyes to somehow find myself on stage with Bruce in Cleveland; and saw my young son pulled up onstage years later in Columbia. I even helped set up the stage for his Super Bowl performance. I have revelled in the nightly marathon of all the shows that lead from one story to the next, one city to the next, and one country to the next.

Once my son was born, he was predestined to be my companion of note on the road to that habitual 'next show.' We have seen more than 106 shows together, counting - or perhaps not - three in Worcester for which he was In Utero. Do you go see a show, or do you go listen to a show?

Our ventures and misadventures have left us buried in snow, sleeping in the streets, waiting in line for days, and cast as homeless - sometimes all at the same time. We've sung happy birthday to Bruce in a thunderstorm; received fuzzy dice from the hands of the man himself; gotten caught between two mobs on a headlong charge to the front of stage; politely convinced Bruce to move an amp stack (or use column of speakers) on the heels of a three hour show to recover a picture; garnering a, 'You've got to be kidding me' look, and even listened to an album so much that we can't remember the title track. Somehow, we always come out the other side with another in the set of lifelong 'Bruce friends', incredible memories, or some undreamt new experience.

I've often been asked, why go all the way to California, Florida, or Minnesota, or Mexico, or Europe, 'Just to see another rock concert.' It seems that it shouldn't take much of an excuse to see someplace new. It shouldn't take much of an excuse to spend quality time with my son. 'Another rock concert' has always been a pretty good excuse, and Bruce isn't even just another rock concert.

My son was hardly the first person I brought along for the ride.

I have felt the pull of Bruce on my life for so long, I have wanted
to share it with anyone close to me. I've had the same running
arrangement with nearly everyone I've met: if they had never seen
Bruce live, I would take them to their first show. My drive to initiate
and indoctrinate has led to many people seeing their first show.

Twenty years working as a middle school teacher in North
Carolina have taught me the value of a proper education. Forty years
on the road with Bruce have taught me the power of rock'n'roll.
One of my most rewarding experiences married the two. In 2000, I
implemented a curriculum designed around Bruce and his music. In
the spring of that year I purchased tickets and organized a trip for
40 students see Bruce play in Charlotte. The trip was such a success,
that I have taken six subsequent classroom concert trips with as many
as 63 students. These trips laid the foundation for the only middle
school Bruce Springsteen Club in the world; 'Jukebox Graduates.'
The club continues to produce a live radio show, to achieve success
in the classroom, and receive messages and support from around the
world. They even earned enough renown to take a trip to New York
City to be featured on E Street Radio and receive a quick phone call
from Bruce himself after a show.

I've had friends suggest no single person on the planet has
introduced more people to live Bruce. With these school trips and
decades of tag-along friends and family members, my best estimate
would approach 500 first-time concertgoers. The joy of seeing so
many people have the opportunity to be energized and inspired by
Bruce makes it easy to forget the travel and ticket expenses.

Sometimes people doubt the value of bringing middle school
students to a rock concert. Do kids even like Bruce? Shouldn't they
be spending that time on the quadratic formula? Unfortunately,
there's no way to explain it without seeing it. You can't tell someone
what it's like to see Bruce for the first time. You can't explain to
someone what it's like to see a middle-schooler walking out of the
show, still pumping his fist and singing the words to 'Born to Run.'
You can't know until you see your student, hoisted on the back of
your son, caught in a pointing match with the Boss, and walking

away with a harmonica. At those times, when people question the logic of the trips, I don't try to explain the inexplicable. Instead, I relay the story of running into a young gentleman while working part time renting construction equipment:

'Hey,' he said, 'You're Mr. T, and you used to work at the alternative school in Hickory.' 'Bruce Springsteen,' He beamed. 'You took me to see Bruce Springsteen while I was at that school, in April of 2000.' We commiserated for a few minutes on the passing of Clarence Clemons. The first thing that struck me was that even 16 years after the fact, he still remembered the date of the show. He claimed that he talks about the concert at least once a month. It is difficult to say what academic value those trips had, but it is impossible to doubt the value of the experience and the memories that it held for that one young gentleman. In many ways I was working an extra job that day so my former student and others like him could have exactly those experiences. That makes it all worth it, and I'm proud of that.

THE SPECTRUM

28 AUGUST 1992 PHILADELPHIA, PENNSYLVANIA

I WAS THERE: NANCY TACCARD

I didn't have far to travel, since I'm from New Jersey, but when we got there it was pouring with rain, so we gave one of the parking attendants $20 and he let us park up front. I've been a fan since *Born to Run* came out.

After the first song, 'Red Headed Woman', I heard all these Boos and I turned and said to my friend 'Pat that's a shame all these people booing him. I thought the song was pretty decent'. She said they're saying 'Bruce!' It must have been that funny cig in the car.

1993

SECC

31 MARCH 1993 GLASGOW, UK

I WAS THERE: BILLY SLOAN

I posted off the letter, written on formal *Daily Record* headed notepaper, more in hope than expectation. My request was short and straight to the point. Would it be possible to interview Bruce Springsteen when he played live in Glasgow?

Over the years, The Boss had never done an interview specifically for the Scottish media. This was my chance to put that right. It was worth asking the question – and only going to cost a first class stamp. Nothing ventured … and all that.

But I could never have predicted the outcome.

Springsteen had slotted in a surprise gig at the SECC in the city to kick off the closing phase of a lengthy US and European tour, which had begun one year earlier. The show was scheduled for March 31, exactly a year to the day since he had released twin albums, *Human Touch* and *Lucky Town* in 1992.

He would perform in the SECC's Hall 4 to an all-standing 12,000 capacity audience, unusual in the normally seated venue. In the weeks leading up to the gig, I gently badgered Jo Donnelly, the wonderful Head of Press at Sony Music in London, to see if there had been any reply to my interview request.

'It's been passed to management. They are looking at it. So fingers crossed,' was her reply. They hadn't said no … yet'.

I took that as a positive sign. Then, just a few days before the show, Jo called to say Springsteen's management, who were based in New York, had approved the interview. I could get five minutes with him, backstage at the SECC – and crucially, be given access to his soundcheck which would take place on March 30 - 24 hours before the actual show.

I couldn't believe my luck. Jo thought she had been cut off mid-call. But I was still on the line. I just hadn't said anything because I was so dumbstruck at my good fortune.

Five minutes is not a long time in which to conduct an interview or extract any relevant information.

But it was better than nothing. And those crucial 300 seconds were all I needed. Five minutes means five good questions - which would surely yield five good answers from one of the biggest stars in rock history.

On the year long string of shows, Springsteen had been working with a group of musicians fans had dubbed 'the other band'. It was the first time he'd toured without the E Street Band, whose keyboard player Roy Bittan was the sole member of the new line up.

At four o'clock on March 30, a photographer from the paper and myself were escorted into the cavernous, empty, Hall 4. There, on stage, was Springsteen and his 'other band'.

By their very nature, soundchecks tend to be rather mundane affairs. The crew repeatedly check the sound mix while the artist runs through a couple of songs until a satisfactory balance is found. It can all be very workmanlike.

But not with Springsteen. The energy and power of his soundcheck was simply breathtaking. You'd have sworn there were already 12,000 fans packing the venue such was the sheer vitality of his performance.

But when Springsteen looked out from behind his vocal microphone all he could see in the vast, vacant floor space was ... me. It soon became clear that this was less of a soundcheck and more a full-scale production rehearsal.

The previous leg of the tour had finished on December 17 in Lexington, USA, so Springsteen and the band had not played together for more than three months. There were a few cobwebs to shake off.

It was like a private gig as Springsteen stormed through classic tracks such as 'Darkness on the Edge of Town', 'Atlantic City', 'Because the Night', Born in the U.S.A.' plus more recent material like 'Lucky Town', 'Better Days' and 'If I Should Fall Behind'.

He punched the air, spitting out his lyrics, danced the tango during guitar breaks in song and lay on his back across Roy Bittan's piano while playing a solo. The only thing missing was thunderous applause at the end of every song. He certainly deserved it.

When it comes to playing live, Springsteen is a man who never cuts corners. The soundcheck began at four o'clock … and didn't conclude until 10.30pm.

I had stood there, quite happily I should add, for six hours and thirty minutes. The only time he didn't see me from the stage during that period was when I'd nipped away for a brief toilet break.

My devotion would prove significant. It was time for my five-minute interview. To say I was nervous would be an understatement. What made it worse was that a female member of his US management team had forcibly briefed me saying: 'Remember, you've only got five minutes. Five minutes. No more. Do NOT run over time.'

Springsteen greeted me and said: 'Let's find a quiet room backstage.' He located a tiny production office, no bigger than a walk-in wardrobe, turned to his management 'minder' and said: 'See you in 20 minutes.'

I'm certain Springsteen felt guilty that I'd waited for more than six hours to get my interview, so he'd decided he would grant me four times longer than my allotted period in which to talk to him. He closed the door, we sat down, I took a deep breath and went straight into my carefully compiled list of questions. And there lay a challenge because, of course, I had only prepared for a five minute long chat. But as our conversation progressed I had to improvise … plucking extra questions out of thin air, reacting to his conversation.

As we neared the 15-minute mark, I wound up the interview, not wishing to abuse the great man's hospitality. He asked me which of his songs was my favourite. I told him, 'Thunder Road' … but it HAD to be the stripped down, acoustic version recorded at the Roxy Theatre in Hollywood which kicks off the *Live: 1975-85* triple album box set.

With minutes to spare, I decided to go for it. As he signed a couple of autographs, I said: 'Bruce, as you can maybe imagine, I am such a fan of your music. I'll probably never get the chance to interview or meet you ever again. Would it be possible to have a photograph taken with you as a souvenir of this amazing experience?' 'Sure,' he said, as we got up to leave the room. By this time, the female from management had returned and began to lead him away. The chance of a photo opportunity had gone. Or had it?

To my amazement, Springsteen approached a lone SECC security guard, stationed at the production door, and said: 'Hey, buddy, can you please take a picture?' The snap you see on this page was taken on my trusty Canon Sure Shot.

It was now 11pm. I raced back to the office and quickly told the night editor what had happened.

'Sit down and start writing,' he ordered. In the following morning's edition of the *Daily Record*, I wrote a first-person piece which began: 'Last night, rock superstar Bruce Springsteen played a surprise concert to an audience of one … me.'

Billy Sloan backstage at the SECC with Bruce

My picture standing shoulder-to-shoulder with The Boss was worth a thousand words.

The gig the following night was a triumph. I've seen Springsteen perform on numerous occasions from The River tour of 1981 to the present.

I don't think I've ever seen him live and not been totally thrilled by the experience. This show was no different.

In between songs, I exited the venue to file my copy via a pay phone in the foyer. Remember, this was in the days long before laptops and emails.

My review was very positive, but I did point out a couple of constructive criticisms.

At the end of the show, I returned to the office and waited for the first 'Streets'' edition of the *Daily Record* to roll off the printing presses. The coverage looked great with a stunning picture of the singer on the SECC stage.

I grabbed 30 copies of the paper and went straight to One Devonshire Gardens, a posh boutique hotel in Glasgow's leafy west end, where Springsteen was staying during his visit to the city. There was tight security at the front door. Sony Music and gig promoter Harvey Goldsmith were hosting an after-show drinks party for the singer and his entourage.

When Harvey spotted me with copies of the Record, he nodded to the guards and they let me through. 'Let's see what you've written,' he said, and began passing copies round to his fellow guests.

I could see Springsteen across the room talking to friends. But suddenly, all conversation hushed as people began to read my review. It was like the first night opening of a new Broadway show. I was suddenly gripped with panic. What if Springsteen doesn't like – or agree – with my minor criticisms? Don't get me wrong, the review was glowing … but I had made what I felt were a couple of honest points.

Harvey complimented me on my review. Others were also fulsome in their praise. I wasn't going to get lynched … and began to breathe more easily.

I chatted to some more guests, including Ricky Ross and Lorraine McIntosh of Deacon Blue, who were also signed to Sony. The party was in full swing.

After about 30 minutes, Springsteen began to say his goodbyes. He was turning in for the night. I could see him walking towards me. 'Thank you very much for your kinds words. It was great to talk to you,' he said, in all sincerity, 'see you next time.'

I almost slid down the wall. Jo Donnelly put an arm around me to help prop me up. 'Well done. He enjoyed the interview and loved your review,' she told me.

For a music fan, it just doesn't get much better than that. From posting the initial letter to walking on air out of the after-show party, it had been an experience I'll never forget.

A couple of lines of lyric from his 1992 album perfectly sum it all up: 'When it comes to luck you make your own, Down in Lucky Town.'

NATIONAL BOWL

22 MAY 1993 MILTON KEYNES, UK

I WAS THERE: ROB & JEAN PARSONS

We first discovered Bruce's music in the early Nineties, which in retrospect, probably wasn't his best period as he had disbanded the E Street Band and recorded two albums (*Human Touch* and *Lucky Town*) with a new group of musicians. We didn't realise the significance of this decision at the time and really liked both of the albums (especially *Lucky Town*), so when a tour was announced we couldn't wait to see him live.

The concert started with Bruce performing three acoustic songs – 'Seeds', 'Adam Raised a Cain' and 'This Hard Land' and we immediately thought he was on a different level to anyone we'd seen before but were disconcerted to hear what we believed to be booing coming from the crowd. We couldn't understand what was happening and then it dawned on us that the crowd was shouting 'Bruuue!' What followed was a three-hour set comprising songs from the new albums, old classics and a smattering

of covers. My wife Jean describes herself as a 'bit of a short arse' who doesn't enjoy being in large crowds, but quickly forgot about all that. We were mesmerised from start to finish by Bruce's performance, with him interacting with the crowd and telling stories between some of the songs.

People describe seeing Bruce live as a 'drug' - the more you see him the more you want to see him. This is where our addiction started.

MEADOWLANDS ARENA

24 JUNE 1993 EAST RUTHERFORD, NEW JERSEY

I WAS THERE: STAN GOLDSTEIN

The loudest crowd cheer I have ever heard at any sporting event or concert was at this show. It was when Clarence Clemons came out for the encores. I thought the roof would blow off the arena.

Clarence had been on WFAN radio that afternoon with Mike Francesa and Chris 'Mad Dog' Russo and gave the scoop that he would be playing that night. When he came onstage during the encores for 'Tenth Avenue Freeze-Out', the place went nuts. It was the fans' way of saying 'We want our E Street Band back!' and they got it for a bit that night, as Max Weinberg also was a guest.

This was billed as the 'Concert to Fight Hunger' to benefit World Hunger Year, The Food & Hunger Hotline and The Community Food Bank Of New Jersey. Joe Ely, Steve Van Zandt, Clemons, Weinberg, The Miami Horns and Southside Johnny were guests.

Bruce lost his boot while going into the crowd during 'Leap of Faith.' Some fans started throwing their shoes onstage and he said, 'I got that one, I need the other.' A woman then came up from the audience with the boot. Bruce sat down on the stage, let her put it on, then she proceeded to try to make out with Bruce. Pretty funny.

1995

TRADEWINDS

22 JULY 1995 SEA BRIGHT, NEW JERSEY

I WAS THERE: TERENCE REILLY

As a guy from New Jersey, seeing Bruce at Giants Stadium or Brendan Byrne arena was always a coveted ticket. But the holy grail, the coup de grace, Christmas morning, the Rose Bowl and Festivus all rolled into one was the dream of seeing Bruce at one of those surprise appearances at a Jersey shore bar.

I'd only read about them in the local newspaper or *Rolling Stone*. 'Bruce Springsteen surprised crowd at (insert bar here) on Friday night with a few songs,' was how the story always went and I'd always dreamed one day I'd be there for my eyewitness account.

Between my first show on August 19 1985, and my latest, Springsteen On Broadway, I've seen Bruce over 50 times but only once was lucky enough to be in the right Jersey Shore bar on the right night. That was July '95. Joe Grushecky & The Houserockers were headlining at Tradewinds in Sea Bright, NJ, on a hot and steamy summer night. As always, they played their asses off until Joe disappeared off stage, coming back to say, 'I'd like you all to put your hands together for a friend of mine'. And out from stage left walked Bruce. There he was. My hero. Denim shirt, baseball cap, striding towards the mic. with that familiar Fender.

'1,2 … 1,2,3,4!'

It was happening. I'm in the house. That's Bruce Springsteen! My dream is coming true. Bruce is counting down. It's 'Lucky Town'. Talk about a dream, try to make it real. It is real. I'm going to read about this in the *Star Ledger* and *Rolling Stone* but for once, I'm here. 'Lucky Town' is the first of 15 songs, played only 15ft away from me.

As if it couldn't get any better. It does. Max Weinberg appears

halfway through the set and takes his rightful place behind
the Boss. Then Little Steven, a few years away from becoming
Tony Soprano's consigliere, takes his place as Bruce's on-stage
consigliere and before my eyes it's a mini E Street reunion, four
years before the official re-dedication of the band and their
reunion tour.

'Atlantic City', 'Cadillac Ranch', 'Murder Incorporated',
'Darkness on the Edge of Town' interspersed with covers,
Houserockers tunes, and finally a blistering close with 'Ramrod'.

Finally, it had happened. There was something in the night and
I now have a seaside bar tale of hearing Springsteen deliver seaside
bar songs.

1996 The Ghost of Tom Joad tour was a 128-date
worldwide tour featuring Springsteen performing
alone on stage in small halls and theatres that ran off and on from
late 1995 to mid-1997. It followed the release of his 11th studio
album, 1995's *The Ghost of Tom Joad*, which won the 1997 Grammy
Award for Best Contemporary Folk Album.

After the title track, featuring audience members whooping and
'Brooocing' by habit, Springsteen regularly addressed the audience
with some variation of this speech:

'This is where I get to set the ground rules a little bit ... a lot of
these songs tonight were composed using a lot of silence. Silence
is a part of the music, so I really need your collaboration tonight
in giving me that silence, so I can do my best for you ... if you feel
like clapping or singing along, you'll be an embarrassment to your
friends and family ... if someone sitting next to you is talking, politely
ask them to shut the fuck up. Don't make me come down there and
smack you around, it'll mess with my man-of-the-people image.'

NEWCASTLE CITY HALL

2 MARCH 1996 NEWCASTLE-UPON-TYNE, UK

I WAS THERE: KEVAN HUNTER

I saw Springsteen's The Ghost of Tom Joad solo tour at Newcastle City Hall, taking my seat on the balcony on the extreme right. The equipment was set up onstage but was out of sight by the speaker stack, which rose above the balcony. I rued my luck but was just happy to be in the venue and able to hear him.

About 10 minutes before the concert was due to begin, a large man with an American accent asked to see tickets, me and five others. After closely inspecting them he asked us to stand up and follow him. My immediate thought was that we'd somehow ended up with forged tickets and were being escorted out. The portly gentleman escorted us to the third row from the front, bang in the centre. 'These are your new seats, enjoy the concert.' We had just taken our new seats when Bruce came on and played a fantastic set.

I hung around while the crowd were streaming out and spotted the guy who had given us our new, brilliant seats. I went over to him and asked why we had been moved; he looked up and said, 'Courtesy of Mr Springsteen'. What a guy.

ROYAL ALBERT HALL

17 APRIL 1996 LONDON, UK

I WAS THERE: PETER HELLYAR

I've seen Bruce around 30 times - my absolute favourite gig was at the Royal Albert Hall on The Ghost of Tom Joad tour. He played 'The Angel' for the first time live, after someone sneaked into the soundcheck earlier that day and requested it when Bruce asked the crew if they wanted to hear anything. Bruce told the story on stage in the evening, saying he had to refer to his songbook for the chords, dedicating it to the interloper. I had fantastic seats, just three rows from the front and right in the centre. I was sat about six feet from Bruce.

Getting the tickets is quite a story. My father and a work colleague travelled to London to queue at the box office, my brother and I at home in South Wales, phoning the ticket-line. We were all unsuccessful. My father and his mate were 10 people from the box office when they closed, saying all the tickets had been sold. Most people left but a few, my father included, stayed, complaining that they had queued all day and should have been rewarded with the opportunity to buy tickets. The manager took contact details and said they would be first in line for any returns.

My father phoned the Albert Hall weekly, got very friendly with the manager, on first-name terms, but still no joy. I worked with someone who shared my taste in music. We'd been to loads of gigs together, including many Bruce gigs. He was the internet before the internet existed and got wind of another Albert Hall date. I told my father and he was straight on the phone to the manager, who was shocked he knew about the date. 'That date hasn't been announced, but I've got eight tickets sorted for you, including two special seats.'

I've seen Bruce with the E Street Band many times and seen him with the Seeger Sessions Band twice but seeing just him on stage doing an acoustic set was the pinnacle.

BRIXTON ACADEMY

24 APRIL 1996 LONDON, UK

I WAS THERE: ROB & JEAN PARSONS

The Ghost of Tom Joad tour or the 'Shut the Fuck Up tour' as it became known, as Bruce demanded silence while he was performing the songs - something that was slightly alien to his fans!

Bruce's music took a different turn in 1995 with the release of the low-key acoustic album *The Ghost of Tom Joad* - basically a set of stories set to sparse music. We personally loved it as it really highlighted Bruce's lyric-writing strengths and his ability to weave true-life struggles into captivating songs.

When the tour was announced we were slightly sceptical as to how

it would work live as the songs
demanded close attention. Our
worries were unfounded as the
concert was truly spellbinding,
Bruce performing the new
songs and explaining their
meaning between, adding to
the depth and empathy. You felt for the characters
involved. He also performed many classics, reworked acoustically, and
this again meant you could really hear the lyrics. The meaning of the
songs came to the fore.

To see Bruce in such a small intimate venue was a real privilege.
He's usually a distant dot on a huge stage. It was something we'll
never forget.

During The Ghost of Tom Joad tour Springsteen played a show in
the gymnasium of his old Catholic grammar school to around 1,300
fans. Sales for the November 8th show were restricted for residents
of Freehold Borough who were allowed to buy the $30 tickets. All
proceeds from ticket sales were donated to St. Rose of Lima's
Hispanic community center. Springsteen dedicated The Ghost of Tom
Joad on the night to Sister Charles Marie, saying she taught him a
lot about kindness.

LOWELL
MEMORIAL AUDITORIUM

14 NOVEMBER 1996 LOWELL, MASSACHUSETTS

I WAS THERE: SCOTT GREENE

I was a late bloomer. I didn't become a Bruce Springsteen fan until
late in high school, before my first year in college. The first time I
saw him live in concert was in August 1992 in Worcester, MA on the

Human Touch/Lucky Town tour. I was in between Junior and Senior year at Syracuse University and my friend Jeremy, Jon and I scored free tickets from college radio station Columbia Music rep Charlie Walk. It was an awesome four-hour event (with an intermission) and I was hooked. And that wasn't even with the E Street Band!

In 1996 Bruce came to Lowell, MA on the acoustic Tom Joad tour.

I didn't have a ticket but read on the emailed *Lucky Town Digest* at the time that there was something called a 'drop line' at Springsteen shows, the day of the concert. I left work early that afternoon, drove over to Lowell and got in the line outside the Lowell Memorial Auditorium. I was number 87 and figured I probably didn't have a chance because the Lowell Auditorium is such a small venue and was sold out anyway.

As the hours went by, closer to show time, the line started moving and people ahead were getting tickets. I was probably 10-15 away from the front when 8pm came around and the show started. Finally, within 10 minutes of the show starting, I got called to the lobby/ ticket window and there was a seat for me - at face value. I hurried to the entrance to the auditorium and was told I had to wait until he finished performing his current song. No big deal. I looked to my left and at the next set of doors waiting to enter was Peter Wolf from the J. Geils Band. Bruce finishes the song, I head in to find my seat, and I'm on the aisle, 20th row center. Perfect, and I only missed the first three or four songs. But my next experience is still the one, which ranks as my all-time No.1 Springsteen concert.

I worked in Boston in the late Nineties and got into work one Monday morning in March 1999 and checked my email. Once again the old *Lucky Town Digest* email comes through and I read a post that announced Bruce and the E Street Band were going to perform two rehearsal concerts at Convention Hall in Asbury Park, NJ before they set off on their historic Reunion tour. Tickets were going on sale that Monday at 10am. Wait a minute, that was 15 minutes ago! The post was from Saturday over the weekend but back then I didn't have access to my work email outside of work, so the first time I was reading this digest was Monday morning.

These tickets were not on sale online and you had to call Ticketmaster. I didn't even know if I could get to New Jersey or if tickets were gone already, but I had to try. I called and it rang and I got an operator on first try and asked about Bruce Springsteen for that Thursday or Friday night. After about 30 seconds she tells me she has two reserved tickets for Bruce Springsteen and the E Street Band, that Thursday, March 18th in Asbury Park, NJ. I just about fell off my chair. How could it not be sold out? It was almost a half hour since they went on sale and Convention Hall, from what I understood was very small. She confirmed and I bought two tickets, not even sure who would go with me or how I would get there.

Long story short, my buddy Kramer and I drove down to NJ (with an 'Asbury Park or Bust' sign in my car window), we had dinner at a small pizza place across the street from the Convention Hall, and we got our bracelets and waited in line on the Asbury Park boardwalk! When we got in we went to our seats, directly straight back from the stage in the wooden bleachers, and I noticed the floor in front of the stage was general admission. I had never seen that at a concert before but have now come to learn that's 'the pit,' the general admission section that many Springsteen fans strive to get when they go to shows. As for the concert, I was transported to another dimension. That performance was unlike any I had ever seen before. The band was having so much fun and it was an experience I'll never forget. My friend and I drove back to Western Massachusetts that same night (a long drive!) but we were wired and high on adrenaline, and that show gave me memories for a lifetime.

1997

PALACE THEATRE

15 FEBRUARY 1997 MELBOURNE, AUSTRALIA

I WAS THERE: TINA HORVAT

My very first concert was at the Palais Theatre, St Kilda, Melbourne. I didn't have a ticket as we lived in Europe at the time. I spontaneously decided to come home to Australia to see family. My husband, Steve, was a Socceroo and we lived wherever the game took us. He knew how to make me happy. He rang a music-mad friend in Perth, who flew to Melbourne, found a couple of tickets and took me to the gig. You can't tell me I'm not blessed to have such people in my life.

I'm a spiritual girl and was brought up a Catholic. My mother was the only one that really practiced the faith in the family and it got her through our hardships. Being the youngest of five girls I was the one who got dragged to church every Sunday with

Tina Horvat with Tom Morello, Melbourne 2013

Mum, to pray for better days. I would have preferred to just listen to Bruce.

My sisters were old enough to go to concerts, party and sleep in on Sunday. She never bothered to drag them. They had other chores and they were a challenge. Special church-going occasions only for them. One of my sisters unintentionally made me envious when she went to the 1985 concert at Melbourne Showgrounds while I nursed my terminally-ill father with my mother. I was only 13 and could only dream of attending concerts at that age. He passed that year. But I was happy for my sister's passion and grateful she influenced me to love Bruce's music. She bought all his CDs, which in turn I listen to.

Tina Horvat with Steve Horvat Jr and Bruce, Melbourne 2013

Our family and friends have also joined us on the journey of enjoying Bruce. Cousins from Croatia, and sisters joined us to celebrate sister Mary's birthday. We went to the concert and Bruce played our sheet request of 'Meet Me at Mary's Place' in Brisbane on 17 February 2017, a birthday she'll never forget.

My sister still has the sheet we made, hanging in her Surfers Paradise apartment. That made her feel so special. She reminds me of it all the time. I have faith and believe we sometimes have an unforeseen connection to people, in some way or form, and they may feel each other's support somehow. Not directly, but somehow - then they glance at you and play your request.

It could be because thousands come out to support, many like ourselves that often go to the concerts, increase the chances of requests. I suppose after losing both parents to terminal illnesses, maybe that's what I've learned - to value life as being precious, to hang on to some form of connection to people, the past, artists, spirituality and hope to unite in life or an afterlife.

From our hometown, Geelong, we've attended concerts in various cities of Australia, and in London while I was pregnant. I met an inspirational woman on numerous occasions that became a friend just by dancing beside her and chanting the words to his songs. Later that night we bumped into each other again at a bar where the whole band was, including The Boss himself. We were so glad we stopped there.

Tina Horvat with Steven Van Zandt, Hard Rock Café, Surfers Paradise, 2017

We met most of the band, and they were happy to converse and let us hang with them. An absolute highlight. To engage in a conversation with the legends of the E Street Band over drinks …

The last concert we attended made such an impact it made Steve and I cry. Not only did we conquer difficulties in getting tickets to the Broadway show on our 21st wedding anniversary, but Patti and Bruce played our first-dance wedding song. I have to give my husband major brownie points - he knew those tickets would excite me more than a designer handbag.

Bruce has a way of telling captivating stories and making people feel they can connect, relate and feel special. And he's so down to earth, with a strong family bond. A perfect idol.

1999

CONVENTION HALL

18 MARCH 1999 ASBURY PARK, NEW JERSEY

I WAS THERE: STEVE TROY

I was raised a Bruce fan by my older sister Denise. I'm 40 now
and she is 12 years older. The first time I ever got to hear him live
was in Asbury, winter 1999. It was when he was rehearsing for the
upcoming reunion tour where the E Street Band was back in the fold
and they had that one show at the convention center.

We didn't have tickets but me and my brother hung out all night at
The Pony then went to the back of Howard Johnson's, where us and
about 200-300 waited all night drinking till the next day to hopefully
hear something from the Convention Hall. The next day my sister,
my girlfriend, and at least another 1,000 or so people showed up on
the beach outside the hall. They opened the doors on the Convention
Hall and I got to hear The Boss for the first time. It brought tears to
my eyes.

I've now seen him 40-plus times and had many other amazing
stories, including getting brought from the nosebleeds to front row by
the 'Men in Black' at a show in Connecticut. But nothing will ever
beat that night on the Boardwalk in Asbury.

EARLS COURT

21 MAY 1999 LONDON, UK

I WAS THERE: MARK HOLBURN

This was the first Springsteen concert I took my wife (my
girlfriend at the time) to. I needed to impress, so who better than
The Boss? We were lucky to get great seats at the front and side
of the stage. Still the best seats I have ever had to a Springsteen

concert. This was the reunion tour of the E Street Band, guitarists Nils Lofgren and Steve Van Zandt now on board together.

To me this was the best I had ever heard Springsteen and the band. His voice seemed better than ever. So many of his great songs: 'Promised Land', 'Prove it all Night', 'Badlands', 'Hungry Heart' and the great 'Born to Run' (with all the lights up on the

Mark Holburn and wife Tracey

audience) were delivered, with so much power and musical precision. Just amazing. And 'This Hard Land' - wow! This song just gets better each time I hear it live.

A fantastic new version of 'The River' with such a haunting high-pitch ending by Bruce, it gave you goose-bumps.

'Youngstown' had always been one of my favourite songs off *'The Ghost Of Tom Joad'* album. To hear it played as a full band song with what has become one of my all time live guitar solos from Nils Lofgren was something else. An angry song about the collapse of a steel mill plant, and its community in Ohio. This was the highlight song of the night and every time I hear this song it stirs so much passion.

He also performed a solo and haunting version of *'The Ghost of Tom Joad'*. Such a beautiful song and I love both versions: the original acoustic folk and the power and anger of the full band version.

This is the first time I heard 'Jungleland' live. What an amazing song and story of young people struggling yet enjoying moments in street gangs, told through stunning lyrics. I don't pretend to be a connoisseur of the saxophone but defy anyone not to be moved by Clarence's solo on this live version. I would say it's the greatest sax solo ever, but I may be biased. Just watch and listen to the *Live in New York* DVD. You'll see what I mean.

He finished up with new song, 'Land of Hope and Dreams'. A song about hope for everyone, no matter who you are, to reach your dreams. It is a tremendous song which seems to mean more and more as you get older.

What a fantastic night. Great seats and a stunning performance in a great venue emphasised that Bruce Springsteen and the E Street Band were back together with a vengeance. Long may it continue.

I have seen Springsteen live only 18 times, but he inspired me to write a story of my life and Springsteen based on all his concerts that I have seen. His concerts are just awesome. They are like a drug; a shot in the arm that keeps you going through the daily routine of life and take you away from the strains and worries of everyday life. It puts a permanent smile on your face during the whole show.

My thoughts on the closing stages of a Springsteen concert are the same to the ending of summer. You want it to carry on and on and can't wait for it come back.

I have had so much fun and happy times conversing with fans and listening to his stunning live performances, alone or with the great E Street Band.

I was there at Hyde Park, London in 2012, singing and dancing in the rain when they pulled the plug on Springsteen and Paul McCartney because they had passed the curfew. I was at Queen Elizabeth Park, London, when he danced with his Mum, Adele, on stage, accompanied by his sister Pam on guitar.

I was at the Albert Hall when he played a beautiful solo acoustic set only to be initially interrupted by some idiot fan hollering between the songs. Springsteen's reply was to tell the guy to 'Relax, sit down and shut the fuck up!'

I remember one concert when a confused elderly gentleman next to me asked why the crowd were booing him only for me to realise and explain to him they were crying, 'Bruuuce!'

I have been privileged on numerous occasions to witness the great Clarence Clemons' mesmerising sax solo on 'Jungleland.' Most of

all I have had the sheer joy of seeing Bruce Springsteen live and
never tire of hearing those legendary words, 'You've just seen the
heart-stopping, pants-dropping, house-rocking, earth-quaking, booty-
shaking, Viagra-taking, love-making, legendary E Street Band.'

CONTINENTAL ARENA

20 JULY 1999 EAST RUTHERFORD NEW JERSEY

I WAS THERE: SCOTT SCHNEIDER

I knew that my first trip to see Bruce in New Jersey would be special
but had no idea how spectacular the night would end up being.

I went with my wife and two friends to the show after a few days
in New York City. We arrived very early and found our seats. They
were about as bad as they could be, in the top and back of the arena.
Having travelled from Kentucky, we were happy to just be in the
building. A guy approached us and said he worked for Springsteen
and if we wanted he would trade us tickets for an upgrade. My wife

Scott Schneider (on the right) with Charlie and Anne

was especially sceptical. Did I mention she was a native New Yorker? After much deliberation, we decided to go for it, as our seats couldn't get much worse. We were instructed to go down to this person and they would direct us to our new seats. After three such, 'Go see that guy', I was beginning to lose faith. Then, finally, we were given wristbands and walked to the front row of the floor, center of the stage. Unbelievable.

The show was amazing. The band had recently reunited for the Reunion tour and they were on fire. Seeing Stevie Van Zandt back with the band was better than I could have imagined. I've seen Bruce somewhere near 50 times and this was the best show ever. When he sang 'Spirit in the Night' I turned around to watch the crowd sing along and it was a magical, mystical experience. I could feel the spirit for sure. At one point in the show Bruce stopped directly in front of us as he slowly danced across the stage and called upon the spirit of Tom Jones. After a few pelvic thrusts syncopated to Max's drum snares, he sent one straight to my wife. What a moment. The show also featured my first hearing of 'Freehold', a song my friend Anne described as a great way to tell an entire town off! The show ended with 'Land of Hope and Dreams' and my friend Charlie and I agreed that this truly is the place 'where faith is rewarded.'

MEADOWLANDS ARENA

29 JULY 1999 EAST RUTHERFORD, NEW JERSEY

I WAS THERE: STAN GOLDSTEIN

Bruce is loose as he and the band celebrate Patti Scialfa's birthday, Tom Hanks and his wife Rita Wilson are sitting just off to the side of the stage, and that adds up to a great evening. The show begins with 'The Ties that Bind,' the first time played since the final night of The River tour (September 14, 1981).

A tour debut of 'Red Headed Woman' played in a country-swing style is followed by a fun 'Give the Girl a Kiss,' only previously performed at the March 19 Asbury Park rehearsal (and to this day only played four times live). After 'Tenth Avenue Freeze-Out,' many in the audience held up signs for 'Rosalita' (someone had run off hundreds of copies of the sign and handed them out to fans) and Bruce wasn't too pleased. 'Put them fucking signs down! I got a job to do!' he said. Bobby Bandiera and Max's daughter, Ali Weinberg, were guests on 'Hungry Heart.' Tom Brokaw was also spotted in the crowd.

I also went to the finale of the 15 shows on 12 August 1999. You know you're in for a special night when the show opens with 'Jersey Girl.' It was the only time it was played during the entire reunion tour.

Before the final song, Bruce says: 'I want to thank everyone for coming down to these shows that we've done here in Jersey. There were some very special nights for us. It's been a great gift being able to stand up here and make this music come alive and to look out into your faces. Thank you. It's been the rebirth and a rededication of our band, of our commitment to serve you. Let me see, how could I say thanks? I know there's a way. I'm sure there's a way. I haven't seen any of those stupid signs. So maybe just once.' And he plays the much-wanted 'Rosalita.'

MEADOWLANDS ARENA

6 AUGUST 1999 EAST RUTHERFORD, NEW JERSEY

I WAS THERE: CHARLIE MCMOHAN

I first discovered Bruce Springsteen back in 1980. I was nine and remember that period very vividly. The US hostages being held in Iran was the top news story every night, John Lennon was senselessly murdered in NYC, Ronald Reagan defeated Jimmy Carter and was President-Elect, and I heard magic come through the tiny speaker of my transistor radio - the sound of Bruce Springsteen and 'Hungry Heart' off the recently-released album *The River*. I was hooked. I started looking into his older music and bought every album. As a matter of fact, a few years later, *Born in the U.S.A.* was the first cassette I owned once I started making the transition from vinyl. Unfortunately, I was always unable to get tickets for his shows in my early teens and during the Born in the U.S.A. tour. They would sell out too quickly, and I was too young to be allowed to sleep out all night in line for tickets.

In the later part of the Eighties, Bruce went solo and the E Street Band took a decade-long break. I really thought I'd never get the opportunity to see them together until 1999 when it was announced that Bruce and the band were reuniting, going out on tour. I was born and raised on Long Island, New York, and was still there in 1999. By then I was 28. I heard that Bruce and the band were coming to NJ in early August. I was beyond excited. Would this be the first time I finally got to see them? When tickets went on sale, they sold out almost immediately. As summer went on, I still hoped to somehow get a ticket. Then one day in late July, the girl I was dating told me her close friend had an extra ticket and would be cool with me going with her friend, her sister and brother-in-law.

Finally, the day arrived. It took us well over two hours to drive to NJ in Friday afternoon/evening rush-hour traffic from Long Island. But we blasted Bruce CDs, sang along, and were all so excited, regardless of the NY Metro traffic. When we got to the Arena around 6pm, the lot was packed with tailgaters, Bruce cover bands on makeshift stages along the perimeter of the parking lots, and Bruce songs blasting from every direction. The electricity in the air was unlike anything I'd ever experienced, and I'd been to dozens upon dozens of concerts, play-off hockey games, and World Series games.

When we finally got inside it was about 30 minutes before the show was set to start. The crowd was chanting 'Bruce! Bruce!' non-stop. Finally, the house lights went off and the PA announcer introduced them. One by one, they filed onto a dimly-lit stage - Steve, Roy, Patti, Gary, Max, Nils, Danny, then the Big Man and Bruce together. The place went insane. Then the first chords of 'Adam Raised a Cain' were struck. I was mesmerized, overcome with emotion, with goose-bumps all over. The moment had finally arrived.

Words can't describe how amazing that show was. It was uplifting, energized, emotional, and spiritual on many levels. I left the venue

emotionally drained, happy beyond words. Who knew that would
be my first of 33 Bruce concerts in eight different cities? I leave
every show with the same feeling I had that day. When it comes to
a live performance, there's Bruce and then there's everyone else.
Like he says, 'Tonight we're going to throw a rock'n'roll baptism! A
rock'n'roll exorcism!' Boy, does he deliver. I'm 46 now, married and
living in the suburbs of Atlanta, GA, but his songs still resonate with
me. Bruce and his music have been there for me ever since I heard
'Hungry Heart' come out of that little transistor radio speaker in
New York at the age of nine. I am a fan for life.

UNITED CENTER

27 SEPTEMBER 1999 CHICAGO, ILLINOIS

I WAS THERE: NICK LAVALLE

I've been a Springsteen fan since I started High School back in 1984.
While it was the *Born in the U.S.A.* album that made me a fan, it was
getting the opportunity to listen to his earlier work and really sit down
and follow the lyrics off of the record jackets that really spoke to me.
I found myself able to relate and learn about life in general by simply
sitting in my basement, blasting through different albums on different
days - based on my moods and emotions at that time.

I was unable to get to any concert on the Born in the U.S.A. tour,
being a young kid, with older parents who were not concert-goers. I
didn't have any older siblings, so I listened and learned about music
through the radio, MTV, and taking a chance on buying albums for
$2.99 in the discount bin at Rolling Stone Records.

I was fortunate enough to attend a Springsteen show during both
the Tunnel of Love and Lucky Town/Human Touch tours. I've
also been fortunate to have attended shows at every tour thereafter,
including The Rising, Magic, Working on a Dream, and The River
Box Set tours, all spectacular experiences. However, the Reunion
tour, specifically the September 27, '99 show, stands out.

At that point, my wife Julie was full-term during her pregnancy with our oldest daughter, Tianna, due on October 12th. We were nervously awaiting this new world and most everything around us was on hold. Julie was one of the lucky people able to get through to Ticketmaster when the tickets went on sale, scoring third row tickets on the main floor. While I was a Springsteen fanatic, Julie was still growing in her fandom. We were both excited about seeing the show and being so close, but as the day neared, we grew concerned about the potential conflict with the concert and birth. As first-time parents, we were unsure whether it would be wise to be in a crowd of that size with her less than two weeks from her due date. We also were concerned that the noise. We checked with the obstetrician and she just laughed, making us feel at ease. She said, 'Go to the show! Maybe the sound will help the baby come out sooner'. She assured us that the music would not be damaging to our unborn baby and that we should go and have a great time.

We went, and it was truly a mind-blowing experience. My wife couldn't stand for most of the show but stayed on her feet as much as she could. We cherished everything about this show, and my daughter still acknowledges being at this concert when we talk about Bruce. The most memorable part of the evening was the band's presentation of 'If I Should Fall Behind', where every member of the band sings a few bars. That was the song we danced to at our wedding, three years earlier, and it kind of brought everything full circle for us - for that period of our lives.

My daughter was born 14 days later, on October 11. Since then, she has been to two other Springsteen shows with me and at the age of 18, listens to and analyses lyrics more than ever, and there are many Springsteen songs on her playlist. As with most of Bruce's music, it is the events in your life that may relate to a given song or given moment. For me, it was that night where I figured out that fatherhood was right around the corner and that my life would be changing. As the song 'If I Should Fall Behind' says, I knew that my wife and I would be walking together, through whatever comes our way, side by side. We are now blessed with four awesome children - Tianna, Nico, Natalia, and Lucia - and our world is chaotic, but completely gratifying. To this day, through anything that comes our way, I wait for her, and when I fall behind, she waits for me.

2000

NASHVILLE ARENA

12 APRIL 2000 NASHVILLE, TENNESSEE

I WAS THERE: TERRY HAYES

The first time I saw Springsteen was during the reunion tour. I've seen him about eight times since, but this was the best. I'd been a fan for 20 years but never able to see him live. I scraped up every penny I could get, bought two tickets, lucked out and got floor seats (12th row right in front of the stage). The problem was, I didn't have transportation - I live about 120 miles away and wasn't doing that well financially. A buddy that was going to drive me backed out last minute. A woman I worked with stepped up and said she'd drive me. We went to the concert, and that woman is now my wife of 13 years .... thanks to a Springsteen concert.

2001

CLEARWATER FESTIVAL

18 AUGUST 2001 ASBURY PARK, NEW JERSEY

I WAS THERE: CRAIG MCKEOWN

The Clearwater Festival in Asbury Park was sparsely attended, with various eco-booths and a small bandstand where local folk singers were performing. Suddenly, Bruce arrived, his young son on his shoulders. He was invited on stage and played about six acoustic songs to a crowd of maybe 30 people; then he left and toured the booths. This was a few days before 9/11. The only other time I saw him was when he performed opening night at the new Brendan Byrne arena in the Meadowlands, NJ.

SETLIST:

01. Does This Bus Stop at 82nd Street?
02. Bobby Jean
03. This Hard Land
04. Blinded by the Light
05. My City of Ruins
06. Land of Hope and Dreams

2002

ISLE OF WIGHT FESTIVAL

14 JUNE 2002 SEACLOSE PARK, ISLE OF WIGHT

I WAS THERE: MAXINE HOWSON

This was my 20th time seeing Bruce live. I took my 17-year-old daughter, who's 'suffered' his music all her life (her words not mine!). We managed to get on the barrier and at one point, Bruce briefly held my hand. I texted my Dad to tell him this. His reply? 'He doesn't know how lucky he is.' At the end of the show my daughter turned and said, 'I understand it now'. Proud mummy moment.

2003 The Rising Tour kicked off in August in East Rutherford, New Jersey and ended after 120 shows in 82 cities over a span of 14 months with a three-night run at Shea Stadium, New York City. This tour took in dates in North America, Western Europe, Australia and New Zealand, and grossed $221.5 million.

The first half of the October 16, 2002 show in Barcelona's Palau Sant Jordi was televised live across Europe on MTV and VH1 UK. A tape of the broadcast was aired by CBS in the United States on February 28, 2003, prior to the United States summer stadium show tickets going on sale. That entire concert was then released as a two-disc DVD, *Live in Barcelona*, in November 2003, the first time any Springsteen concert had been officially released in full.

TELSTRA DOME

20 MARCH 2003 MELBOURNE, AUSTRALIA

I WAS THERE: CAROLINE ZERAFA

Life is all about timing. Right? Well, this gig, The Boss at Telstra Dome, was a long time coming. Bruce toured, I didn't go, Bruce toured, and I didn't go. It wasn't that I disliked Bruce; it was about a pair of horrible girls who bullied me at secondary school. They loved Bruce, but they hated me. Every time I heard 'Born in the U.S.A.,' I remembered their pock-marked faces, windcheaters, and their cruelty. In the end, they failed year 11, and years later I bought a copy of *Nebraska*.

On the day of the concert, Melbourne was stinking hot. I remember walking across to Telstra Dome gazing up at the sky. Would it rain? I thought I could smell rain. I looked down at my feet - glad I'd worn sneakers. When we finally arrived at the venue, I felt a buzz, a hum. All those clichés about the air being electric, and the suspense and adrenaline building, were true. I had never seen Bruce live, but I knew, I just knew, this would be a great gig. Yeah, yeah - I'd read and heard about his marathon shows, but after listening to Bruce over and over, I felt performing was not his 'job' but his calling.

Something else happened that day - the United States invaded Iraq. My friends and I discussed the invasion, named Operation Freedom, as we sat waiting for The Boss. Would Bruce reference the invasion during the show? What would the set-list include?

Then - he was there. Bruce casually strolled over to his

microphone. Silence. No E Street Band, just Bruce, a microphone, an acoustic guitar. He began to speak about the invasion in a low, sombre voice, while softly strumming his guitar. I can't recall word for word what he said, but he finished by introducing a song he'd written about the Vietnam War - 'Born in the U.S.A.' The song was transformed. It became a dirge - a lament. The original version was nowhere to be heard. It was just Bruce, a guitar, and his words. I leaned forward in my seat thinking of the young people preparing for war. Maybe Bruce was too. The song faded into a full band version of Edwin Starr's 'War.' The Boss sang 'War. What is it good for?' The audience answered, 'Absolutely nothing!'

I've forgotten details of that concert, but I'll never forget the way it made me feel. I was comforted by those songs - by Bruce and the E Street Band. For a while, there was no 'Operation Freedom.' In my world, there is music. There is always music. And on March 20th, 2003, I was there.

OLD TRAFFORD CRICKET GROUND

29 MAY 2003 MANCHESTER, UK

I WAS THERE: IAN J. WINFIELD

I had already had the pleasure of experiencing Springsteen live numerous times before this show of The Rising Tour, but for me its opening moments were a once in a lifetime experience.

Although I had secured tickets well in advance, there had been a disturbing possibility that the show would be cancelled at the last minute due to some concerns about disturbance to the residents around the cricket ground. Thankfully this didn't materialise, and I remember a great sense of relief as we were let into the ground on a perfect late spring evening. Several hours later the usual roar went up as Springsteen appeared on the stage, but surprisingly (to me at least) it was just him with a steel guitar. He then opened solo with his bluesy, delta-country version of 'Born in the U.S.A.' It literally took my breath away and was the most primal experience of my life. The simplicity of the situation was stunning. At that time and place I felt a direct connection back to the troubadours of medieval times. He was doing nothing different from what they had done centuries ago, with essentially the same tools. I was also amazed that this man could come out and captivate such a crowd of tens of thousands with only his song, his voice and his guitar. His lyrical extension on that evening of the number of years that the song's protagonist had now spent burning down the road, conjuring up images in my mind of war veterans perhaps now in their sixties, was both shocking and heart-breaking.

Ian J. Winfield and his wife Denise on holiday in the US

The rest of the show went by in its usual rollercoaster flash of exuberance and cathartic emotion, but those first few minutes are seared on my consciousness forever. The man is a poet and a magician.

RDS ARENA

31 MAY 2003 DUBLIN, IRELAND

I WAS THERE: SHANE HEGARTY

Like every moment when scepticism explodes into fervent belief, there was an epiphany. It was the RDS Arena in 2003; my second time seeing Bruce Springsteen live. The first – at the same venue in

1999 had felt underwhelming. I just hadn't found that connection.
Then again, my understanding of Springsteen was limited largely to
a home tape of *Born in the U.S.A.* as a teen, and an obsession with him
from my future wife, whose depths felt alien to me.

The *Rising* album shifted something, brought me closer. But on
a May evening in Dublin, he strolled on stage, played 'Born in the
U.S.A.' acoustically, followed it with a full-band version of 'The
Rising', and that was the moment of clarity. Over three hours later, I
finally understood the ferocious energy, raw emotion, joy, spontaneity,
craft, rock'n'roll purity, and, yes, connection of a Springsteen show.
The gig had ended but it was only the beginning of my personal,
never-ending tour. Right now, I'm ready for my 15th and 16th shows
(nothing compared to those who follow him practically as a full-time
gig). My only regrets are the ones I've missed.

Each show is different. Each set list has it treats. Every time I think
it's peaked, something magical occurs. There has been the rain
drumming on the roof of the old Point during the Devils & Dust
acoustic show of 2005, the 2012 tribute to the recently-departed
Clarence Clemons in 'Tenth Avenue Freeze-Out', and bleeding
fingers as he ended Kilkenny 2013 with a stunning 'This Hard
Land'. There were tens of thousands there, yet he was speaking to
every individual.

In that time, The E-Street Band shows have stretched longer and
longer, while the pre-encore breaks have disappeared entirely. He
plays like he never wants it to end. Three and half hours? He, and
we, could do another three and a half. In my house, we have a long-
standing fear that each time we see him may be the last. After all, he
plays every show like he has the exact same fear.

A favourite song? There are so many. Too many. But, screw it, this
week I'm going for 'Badlands'. That song is rocket fuel for the soul.

I'm blessed, in that I've met Springsteen twice. Once with The *Irish
Times* over lunch in Toronto, during which I actually stopped to take
in the happy fact that my professional career had peaked. Then, in
Mount Juliet in 2013, when I happened to be in its small bar when
he joined in a session, playing two songs in between eating his fish

supper. When he left the room some hours later, the room collectively exhaled in disbelief.

I WAS THERE: GLEN HANSARD, SINGER, SONGWRITER

I bumped into him when I was about 15 years old; I'd just started busking and was coming into town. The Ballymun bus pulls up in Parnell Square, and I was walking past the Gresham with my guitar on my back when I saw this big Cadillac parked outside.

I bumped into this man, and I'd no idea who it was at first. But I'd been watching MTV USA, so I soon realised. It was around the *Born in the U.S.A.* period, and I was just a kid, but it gave me a real kick. You know, it was a moment where I was like, 'Hey, is that your man from the TV?' I had no real idea who he was at that time.

The next time I met him was years later in Dublin. We'd just won the Oscar. We were at his show at the RDS and we got word from someone in his camp who came out into the crowd and said, 'Hey look, do you want to come back and say 'hello'? Bruce would like to congratulate you.' Which was really special of him to do right before he went onstage. So I went back and I shook his hand.

What a normal, straight ahead, fuckin' legend of a dude! Forget about a genuine rock star, he's also one of the most genuine human beings I've ever met. Regardless of what he's done in music. He invited us back for a drink afterwards at the hotel, so we went back and we talked. He was incredibly gracious and generous with his time and his advice. I was lucky to get the chance to spend some hours with such a master and ask him

Glen Hansard

simple things like, 'How do you keep your voice in shape?'

It's one of those things. If you had an hour with your hero, what would you ask them? There's so much, so I thought I'd remain practical. There'd be no point in asking him 'How'd you write this song?' or 'How did you write that?' More just, 'What do you do when you're in the mid-west in arid dry heat and you've got three shows in a row? How do you keep yourself from burning out? If you take a drink after a gig, how do you weigh that up?' Just simple questions, about getting through what it is we all do.

PNC PARK

6 AUGUST 2003 PITTSBURGH, PENNSYLVANIA

I WAS THERE: KRISTEN SEGINA

My first Bruce Springsteen concert was in August 2003 at PNC Park in Pittsburgh, Pennsylvania. It truly was a wonderful show; I had never seen fans reacting that way at a concert. There was so much happiness, energy and enthusiasm in the crowd. People on the floor level were going berserk - waving towels, jumping up and down, and dancing like there was no tomorrow. I saw a father and daughter near me dancing and it was so sweet - she must have been 11 or 12 and he was twirling her around like a princess. They were having their own moment and to see every age at a Bruce show is definitely the norm - young, old, kids, grandkids, they all show up to see him.

Bruce was terrific - he was 53 at the time and he looked like 29 on the jumbo screens they put up. Loving the music, the reaction from the crowd, it truly makes him happy I believe. At one point he locked his ankles to his microphone and was hanging upside down again, something I had never seen from a performer - nor have I seen it since. The band was so together - so in sync. I can't put it in words.

At the end of this lengthy, memorable show, we were sitting in the stands, waiting for the place to clear out before heading back to the parking lot. Bruce and the band were walking around to the back of the stage, on the grounds, and we all started waving at them. Bruce waved right back in the same manner we were all waving. I felt like he acknowledged us, even up in the peanut heaven seats, and it was a cool moment.

I had lost my job literally days before this concert, and Bruce made everything all right that night. I would listen to the song, 'Lonely Day' from *The Rising* album, also the name of the tour, and get this feeling that yes, everything was going to be all right. It was true. I found a new job and am still here 14 years on. Bruce's music/ concerts do that to you - put you in a different place. A 'zone', I call it. He lifts you up and keeps you there.

I last saw Bruce in January 2016 on The River tour and again he was terrific - it felt like a spiritual revival at the end, Bruce yelling, 'Let's keep going! Does anyone have to get up tomorrow? Do you have to be at church early tomorrow?' I was buzzing after that show.

Those are my memories of Bruce Springsteen and the E Street Band. I cherish them.

LINCOLN FINANCIAL FIELD

8 AUGUST 2003 PHILADELPHIA, PENNSYLVANIA

I WAS THERE: BRANDON THOMPSON

As a young Springsteen fan, it's usually assumed your parents forced Bruce on you. Being from New Jersey, I see how that makes sense. But I remember I was about to head into the fourth grade (about 10 years old) and he was on an early morning show playing songs from *The Rising*. I heard the TV in the background and Springsteen was in the middle of 'My City of Ruins.' I was instantly drawn to the screen and sat there throughout. Later that day I remember going to the mall with the family and kept singing over and over, '*Come on, rise up!*' to a point where my mother asked me to stop. I still laugh about that moment. But it was the start of a musical journey that would change my life.

The following summer, he was rolling through Philadelphia's new football stadium, Lincoln Financial Field. I knew, and my parents knew we had to go. This would end up being my first Springsteen show. I still remember the days leading up. I couldn't wait. Springsteen was playing three shows and I remember vividly I thought we had tickets to opening night, but it turned out being the second show. I was devastated I had to wait that extra day.

Being a young kid, having your hopes build up all day to realize you have to wait another 24 hours, was terrible. But the time finally came - and it's a memory I'll never forget. I knew his new material (*The Rising*) most, and the original performance of 'My City of Ruins' drew me in to pick up the album. To this day, the feeling one gets the day of a Springsteen show is something that will never be beaten. The anticipation builds up all week, then what seems like the longest day of your life until 8pm. It's what us Springsteen fans live for - to see the legend live and in person.

Everyone always asks what my favourite song is. It changes often. It really depends where you are in your life. Springsteen's music has the magic to adapt to your life. That's how great his writing is. Right now, I'm loving, 'Darkness on The Edge of Town' and 'Living Proof.'

SKYDOME

10 SEPTEMBER 2003 TORONTO, CANADA

I WAS THERE: ROB FAULCONBRIDGE

I saw him for the first time at the Skydome, Toronto. It was a beautiful late summer evening with a huge, bright full moon hanging low in the sky. They decided to keep the roof open. Bruce stepped on stage with guitar in hand, Danny Federici had the accordion going, and Bruce said, 'I want to start the night with a song in memory of my great friend, Warren Zevon'. They played 'My Ride's Here' with Suzi Tyrell on fiddle. Magical. Then later in the night he would hang off the microphone stand and had us all howling at the full moon! Another memorable song that night was 'Seven Nights to Rock', if the roof was closed, he would have blown it off with that song! A perfect rock'n'roll night that will always be remembered.

KENAN STADIUM

14 SEPTEMBER 2003 NORTH CAROLINA

I WAS THERE: RONNIE HOWELL

One of the most memorable Bruce shows ever for me was in North Carolina in 2003 immediately after Johnny Cash died. To start the show Bruce came on stage with an acoustic guitar and under a single stage light sang 'I Walk the Line.'

I have never been in a crowd of thousands where absolutely everyone was quiet. You could have heard a pin drop in that football stadium. My most magical music moment anytime, anywhere. I looked at my wife after that song and told her we could leave now, I had seen Bruce at a show I would never forget. We stayed of course.

SHEA STADIUM

3 OCTOBER 2003 NEW YORK CITY

I WAS THERE: MARK PALACE

Armed with a pair of floor tickets for the first Shea Springsteen show, I mustered my nerve and asked the pretty blue-eyed brunette I worked with to join me. Much to my chagrin, she couldn't, but the experience was still memorable.

The impressiveness of standing behind the mound and looking up ... and up ... and up, and the bizarreness of using the port-o-lavs lined up between the mound and home plate thinking, '90 mph fastballs usually whiz by here' come to mind.

The second night, a seat in the upper deck provided an amazing panoramic view of 50,000 people dancing to 'Twist and Shout' and having an absolute blast. I'll never forget it. And everything worked out in the end. I married the pretty brunette last October and our first baby's due.

I WAS THERE: MONICA ZICOLELLA

My memory of Bruce Springsteen's Last Dance Concert in 2003 at Shea Stadium can't be beat. The concert started off so slow, dark and kind of depressing, that at one point we actually considered leaving, but I refused until I at least heard 'Born to Run.' I can't tell you how happy we all were that we decided to stay, because once the house lights came on and the darkness was lifted, the Stadium turned into one big, happy party - everyone got on their feet, dancing and singing to song after song.

I WAS THERE: ESTER BECK

I saw all three shows at Shea. I was on the field each time, but the best experience was when I was front and center in the pit and Bruce did 'New York City Serenade'. A rare treat and one of my favourites.

Seeing Al Leiter (Major League Baseball pitcher) on stage with Bruce was another treat, even though he really didn't know the words to 'Rosalita'.

The shows were early October, and Christine, a New Jersey friend, had brought a cake to the tailgate party, which said 'Happy Birthday Maryann, Esther and Bruce', (we all had late September birthdays). Maryann was there from Texas and I was there from Coram (born in Asbury Park), but Bruce stayed inside the stadium and was a no-show to the birthday celebration. It was a memorable three days.

SETLIST:

01. Roulette
02. Candy's Room
03. The Rising

04. Lonesome Day
05. The Ties That Bind
06. Brilliant Disguise
07. Empty Sky
08. Waitin' on a Sunny Day
09. Rendezvous
10. Another Thin Line
11. Souls of the Departed
12. Because the Night
13. Badlands
14. Prove It All Night
15. Mary's Place
16. New York City Serenade
17. Into the Fire
18. Janey Don't You Lose Heart
19. Pink Cadillac
20. Born to Run
21. Seven Nights to Rock
22. My City of Ruins
23. Born in the U.S.A.
24. Rosalita (Come Out Tonight)
25. Dancing in the Dark
26. Twist and Shout

MILLER PARK

27 OCTOBER 2003 MILWAUKEE, WISCONSIN

I WAS THERE: SANDY TAPP

The second leg of The Rising Tour. Tailgating in the parking lot, we hear the soundcheck, then the unmistakeable sound of the retractable roof closing. The Boss has spoken. This will not be an outdoor show. Minutes before show-time, my friend Patti chooses the men's bathroom line, which is much shorter. We stay in the women's line. We wait and wait. She doesn't come out. She has been taken to the jail in the basement of Miller Park; it's illegal to use the opposite sex bathroom in Wisconsin! Who knew? She isn't arrested and appears at our seats a few minutes into the show. We still pee our pants recounting this story today! Oh, might have been my first time hearing 'Jungleland' live.

2004

The Vote for Change tour was a politically-motivated American concert tour presented by MoveOn.org to benefit America Coming Together. The tour, which started in Seattle on September 27, was held in swing states, designed to encourage people to register and vote. Many of the performers urged people to vote against then-President George W. Bush and for John Kerry in 2004's election campaign. Bush would defeat Kerry that November. Bruce's shows were compressed to two hours in length due to the multi-act nature of the concerts, accomplished by removing elongated outros and false endings from songs like 'Born in the U.S.A.' and 'Badlands'.

Talking about his move on joining the tour Springsteen stated: 'I've got 25 years of credibility built up, and this isn't something I've moved into lightly. But this is the one where you spend some of that credibility. It's an emergency intervention. We need to get an administration that is more attentive to the needs of all its citizens, that has a saner foreign policy, that is more attentive to environmental concerns.'

CONTINENTAL AIRLINES ARENA

13 OCTOBER 2004 EAST RUTHERFORD, NEW JERSEY

I WAS THERE: STAN GOLDSTEIN

Bruce entered the political arena with a group of shows designed to encourage people to register and vote in the upcoming elections, with each of the seven concerts held in swing states in support of Democrat candidate John Kerry. The final sold-out show attracted a 19,000 crowd, Patti Scialfa and her band opening, followed by Jackson Browne.

Bruce and the E Street Band were joined by former Creedence Clearwater Rival main-man John Fogerty (who played 'The Promised Land') and Eddie Vedder from Pearl Jam. The best part was Bruce and Vedder performing Pearl Jam's 'Better Man'. Also cool to see Bruce sing 'Running on Empty' with Jackson Browne.

2005 The 2005 Devils & Dust 76-date tour saw Bruce Springsteen performing alone on a variety of

instruments and followed the release of 13th studio album Devils & Dust. Audience members at some venues were greeted by a paper hand-out, which stated, 'All guests must be seated by the start of the first song and please turn off all mobile phones and pagers during the performance.' Bruce sometimes called for quiet during the show, humorously threatening audience members with mayhem if their cell phones went off.

During tour rehearsals Springsteen had experimented with a small band line-up, with Nils Lofgren (guitar and keyboards), Danny Federici (organ), Soozie Tyrell (violin and vocals), and Steve Jordan (drums), all of whom had appeared on the album. However, Springsteen decided it was not what he wanted and would perform on the tour

all by himself. The Devils & Dust
tour was named the Top Small
Venue Tour of 2005 by the *Billboard*
Touring Awards.

FOX THEATER

25 APRIL 2005 DETROIT, MICHIGAN

I WAS THERE: JAMES YOUNG

Opening song 'Reason to Believe' set
the scene for the night – you never
knew what was coming next. He
played it as a Delta blues, just playing
harmonica, stomping the beat with his
foot on the stage and singing through a
distorted harp mic that made his voice
sound like something from 1940s' radio. Almost every song was
a fresh listening experience, making it challenging but extremely
satisfying. Throw in his storytelling between songs and this was a
brilliant night.

COLORADO CONVENTION CENTER

7 MAY 2005 DENVER, COLORADO

I WAS THERE: RICHARD ROBERTS

This was my one and only Springsteen show, and what a thrill to see
him solo, playing acoustic versions of about two dozen songs.

He walked on to an almost-empty stage and apart from his
instruments were two chandeliers and indigo-light streaming through
the darkness. He opened with 'My Beautiful Reward,' playing both
the keyboard and harmonica segments. The audience was with him
all the way, relishing every anecdote he shared before performing

another song. One of the many highlights was his tales of the joys and pitfalls of parenthood before performing 'Long Time Comin', indicative of the connection he forged with this crowd throughout the show.

ROSEMONT THEATER

11 MAY 2005 ROSEMONT, ILLINOIS

I WAS THERE: MEGAN KEEN

On reflection I think this was the best concert I have ever been to. You maybe don't think that on the night. There was so much to take in. The highlights of the show for me were, 'Part Man, Part Monkey' and 'Reason To Believe'. I knew he was a great guitarist, but I didn't know that he played a pretty mean piano too.

THE THEATER AT CONTINENTAL AIRLINES ARENA

19 MAY 2005 EAST RUTHERFORD, NEW JERSEY

I WAS THERE: STAN GOLDSTEIN

Most of the shows on the first leg of the tour were held in theaters, but some tried the half-arena approach. The CAA became 'The Theater at Continental Airlines Arena' when half of it was used, a giant curtain draped behind the stage.

There were three shows on this tour in East Rutherford. The first, on May 19, almost turned into a disaster when a bank of speakers on the upper right column (facing the stage) blew out early on and many in the low 200 sections were left without sound. They started making a lot of noise ('We can't hear you!') and Bruce, not knowing what the commotion was, got upset and said sarcastically 'It's good to be home' and told the screamers that if they had a problem their 'money's at the door.'

The problem was fixed and Bruce joked about his family causing the disturbance, calling the show, 'Attack of the Relatives'. During his intro to 'The Wish,' Bruce offered, 'It's kind of boring without the shouting.'

POINT THEATRE

24 MAY 2005 DUBLIN, IRELAND

I WAS THERE: TARA KENNEDY

This was my favourite Springsteen tour since 1985. I paid way over the odds for my ticket, but have no regrets, it was worth it. Just Bruce alone on stage playing those rare songs for us - it all felt very intimate, the atmosphere amazing. I loved it when he took to the piano. You knew you were about to get something special. This tour showed Bruce at his best.

ROYAL ALBERT HALL

27 MAY 2005 LONDON, UK

I WAS THERE: NICK HORNBY

The first time I met him was after his Friday night show at the Royal Albert Hall, at a party in an upmarket West End hotel. He talked with an impressive ferocity and fluency to a little group of us about why he demanded restraint from his fans during the solo shows. The following afternoon I went to the soundcheck for the Saturday show, and sat on my own in the auditorium while he played 'My Father's House', from *Nebraska*. It wasn't the sort of experience you forget in a hurry.

VAN ANDEL ARENA

3 AUGUST 2005 GRAND RAPIDS, MICHIGAN

I WAS THERE: HANNAH LOVETT

I believe this was his one and only concert ever in Grand Rapids. Part of the seductive appeal of seeing Bruce in concert is never knowing what song you might get to hear – and this was defiantly the case on his Devils & Dust tour.

Without the safety net of the E Street Band, Springsteen was at his most spontaneous and fearless, not merely adding unusual songs to set lists, but often performing them in a one-of-a-kind manner.

Standout songs included 'Racing in the Street', his playing as majestic as the song warrants, especially the long outro. Later in the night, his final performance on piano, 'Jesus Was an Only Son,' was another highlight, which Bruce set up with a wonderful story of his family, sung with conviction and tenderness.

ST. PETE TIMES FORUM

4 NOVEMBER 2005 TAMPA, FLORIDA

I WAS THERE: MIKE MULROY

I took my eight-year-old daughter to see Bruce in Tampa on the Devils & Dust tour. We were on the floor in our seats when he played 'My Hometown.' That song always meant something to me, thinking about my father when I was a kid, sitting on his lap, driving through town. As the song ended, my daughter fell asleep on my chest. I realized this song has taken on a new meaning. Here I am 30 years later, same song but the only thing different? I'm driving.

2006

Bruce Springsteen's 14th studio album *We Shall Overcome: The Seeger Sessions* was released in April 2005, the first and so far only album of entirely non-Springsteen material, his interpretation of 13 folk music songs made popular by activist folk musician Pete Seeger. The album won the Grammy Award for Best Traditional Folk Album at the 49th Grammy Awards.

The 2006 Bruce Springsteen with The Seeger Sessions Band Tour (sometimes referred to simply as the Sessions Band Tour), was a 62-date tour with the 18 strong band playing what was billed as 'An all-new evening of gospel, folk, and blues'.

POINT THEATRE

5 MAY 2006 DUBLIN, IRELAND

I WAS THERE: DARREN AHERNE

In 1985 Bruce Springsteen set foot on stage at Slane Castle to perform what would become one of his most renowned concerts in Ireland. I wasn't there, why? I was only 13 and didn't really know who he was. It was shortly before this that my interest

(I call it interest - some call it obsession) in his music began. An uncle gave me a cassette bootleg of *Born in the U.S.A.* I loved it. I didn't understand it but played it over and over until the tape broke.

That Christmas I got a record player

Darren Aherne and friends give the camera a thumbs-up

and one record. As I unwrapped it I hoped it would be *Born in the U.S.A.* Result. It was, and I still play it to this day.

Around the same time I picked up a second-hand 'Hungry Heart' single, and along with the cover and a sketch I had drawn (badly) of the Boss I marched across town to his hotel, walked up to the desk and with as much confidence as a 13-year old could have I asked to see The Boss, in the hope of getting an autograph. It didn't happen and I'm still waiting. He wasn't there. It nearly happened in Dublin in 2016 when I brushed shoulders with Bruce while leaving the Merion Hotel. It will happen someday, I'm sure.

On the bright side I had a record collection, well, two records, and felt I was a certified Springsteen fan. It rolled on from there for another 33 years. But I'd never seen him live.

When I finally got the chance to go to a Springsteen gig it was the Seeger Sessions tour and I was wary at the thought of a folk tour without the E Street Band, a big part of what I loved. Along with my brother Brendan, I aimed to go, although we didn't know anything about the Seeger Sessions Band. It could only go two ways - either totally ruin what I loved or send me deeper into Boss world. We missed out on tickets and our only way was to pay over the odds to a tout. And to this day I don't regret paying for an overpriced ticket.

It was a fantastic gig, so much so that we went again on the return leg of the tour. That's more or less been the pattern ever since. It's never a choice about which night.

May 2008 at the RDS, and the magic kept going. The opening setlist on the Magic tour was indeed a fantastic moment in my Boss life, the encore bringing the show to an electrifying end with some of my favourite songs - 'Born to Run', 'Bobby Jean' and 'American Land' blasting out into the Dublin night.

In July 2009 at the same venue on the Working on a Dream tour, on a cold wet evening, we knew the only place to be was standing on the pitch. As the security guard directed us to our seats we quietly slipped by on to the crowded pitch. As the rain poured down we offered our seats to an elderly couple, who were only too happy to accept. Bruce opened with Creedence Clearwater Revival's 'Who'll Stop The Rain'. We pissed ourselves laughing. The rain didn't stop, but we were at a Springsteen gig. That's all that mattered. The fact we were coming back with our wives the next night made it better, because we had another gig to see.

A pattern had well and truly formed. When Bruce played Ireland myself and my brother (and now my nephew Dean too) would go one night and next we'd go with Nathalie and Michelle too.

In 2013 we manged Limerick, Belfast and Kilkenny on a return leg, only failing to get tickets for Cork. To kick off was Thomand Park. It was a warm July day cruising down the N7 from Dublin, the radio blasting out one thing only, for what was anticipated to be the biggest Springsteen gig ever. At 5pm we rocked up to the ground, a young lady issuing wristbands for the pit. Extremely lucky - some fans had queued for three days.

Sipping on a cold one, our banter with other fans was interrupted by music from the stage. Just a soundcheck? It was of sorts; Bruce appeared on stage prior to his three and a half-hour set, early arrivals rewarded with a three-song acoustic performance of 'Does This Bus Stop at 82nd St', 'For You' on the piano, and a rarely-played stunning 'Harts of Stone'. He was in fine form and ready to rock the very foundations where the stadium stood.

The main set opened with what I describe as an upbeat gospel tune, 'This Little Light of Mine', a heart-stopping song reminding of my children, Katelyn, Emily and Nathan (all Bruce fans).

As it went on the hits just oozed out - 'American Land', 'Badlands', 'Death To My Home Town' … jaw-dropping performances to drive the crowd wild. 'American Skin (41 shots)' became the second requested performance of the night, and possibly the most angrily-emotional version I'm likely to hear.

There were dedications as he made reference and congratulations to local hurlers on ending their 17-year famine for success. But probably one of the most outstanding moments saw a 12-year-old whose sign read 'Ross with the Boss' pulled up on stage to duet with Bruce on 'Waitin on a Sunny Day'.

By now it was almost dark, and out of the darkness came 'Jack Of All Trades', 'Land of Hope And Dreams' and one of my all-time favourites, 'The River', performed with ambience of dusk and soft light, the mouth-organ sounding out like a thousand brass bands but still silent and sweet to hush the entire crowd into a sweet hum. Magic.

We knew the show was coming to an end, but it had been an excellent mix of emotions and reflection and wild times for both the audience and those on stage. It needed to finish with a bang though, and the final encore consisted of 'My Hometown', 'Born in the U.S.A.', 'Glory Days', 'Bobby Jean' and 'Dancing in the Dark.' It was 1985 again, Slane Castle, I was 13 but this time I was at the gig, back where it all began. I walked out of Thomand Park to the sound of 'This Little Lite of Mine' playing for a second time, and I was completely at home.

TWEETER CENTER

27 MAY 2006 MANSFIELD, MASSACHUSETTS

I WAS THERE: MARK SALESKI

Driving back from Foxboro the morning after the Seeger
Sessions show, me and the wife were listening to Pete Seeger's
We Shall Overcome, The Complete Carnegie Hall Concert. I was struck
by the sense of community in that audience. He would begin
a tune as simple as 'Skip To My Lou' and the crowd not only
joined in but also seemingly invited communal past experiences
with the song into the hall as an extra participant.

Looking back at that 1963 show, perhaps that sense of
togetherness shouldn't be surprising: 'We Shall Overcome' was
a very important song for the Civil Rights movement. But what
about my Bruce Springsteen and the Seeger Sessions concert
experience in Boston? It was a communal happening. A
surprisingly intense one at that. But what we don't have today
is a tight connection to most of this music. So how is it that we
were all singing along as though our lives depended upon it?

You'll get no straight answer from me - I'm still trying to
work out what the hell happened that night. I don't sing along
to anything, not even 'Happy Birthday.' Yet here I was belting
out the chorus to 'Pay Me My Money Down,' 'Jacob's Ladder,'
and 'Buffalo Gals.' I even shouted, 'It Blowed Away!' during
'My Oklahoma Home.' Go figure!

One thing's certain: musically, Springsteen pushed all the
right buttons. The Seeger Sessions live band packs quite a
punch. Folk music? Yeah ... jazz, blues, and soul too - all
filtered through the spirit of New Orleans. Bruce's own
songs, reworked for the tour, surprised and delighted. 'Open
All Night' as a bluesy rave-up, an upside down (or maybe
sideways?) 'Cadillac Ranch' giving way to 'Mystery Train.'
Then there's the 'Polka/Mariachi/Ska' version of 'Ramrod.'

Heck, even the mistakes were glorious. Trying to add one

more rising key change to 'Jacob's Ladder,' only about a half of the band went ahead, resulting in a bar or so of giant sour notes. Somehow, it only added to the raucousness. After the song, Bruce noted, 'We tried to climb too high … and we fucked it up!'

The more thoughtful/spiritual side of the material was represented by a slow, soulful 'When The Saints Go Marching In', 'We Shall Overcome', 'Bring Them Home (If You Love Your Uncle Sam)', Springsteen's own 'If I Should Fall Behind', a mournful 'Mrs. McGrath' punctuated by a bodhran-like bass drum, and an amazing tribute to New Orleans, 'How Can a Poor Man Stand Such Times and Live?'

The final encore, a Peter Wolf-aided 'Dirty Water' followed by the stomping 'Buffalo Gals', bringing to mind the E Street finale of yore - the Detroit Medley. Knees were knockin' and everybody was rockin'. To those who decided to sit out this tour -you had no idea what you passed up.

SPORTPALEIS

7 NOVEMBER 2006 ANTWERP, BELGIUM

I WAS THERE: JAN VERBRAEKEN

His 17-piece Seeger Sessions Band provided an unforgettable evening in Antwerp. At nine o'clock The Boss, preceded by his band, walked on stage. 'Good evening Antwerp!' Springsteen was welcomed as one of the greatest artists of his generation. Resounding applause blared through the Sportpaleis, and not one note had been played.

He opened with 'Blinded By The Light' from the first album, completely unrecognisable. Springsteen sang it rapidly and almost staccato. An impressive start. This was anything but a one-man show. All musicians displayed their talents.

2007

VERIZON CENTER

12 NOVEMBER 2007 WASHINGTON DC

I WAS THERE: ERIN KALBARCZYK

I think I can safely say I have seen Bruce about 40 times since my first show in 1979. I can still remember jumping up and down with my arm around my best Bruce friend, and her arm around me, shouting the lyrics to 'Badlands' all those years ago.

A number of shows stand out, as it should be if you are a returning fan. At any given time, different ones are my favourite, depending on my mood or the issues of the day when pondering my memories. The Magic tour show in Washington D.C. in 2007 is memorable for a number of reasons. It was my first time in the pit, and I was one warm body from the stage for the entire night. The set-list rocked out loud. 'Backstreets' was stunning. 'Reason to Believe' took my breath away. And I got to help Bruce out during 'Born to Run.' He had been standing off to my right, about two feet too far away for me to reach, so I was happy for the folks who could reach. Then, inexplicably, he took two steps to his right, my left, and I reached up just in time to touch strings and his fingers as his hand swept down to play. It took all of maybe two seconds, but that's all that was needed.

Another standout was Chapel Hill, North Carolina, 14 September 2003. I was in the 14th row on the field. Academics must have been sitting in the first 13 rows, because they didn't stand up when the band came out, and when Bruce came out, they didn't stand up. My line of vision was clear for the first time in decades. Unbelievable. Another kick-ass set-list - of course, because it was The Rising tour - my sixth show of that tour. I had seen them in Washington DC the night before at FedEx. 'Pink Cadillac' was a highlight that night. I probably listen to the boot of this show as often as I listen to the Baltimore show of the Wrecking Ball tour - the last time I saw and heard Clarence. His brilliance during 'Jungle

Land' in Chapel Hill was pure. 'Jungle Land' came right after a beautiful 'American Skin (41 Shots)'. I stuck my right fist in the air each time Bruce sang, 'You get killed just for livin' in ... your American skin.' Hell, yes.

My first North Carolina show, November 16, 2002 in Greensboro, turned my husband into a believer. He and my youngest daughter had taken to calling Bruce 'Mooooose' just to annoy me. But he came with me to Greensboro and the Bruce universe turned on its exquisite axis once again. Our seats were stellar - lower level, maybe 20ft from Clarence. The sound was outrageously clear. From the second the stage went dark, a low roar rolled through the Coliseum from the rear and caught everyone in its path. We sang along all night, but my clearest memory of the crowd-sing, and you can hear it on the boot, was during 'My City of Ruins'. Exquisite. And when I want to hear the most perfect 'She's the One', I turn to that boot. It had rained that day, so I knew to expect something stellar. What we got was beyond stellar, in part because the crowd was as one. We had our you-are-us and we-are-you thing going on with Bruce and the band that night, no doubt about it. My best Bruce friend had driven down from Baltimore for the occasion and her seat was nearby. When the band left the stage, I turned and looked at her, and she looked at me - our mouths hung open as if to say, 'What did we just witness?' But we knew.

I was nervous about taking my husband to that show. He'd been to one years before in nosebleed seats at the Cap Center, Largo, MD. Not optimal. No bonding there. But in Greensboro, Allan saw what I had been seeing. Finally.

Those are three distinct memories of love, inspiration, sweat, and sweet reunion with old friends who have been with me since 'Born to Run' blasted through the tiny tinny speakers of whatever little car I drove in 1975. Long Live Rock, and many thanks to Bruce and the E Street Band - one and all. I grew up with The Beatles, was lucky enough to see them three times, but they only toured for two years. It was over in a New York minute. Just 'Imagine' how lucky I feel to have had this band since 1975, given that my heart was broken in 1966 by the Beatles. Who knew it could be this good, this educational, this sincere, this heart-rending, this much fun.

2008

The Magic Tour kicked off on October 2, 2007 in Hartford, Connecticut after three rehearsal shows the previous week, closing at the Red Bull Arena in New Jersey on December 22, 2008. Playing 100 shows in total, it was Springsteen's first tour with the E Street Band since 2004's Vote for Change shows and the first prolonged outing with them since the 2002–03 Rising Tour.

The tour won the 2008 *Billboard* Touring Awards for Top Tour, Top Draw, and Top Manager (for Jon Landau), and over its two years, grossed more than $235 million.

Keyboardist Danny Federici would take a leave of absence from the tour to pursue treatment for skin cancer. He made his only return to the stage on March 20, 2008, when he appeared for portions of a performance at Conseco Fieldhouse in Indianapolis. Federici died on April 17, 2008 aged 58 at the Memorial Sloan-Kettering Cancer Center in New York City. Springsteen said: 'He was the most wonderfully-fluid keyboard player and a pure, natural musician. I loved him very much.' The album, *Working on a Dream*, is dedicated to him.

RDS ARENA

22 MAY 2008 DUBLIN, IRELAND

I WAS THERE: ALEX LIPINSKI, SINGER, SONGWRITER

I attended my first Springsteen concert at the RDS Showground. Having attended nine shows since, I will attempt to put into words why I'm drawn to them like a moth to a flame.

Going to see Bruce Springsteen and the E Street Band is not merely a form of entertainment. It's an experience. A religious experience. Not that I can put my finger on what a religious experience is exactly. A sense of enlightenment, if you will. More so than any artist I've seen perform live, the concert is completely communal. Whether it's a capacity of 2,000 or 80,000 people, the band and audience are together as one. It is completely personal. The singer has the ability to create intimacy, whether you're sitting in the back row or the very front. There is a connection, a bonding, a togetherness, a transfer of energy between audience and performer that I have yet to experience to such a degree in any other live performance or any other walk of life for that matter. Going to a

Bruce Springsteen concert has been likened to going to Church. Not for any religious reason, but a spiritual one. He's called The Boss for good reason.

Every time I come out of a Springsteen gig I feel revitalised, restored, fulfilled, inspired; a shot in the arm. A fresh outlook on life. It's the reason I keep going back. It's the same reason thousands of other fans travel round the world to follow each concert - to recapture that same feeling. After every Springsteen gig I have attended, whether it's in Dublin, London, Milan, Cardiff (just some on the list), I am always left with the same feeling of wholeness. Everything in my mind is simplified and makes complete sense. It's a drug. Everywhere I travel to a Springsteen concert, I meet other people from many different walks of life who have travelled either from near or far, who are there for the same reason as myself. People travelling on their own or with their partner, or with friends. Stories are shared from previous travels and concerts. There is a sense of community rarely found to such degrees in other fanbases. This is my Soul Place. If I only had one day remaining on this planet, I would choose to be at a Bruce Springsteen gig.

But how does music have the ability to do this? How does it have the ability to change your outlook on life? To shape the way you view the world? It's unexplainable, yet the feeling is familiar to everyone. How can a simple three-minute song have such an effect on our mood, our feelings, our soul? Music has certainly shaped the way I live my life, the way I see the world. It enables me to understand life a little clearer. Music is therapy. It has the ability to heal, to repair, to open the mind to new ideas and enlarge your imagination. Music is escapism. Music is reality. Music is life. All these qualities are epitomised in a Bruce Springsteen concert. Yet it is still impossible to put down in words what exactly it is in a song that can make us have all these feelings. Feelings that can transform us. It's an added element of mystery but we know it's there. To quote a Bruce lyric, 'Show a little faith, there's magic in the night....'

RDS ARENA

23 MAY 2008 DUBLIN, IRELAND

I WAS THERE: SKIP WEISMAN

It was May 2008. My wife and I are attending her Irish family reunion in Donegal. We had been planning to attend this family event for about two and a half years.

In the fall of 2007, Bruce released his *Magic* album and in December announced a world tour. As it was my first trip to Europe and my wife knew Bruce would be on tour, she gave me permission to leave the family reunion to attend a concert if it was in a location that would accommodate a reasonable side-trip.

As luck would have it the tour was in Dublin, with three shows that started the final day of the reunion. We got tickets for night two and my wife went with me. All the tickets for the rugby pitch were general admission, so we got there early to get a good location on the field.

We didn't try to get in to the pit in those days but got there early enough to grab a seat on the railing in front of the

Skip Weisman and his friend Nils Linnecken

stage on the other side of the pit. When we arrived, we sidled up next to a guy sitting with his legs crossed, wearing a *Backstreets Magazine* cap, reading a novel. We introduced ourselves and made some small talk before the show. My wife and I learnt he was from Hamburg and spending his vacation seeing Bruce on this stretch of shows.

As the fans began to crowd in we got physically closer. As the show started the crowd from behind got kind of aggressive as some drunk women tried to breakthrough to get to our rail position. We fought them off and then the three of us enjoyed the show together.

After the show ended we shook hands and bid each other farewell and safe travels. On the way out, we bumped into each other twice and then a third time where we found ourselves side by side in line for the toilets. At that time, we decided to exchange contact info to stay in touch as the tour progressed, so we could share notes.

As with most things when we have the best of intentions, life and business get in the way and we never exchange correspondence for almost a year. In early 2009 as Bruce released *Working on a Dream* and got ready to play the Super Bowl, I emailed Nils (yes, that's his first name, and his last name begins with an 'L') to see if he remembered me and see what he thought of the new music. We exchanged emails.

In mid-July, after Bruce announced he would be performing the final concerts ever at a Giants Stadium, I received an email from Nils. It was 6pm Eastern Time on a Friday, sent around midnight German time, asking if he could stay with us if he were to come to see the shows. A few hours later I email back saying, 'Yes, if I can go to the shows too.' At noon the next day, I receive an email from Nils, his flight already booked, and told my wife, Anne.

We started working on getting tickets to the final two shows of that Giants Stadium run. While we're working on that, Springsteen announces a couple of Madison Square Garden shows about 30 days after those concerts. I get another email from Nils wanting to know if he could come back and stay for those shows. We say, 'Of course,' thinking this guy is even crazier about Bruce than me.

After those two US trips, Nils and I have seen at least 20 shows together between there and Europe, even winning the pit lottery in Philadelphia in February 2016 for The River retrospective tour as the first two into the Wells Fargo Arena. But it's become much more than just a Bruce relationship. We've become true friends, our families have vacationed together, Nils' sister and kids have visited our home, I've taught his son and daughter how to play baseball in our backyard and my wife and I have visited their Hamburg home twice.

May 20, 2018 will mark the 10th anniversary of the night in Dublin where my wife and I made a lifelong friend that truly changed the trajectory of our lives and made our lives richer than we could ever imagined. It never would have happened without Bruce. Nils and I are forever grateful for the meaning Bruce's music has brought to our lives and the opportunity to build a friendship around that.

MILLENNIUM STADIUM

14 JUNE 2008 CARDIFF, UK

I WAS THERE: ALISON HOLLY

The first time I saw Bruce was in Cardiff. As we were leaving, I heard a lady comparing her husband's lack of moves compared to Bruce's. I would love it if they played my hometown of Bristol. The music is intoxicating, their ethos is amazing.

The following year I read about Bruce and the E Street Band playing the last concert held at Giants Stadium. Read about it, thought about it, left it too late. Then they added extra dates. So we got tickets for the very last night. People said I was mad going that far just for a concert.

We were also at Hyde Park, when Sir Paul McCartney came on to the stage and the plug was pulled after the show ran over time. Stevie Van Zandt tweeted about the UK being a nanny state. I completely agreed. Not a huge fan of Sir Paul, but an epic event all the same.

I flew to Milan for a concert at the San Siro. Amazing atmosphere, the ticket including round-trip tickets on the

Alison Holly shows off her Bruce tattoo

Metro. And the most recent was in Paris, 2016, where I got the closest ever to the stage. Two hours in there's a power cut, affecting most of the stage electrics. An ad-hoc time-filler took place, with autographs signed and a crowd-initiated sing-along. About 20 minutes later the power came back and the show continued in true style.

I WAS THERE: NIALL BRANNIGAN

It was a baking hot Saturday as my wife, Jan, and Pete, her friend and by the end of a two-hour journey, my best buddy, drove to Cardiff. Bruce and the E Street Band were playing The

Millennium Stadium that night and we had tickets. We dropped Pete at his guest house, checked into our hotel, then met in a bar, a short walk from the stadium. It was sweltering but the mood in the pubs and bars was fun and excited.

In the huge venue, Pete headed to the stadium floor and Jan and I climbed to our seats, halfway back from the stage. I'd seen

Niall Brannigan in his music room, complete with cherished lithograph and Morgan Howell painting of the Born to Run single

Bruce many times since that first time on 29 May 1981 at Wembley, several with Jan, but this was her very first stadium gig. It was just past the anniversary of 'that' gig and our wedding anniversary, just before the anniversary of my Dad's death and six months on from the passing away of my gorgeous Mum. To say I was raw, excited beyond reason, and shaking with anticipation would be to understate and underplay everything about that night.

The sun was starting to dip down below the roof as the band came on stage, a packed audience roaring their joy at seeing their friends in this legendary band on stage, one more time. The lovely Danny Federici had died just two months before and this would be the last time we would see my beloved Clarence, but here they were. And the joint was jumpin'.

The setlist was a brilliant mix of old and new. It had a great version of 'Radio Nowhere', not yet a year old, after a blistering 'Tenth Avenue Freeze Out', already 33 years old. It had songs from every era of Bruce's career, newer songs like 'Gypsy Biker' and 'Long Way Home' perfectly at home among elder siblings like 'The Promised Land' and 'The River'.

'Badlands' ended the main set (no break these days) before the best four-way combination punch you could ever wish to hear; 'Jungleland', into 'Thunder Road', followed by 'Born to Run' and 'Rosalita'. I was in some kind of heaven, 'Jungleland' and Clarence's sax solo reducing me to tears as I remembered my Dad, 'Thunder Road' getting the same treatment from me that it had on an equally-hot night 27 years earlier, 'Born To Run' ringing out into the night sky like a runaway freight train on some distant horizon, and then 'Rosalita', bringing a smile to everyone's face as we danced and sang and cried tears of joy. I thought of Mum, Dad, my lost youth, my happiness at having the love of my life beside me, her face glowing with pleasure, and of a night in 1981 when at the age of 19 I had a whole world in front of me, a world I wanted to dive into, to drown myself in and to never leave - Bruce's world.

BARCLAYCARD CENTER

17 JULY 2008 MADRID, SPAIN

I WAS THERE: DEAN KIRBY

A few friends and myself went to see Bruce in Madrid and as usual I worked my way down to the front (the only place to be at a Bruce gig). The next day we were flying back to Manchester and at the airport met one of the security guys from the gig who had handed us water down in the pit. I got chatting and he mentioned the tour's Scandinavian leg. He gave me his name and said to ask for him. He'd make sure we got in, so a pal and I ended up going to Stockholm, where we met the guy at the back of the stadium as he got off the band's minibus. Turns out he was Bruce's bodyguard. Bruce came over, shook our hands and had a chat, then the bodyguard gave us a guest-pass each and we followed the band into the stadium. What a night, and what a guy.

OLD GIANTS STADIUM

31 JULY 2008 EAST RUTHERFORD, NEW JERSEY

I WAS THERE: ELIZABETH SESSA

I had begged my parents to take me to a Springsteen concert for as long as I could remember. As anyone who knows me now will tell you, I associate my earliest memories with the music of Bruce Springsteen. I had been left home with my cousins to be babysat while my parents, aunts and uncles had all gone to numerous shows, and I was over it. I wanted in on this experience that drew them back time and time again. They finally took me to my first concert in 2007. But being 11 I can barely remember much of it and hardly appreciated the experience. I got to see him again a few months later, as a 12th-birthday present.

I remember sitting in the back of my Dad's Ford Explorer and just observing the tailgate. Springsteen fans have a connection that is in a class of their own, but Jersey Springsteen fans are something special. My family and friends that I had gone with had brought enough food and alcohol to supply a small village and it attracted dozens of people over to our group. Everyone shared their own stories of previous concerts, places they had seen him, and had this connection that blew my mind. It wouldn't be another nine years before I met Bruce during his book tour and saw this replicated. People online sharing their stories, building that connection with each other, all because of The Boss.

Elizabeth Sessa poses with Bruce during his book tour

I would share a fraction of my story with Bruce himself. I wasn't able to tell him how I had a song of his that I associated with each member of my family. I was unable to tell him how his music had gotten my Mom through her divorce. I was unable to tell him how grateful I was for his music to get me through all of the darkest times in my life. I was able to tell him how his music had kept me connected with my Mom, who passed away nearly two years to the day before I met him. And as he always does, Springsteen strengthened that bond with a kiss on the forehead that day.

The concert on this night was delayed because of an overturned tractor-trailer on the Turnpike that prevented fans from getting to the show, which just prolonged the tailgate and built up the suspense of the concert. I remember watching my Dad and my Uncle John blasting 'Born to Run' out of the speakers of my Uncle's truck.

When I was a toddler, I had thought it was them on the cover of the album (my Uncle does look like Springsteen, my Dad, however, doesn't resemble Clarence to any degree). Back to back, they both went for the air guitar-and it was like magic.

'You wanted to come to a Bruce concert with your Uncle John,' my Uncle would say to me after mistaking my reaction for horror instead of awe.

When the show started, two hours later than billed, the energy was amazing. There was magic in the air that only a performer like Bruce could command. Time seemed to stand still as the E Street Band gave there all in a 28-song set. As he continues to do, he took an audience from East Rutherford, NJ on a rock 'n' roll journey that defied the rules of time and space.

HARLEYFEST

30 AUGUST 2008 MILWAUKEE, WISCONSIN

I WAS THERE: CRAIG & STEPH SCHULTZ

From a 200-seat 1975 Theater show in Milwaukee to The River Tour 2016 at the Bradley Center, Milwaukee, with over a dozen shows experienced in between; the penultimate show for us had to be this Harley-Davidson 105th anniversary celebration in Milwaukee.

Set along the lake shore in Veterans' Park on a warm summer evening, we were among 60,000 lucky souls taking in this concert experience, the sound sparkling clear and powerful from a huge custom stage labelled the 'Roadhouse at the Lakefront.'

Bruce and band were in stellar form throughout a 31-song, three-and-a-half-hour show that was the last, and longest, of the Magic tour. Appropriately the show was started to the distinctive sights and sounds of roaring Harley's as the band took the stage, Bruce then launching into 'Gypsy Biker', peppering the set-list with fan requests, including 'Woolly Bully', 'Seven Nights To Rock', and a wide cross-section from his songbook.

Highlights included a stirring 'Spirit in the Night' (including a full stage knee-slide), 'Tenth Avenue Freezeout' (the Big Man in fine form) and a stirring 10-minute 'Racing in the Streets' featuring Roy's moving, astounding five-minute piano intro.

A 10-song encore began with a touching 'Sandy' (Danny's son Jason joining on accordion), a rousing 'Dancing in the Dark' and a fitting cover of 'Born To Be Wild', delighting an ecstatic crowd!

Exhausted and elated, we slowly made our way south on Lake Shore Drive toward the City and our parked lot. As we crossed the Boulevard, freshly in the afterglow of this spectacular show, we heard the distinctive sounds of Harley's coming from behind.

We were awestruck to turn and see a line of bikes escorting a group of Limos away from the site. As they passed, with windows down, Bruce, Steve, and Nils were hooting, waving, and acknowledging the lucky crowd of passers-by, then disappeared across the bridge and roared off into the night. What an amazing ending to our 'best ever' Bruce Springsteen & The E-Street Band concert.

2009

IZOD CENTER

23 MAY 2009 EAST RUTHERFORD, NEW JERSEY

I WAS THERE: STAN GOLDSTEIN

This was the final show on the first US leg of the Working on a Dream tour, with three tour premieres: 'Something In the Night,' 'Cover Me,' and 'Incident on 57th Street.'

I remember an outstanding 'Kitty's Back' in the encores, one of the best I've ever heard. After playing the usual show closer, 'American Land', Bruce asked the crowd, 'Are you trying to test me?' before adding: 'The Turnpike is closed - nobody goes home.' The band then finished with a rousing 'Glory Days', going into 'Mony Mony.'

TIMES UNION CENTER

14 MAY 2009 ALBANY, NEW YORK

I've seen Springsteen 32 times over the past 34 years, with another booked on Broadway. More than just his music, Springsteen has been a bond between my siblings and me. We all love him, break down his lyrics, attend concerts together and

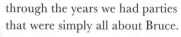

through the years we had parties that were simply all about Bruce.

In 2009, tragedy struck. My younger brother, Jeff, passed away after a sudden stroke. We all lost our best friend and I was absolutely consumed in grief.

One day, working in Albany, I phoned my wife back in Buffalo to say I might not make the long drive as it was getting late in the day. Moments later, she called back and said, 'Bruce is in Albany.' My heart being busted had caused me to lose track as to where Bruce was on the 'Working on a Dream' tour. An hour

later, I had a ticket. I would be alone in the expensive seats, but there was one problem, I was crying too hard to go in. I kept thinking, 'How can I be happy listening to Bruce, without my brother by my side?'

I worked up the courage to go in, and Bruce put on his cowboy hat and pranced around the stage doing, 'Outlaw Pete' bellowing 'Can you hear me?' With tears flowing down my face, I was able to work my way through my emotions as Bruce and the band put me through the paces of a spiritual reawakening.

I've returned to Albany twice more, by myself, to attend at least one show on the tour, knowing Jeff is beside me. Springsteen has emotionally saved me, year after year. At the end of each show, I simply yell out, 'Thank you.' And I mean, 'Thank You' for helping me to navigate. I've spent thousands and thousands of dollars on Bruce clothes, records, cassettes, CD's, downloads, bootlegs, books, concerts, and even car seats!

And I've never regretted even one nickel.

GLASTONBURY

27 JUNE 2009 WORTHY FARM, PILTON, UK

I WAS THERE: UNA MULLALLY

I've only seen The Boss play live once, headlining Glastonbury in 2009, where he and the E Street Band made (in my opinion) the mistake of playing a Springsteen set, not a festival set. That gig was well reviewed, but what I remember is people drifting away at the fringes, realising that Springsteen plays for his fans, and not fair-weather ones.

As someone who finds earnestness incredibly attractive in music, I still sometimes can't quite relate to the very male, heartland rock he brought to the mainstream. But it's the undercurrent of anti-establishment sentiment that makes Springsteen feel of 'us' and not of 'them.' 'Born in the U.S.A.' sounds as vicious as ever; 'Streets Of Philadelphia' is as mournful and searching as it was in 1993 when Hollywood finally began to acknowledge the HIV/AIDS crisis. Springsteen is also a shoulder to cry on. His 2002 record *The Rising* answered a yearning for inspiration and comfort, people were seeking post-9/11, although perhaps Steve Earle unpicked the complexities of that era a little better, two years later with *The Revolution Starts… Now.*

In an Irish context, criticising Springsteen is a bit like criticising Tayto or Brian O'Driscoll. He is a totem of authenticity, a version of America that Irish people love, with all its white, blue-collar masculinity, a shorthand for realness and decency in a fake and corrupt world. He is 'real', although David Remnick's profile of

Bruce in the *New Yorker* in 2012 captured how the showmanship beloved of fans is so expertly rehearsed.

RDS ARENA

11 JULY 2009 DUBLIN, IRELAND

I WAS THERE: ELAINE BUCKLEY

By the time I was born, Bruce Springsteen and the E Street Band had already released seven albums. He is not of my era, nor was he a prevalent feature in my house. Intrigued by the furore surrounding the release of *The Rising* as a teenager, I made a conscious decision to delve into his back catalogue. It was *Born to Run* that started it, *Darkness on the Edge of Town* that escalated it, and *The Wild, the Innocent & the E Street Shuffle* that triggered the full-blown obsession. I spent hours poring over his lyrics and chipping away at his songs on my guitar. The more I listened to and learned about The Boss, the further I fell – this was true love.

My ultimate Springsteen live experience was in 2009 in the RDS. I went to see him twice in the one weekend, queuing for pit bands for both shows. His set lists are pot luck, but on the Sunday night I saw the majestic 'Jungleland', with Clarence Clemons' legendary sax solo moving me to tears. Straight after, the E Street Band launched into 'Rosalita', my favourite song. It will never be topped.

GIANTS STADIUM

3 OCTOBER 2009 EAST RUTHERFORD, NEW JERSEY

I WAS THERE: JOHN HARVEY

For me nothing will come close to seeing 'Jungleland' live the first time I saw him in New Jersey, at the old Giants Stadium. I swear I had goose-bumps and weak knees the entire song. It's incredible to see the entire crowd smiling ear-to-ear, singing every word. I could never make it through 'Independence Day' or 'Drive All Night' without crying.

Adam Brooker enjoyed a full backstage tour and met Springsteen

Springsteen on stage at Allphones Arena Sydney, Australia, 2014, see page 324

Springsteen on stage at Carousel House,
Asbury Park, New Jersey 2010, see page 260

*Lynette Giglio's photo of Springsteen meeting the
crowd at Allphones Arena Sydney, Australia, 2013,
see page 300*

Matthew Finn's photo of Springsteen from Hanging Rock, Melbourne, Australia 2017, see page 376

Matthew Aucoin jams with Springsteen on 'No Surrender' at Citizens Bank Park, Philadelphia see page 362

Jessica Bloom takes her world famous selfie at Qudos Bank Arena, Sydney, Australia in February 2017, see page 374

THE SPECTRUM

20 OCTOBER 2009 PHILADELPHIA, PENNSYLVANIA

I WAS THERE: JOE LEWIN

I've seen Bruce about 110 times since 1985. One of the most memorable was Bruce taking my sign request for '(Your Love Keeps Lifting Me) Higher & Higher' on October 20, 2009 at The Spectrum. Unfortunately, I didn't get a picture of myself with the sign before the show.

ROYAL FARS ARENA

20 NOVEMBER 2009 BALTIMORE, MARYLAND

I WAS THERE: TIM MULLIN

Our daughters Kylie and Cameron first saw Bruce at a concert at the MCI Center in Washington, DC on September 3, 1999, where Cameron, who had just turned five, fell asleep, but was awoken by the crowd singing the opening to 'Hungry Heart' in the encore.

On May 15, 2009, we went to a stadium show in Hershey, PA, on a beautiful night in a small venue. There were changes in the band. It was the first time we'd seen them since Danny Federici's passing, and Max Weinberg's teenage son took over on drums as Max had other commitments. But I was pleased to see that after many years, Bruce was

Bruce holds up Tim's daughter's Hungry Heart sign

once again comfortable with rock'n'roll and seemed to enjoy playing the music I had grown up with.

We were amazed as we witnessed for the first time Bruce taking requests from signs held up by fans. On the way home, maybe inspired by an 18-year-old playing drums, Cameron announced that at our next concert, Bruce would pick her sign and play her request. She pinned the ticket stub to the bulletin board in her room as a reminder.

That summer and fall, Cameron played Springsteen's albums in order, from *Greetings* all the way to *Working on a Dream*. The tour continued and, remarkably, a date at First Mariner Arena in Baltimore was announced.

The band had not played Baltimore's pitiful arena (originally the Civic Center) since 1973 when Springsteen opened for Chicago. Cameron reiterated her plan for Bruce to pick her sign. Ever the sceptic, I doubted the many pieces could possibly fall into place: floor tickets, a spot in the pit, and a sign that struck the fancy of The Boss. I knew I could deliver the first - Stub Hub ensured it was only a matter of cash, and I'd pay what it took to get floor tickets but getting into the pit required luck. And getting The Boss to pick her sign required more than luck.

Good karma abounded. My wife Tricia was known for her skill and patience in acquiring tickets; she was usually the one who spent hours in line or talked to scalpers. But she and Kylie were on a college visit and I drew line-duty that day. Nevertheless, floor tickets were acquired at face value from *Record and Tape Trader*. The casual fans in front didn't want their maximum number, so I bought their extra two.

Unfortunately, it wasn't even clear that the girls could get there. Kylie was a high school senior and Cameron a freshman and they played together on the varsity basketball team. That night's scheduled practice created a serious logistical problem, and our values didn't allow the two of them to skip practice. Approached about the conundrum, Strom, the coach, athletic director and good friend, joked 'If I get a ticket, I'll cancel practice.' Those two extra tickets sure came in handy!

On concert day, we worked on getting into the pit. I knew we would need wristbands for access to the floor and figured I would get some of the first four issued, so the low numbers would get access. Tricia and I were some of the first to get wristbands, but you could only get wristbands for people physically present, and the bands were placed on your wrist then and there. The girls were in school so theirs would have to wait. Tricia managed to slip off her wristband and together with a proxy went through the line again, but the girls' numbers were hundreds higher than ours.

The sign? Cameron had been sick that week. Recuperated, she walked a few blocks to the craft store. Three dimensional hamburgers and battery-lit hearts accompanied the words, 'HELP! I've Got A Hungry Heart.' It was beautiful, creative and sure to draw Springsteen's attention. But I knew it could never be chosen by The Boss. The concert was in Baltimore, where I had 'a wife and kids, Jack.' 'Hungry Heart' would be played and would be all over by the time signs were even needed. I resigned myself to consoling a disappointed Cameron.

The girls raced downtown after school, and we stood in line separately, hundreds of people apart and around the corner from each other. But the pit fans weren't selected by lowest numbers. A random number was drawn, and 200 fans after that number got in. The girls were in that 200, now wearing two wristbands - one for the pit. My goodness. Against all odds we had overcome the first two hurdles. But the sign?

I was right. 'Hungry Heart' was on the set-list and wasn't going to be played by fan request. In fact, it was the third song that night. But after the crowd belted out the entire first verse, and after Bruce had crowd-surfed, as the Big Man's sax wailed, Bruce started pointing at the crowd and frantically waving. It took the girls a while, but they eventually realized The Boss wanted the sign! It was passed overhead through the crowd, and soon Bruce held it aloft like a trophy. A *Baltimore Sun* photographer recorded the moment. Bruce marched across the stage, holding the sign high. As he finished the song, he placed it in front of the microphone stand.

2010

CAROUSEL HOUSE

7 DECEMBER 2010 ASBURY PARK, NEW JERSEY

I WAS THERE: AUDREY HUNN

I have a beautiful jean-jacket with Bruce airbrushed on the back that was a gift received back in 1990. And there began my quest. No.1 on my bucket list was to have it signed by Bruce. He saw it many times through the years when I held it up at shows. He'd point at it, nod and laugh. If I didn't know better, I was starting to believe he knew exactly what I wanted. It became a game I was determined to win.

After a tour promoting his *Magic* album, a phenomenal Super Bowl half-time appearance and a

Audrey Hunn meets Bruce after her Springsteen husband won a Backstreets Magazine competition

Working On A Dream or Magic II tour, Bruce decided

to wake up E Street Nation once again to celebrate the 40th anniversary of the release of *Darkness on the Edge of Town*. There was *The Promise* Box Set filled with outtakes, a DVD, and much more. Contests started popping up, like a chance to win an opportunity to come into E Street Radio at Sirius/XM and ask Bruce a pre-screened question. How could he turn the jacket down there? I thought I had the perfect question. They didn't agree.

Then came the next contest. *Backstreets Magazine* asked us to email an answer to a trivia question. Everyone who answered correctly went into a draw to come to Asbury Park and be present to watch Bruce film a video. I'd get picked for this, right? Entries went in over the weekend, with the draw and e-mail notifications on Monday evening and the filming on Tuesday. I fought to stay awake Monday night as I wanted to hear that ping of my email. Finally, I fell asleep. When I awoke in the morning I pulled up my email, hopeful, but it wasn't there. I was bummed but we all know faith will be rewarded. I got up to get ready for work and noticed my cell phone telling me I had a message from my friend Scott Geller (my 'Springsteen Husband'), left in the wee hours of the morning. All he said was, 'Want to go get your jacket signed today?' OMG! They picked him and he was allowed to bring one other person. Today could be the day.

I needed to plan my strategy, find out exactly what was going to happen and the likelihood of getting close enough for my jacket to be signed. We were going to watch him film a video with the E Street Band in the Carousel House, to be released on *Vevo* as a thank you Christmas gift to fans. I also found out that *Backstreets* picked only 15 people from the draw and each was able to bring a plus one. It kept getting better. My head was spinning.

On arrival, we were ushered into a holding area. The band was rehearsing and we were able to watch on monitors. Then a gentleman came over to explain we would be heading in and individually placed on the stage with Bruce and the E Street Band. Oh, and there are to be no cameras, cell phones or autographs. What? No autographs? No way! I had little time to contemplate. We were on our way in. There was Bruce, Stevie, Garry, Max, Roy,

David Lindley, Charlie, a horn section and Clarence. There was management and family and a total of 61 people in that room, including the band. Wow.

Scott and I were right behind Garry, very close to Roy and the piano. We were behind Bruce as he was performing, but that put us in almost every shot. They did about 11 songs, each at least twice. We were on that stage over four hours.

About halfway through Bruce called for a break, but they didn't leave the stage. The band walked around, thanked everyone for coming out. Bruce was across the stage chatting with fans in front of him and directly across from us. He looks up and we make eye contact. I feel my arm go up but am not sure what I'm about to do. In that second, I wave him over and he's coming. Uh oh, this is it. Scott's behind me and whispers in my ear that if I faint he'll kill me. Bruce arrives and the next five minutes are slow motion for me. This is my first time meeting him and getting to talk to him and I was so happy and relieved. He was very much the generous down-to-earth man I always envisioned. We chatted about animals he rescued and everyday topics when suddenly I think I hear Scott blurt out, 'Bruce, can you please sign this girl's jacket?' What? Twenty years I've waited to ask this, and I think someone just did it for me. Not only that but Bruce as kindly as possible declines because of the rules we were given before we came in and how long of a day it was already. I'm sure I'm screaming internally, 'No, no!'

This was it. This was my shot. I stand up tall, cross my arms in front, look Bruce straight in the eyes and say, 'Bruce, I've waited 20 Fehkaktah years to have this jacket signed. Please don't let me leave here today without it.' Scott turns me around and lifts my hair so he can see it. I turn back to Bruce, standing with arms crossed in front of him, and he says, 'Well, I guess you've waited long enough. Does anyone have a pen?' I reach into my jacket pocket to pull out the sharpie I go nowhere without and hand it to him. He laughs. I turn and lift my hair. He signs. I thank him and on he goes to speak with more fans.

I haven't moved. I'm still trying to process what happened. I realize everyone around is clapping, congratulating me. Scott grabs me by the arms, says, 'You did it!' Holy crap, I did it. I look at him and as reality sets in I burst into tears. Not because I just met Bruce Springsteen, but because I just accomplished something I've been working at for 20 years. No.1 on the bucket list.

I'll never ever forget that day. I still sometimes can't believe it happened. I've since met him several times and danced with him onstage at Madison Square Garden, but that day was incredible. That day, thanks to my Springsteen husband, I was on stage with Bruce and the E Street Band over four hours and got my jacket signed. And when they were done they stayed around, took pictures and signed autographs. I got the rest of the band to sign the jacket, including Clarence. Little did any of us know that would be his final performance with the E Street Band. Not the Buffalo show. The Carousel show, December 7, 2010, Asbury Park, NJ.

2011 Clarence Clemons died on June 18, aged 69, from complications caused by a stroke. He had been admitted to hospital the previous week after suffering a stroke at his home in Singer Island, Florida. Known as the Big Man, 6ft 5in Clemons was credited with helping shape the early sound of The Boss. He began playing saxophone at the age of nine after receiving one unexpectedly from his father for Christmas. He said he wanted an electric train for Christmas, but instead got a saxophone. On the news of his death New Jersey Governor Chris Christie ordered all state flags to be lowered to half-staff in his honour.

He was a member of the E Street Band from 1972, playing the tenor saxophone. His presence as a visual foil to Springsteen made him the most prominent member of the E Street ensemble. He released several solo albums and in 1985 had a US hit with 'You're a Friend of Mine,' duetting with Jackson Browne. He also made cameo appearances in several TV series, including *Diff'rent Strokes*, *Nash Bridges*, *The Simpsons*, *My Wife and Kids* and *The Wire*.

Bruce Springsteen said of Clemons, 'Clarence lived a wonderful life. He carried within him a love of people that made them love him. He created a wondrous and extended family. He loved the saxophone, loved our fans and gave everything he had every night he stepped on stage. His loss is immeasurable, and we are honored and thankful to have known him and had the opportunity to stand beside him for nearly 40 years. He was my great friend, my partner, and with Clarence at my side, my band and I were able to tell a story far deeper than those simply contained in our music. His life, his memory, and his love will live on in that story and in our band.'

2012

The Wrecking Ball World tour reached 26 countries, the most ever for one of Springsteen's tours. Kicking off on 18 March 2012 at Philips Arena, Atlanta the tour coincided with the release of Springsteen's 17th studio album, *Wrecking Ball*, the band playing 133 shows.

This was the first tour for the E Street Band without founding member Clarence Clemons. In an attempt to fill the void, Springsteen added a full horn section, including Clarence's nephew Jake Clemons, three background singers and a percussionist, giving the E Street Band its largest line-up ever at 17 members.

THE MOODY THEATER

15 MARCH 2012 AUSTIN, TEXAS

I WAS THERE: STEVE HARRIS

I was one of the lucky ones to have my name drawn at SXSW in 2012 and see him at the Moody Theater. He had the whole E

Street band and there were also appearances by Eric Burdon and Alexander Escivito. Bruce was keynote speaker that year. The ticket was not transferable and for one person only. My wife was not drawn but went to Antone's and Nora Jones showed up there with the Little Willies. Great memories.

IZOD CENTER

4 APRIL 2012 EAST RUTHERFORD, NEW JERSEY

I WAS THERE: STAN GOLDSTEIN

This was Bruce's final show at what used to be the Meadowlands Arena. Springsteen's appearances included a six-night run to open the arena in July 1981, a 10-night sell-out in 1984, an 11-night run in 1992 and a 15-night sell-out in 1999. I said to a friend after that it would go down as a legendary show. I still stick by that. Even though it was only 24 songs, it was a special night early on the Wrecking Ball tour, highlighted by an off-the-charts 'Racing in the Street.'

The review from *Backstreets.com* said it best: 'Right up top, we've gotta mention 'Racing in the Street.' In its classic incarnation, rather than the alternate from *The Promise* box, 'Racing' was the majestic highlight of the night. Subtle horn fills added colour and the outro soared with Roy's eloquent piano, Garry's bass lines cranked up, and Max building it all to crescendo after crescendo. E Street orchestration at its finest.'

There were three tour premieres - 'The Ties That Bind,' 'Candy's Room,' and 'Johnny 99' - in the first seven songs. 'Racing In the Street' and 'Ramrod' were also premiered. This was the first show that had video montage of the late Clarence Clemons play when Bruce sang, '*The Big Man joined the band*', part of final song 'Tenth Avenue Freeze-Out.'

MADISON SQUARE GARDENS

7 & 9 APRIL 2012 NEW YORK CITY

I WAS THERE: TOMMY BUTLER

It was 2009 when I first listened to Bruce. Glastonbury was the event and since then my life's been transformed, enriched and amazed.

Shortly after he wound down the tour and I scoured through the archive on *YouTube* and my Dad's CD collection. Two years later, a magical moment occurred. He was releasing a new LP and going on tour. I had

Tommy Butler with his wife Emma and son Leo

to get a ticket. I did, to Manchester and Barcelona. There were also two NYC dates. At this point in my life, I had no one else apart from myself. Everybody had heard of the world's most famous arena - what better christening for a Springsteen concert experience than in the Big Apple, at Madison Square Garden? Thanks to my sister's bankcard, a bit of luck and Ticketmaster working in my favour, I got a ticket.

I booked my flight on 31 January and it was confirmed - I was going to New York to see Bruce Springsteen and his E Street Band. I remember my Mum's words when I said I was going on my own - 'I'm worried, please be careful!' I was only 20.

The date arrived, Dad dropped me at Heathrow and I flew to Newark. I was so excited that I told everyone in the airport where I was going. The border control guard who checked my passport asked me, 'Where was The Boss born? My mind went blank. I didn't know. He said, 'It's Freehold, NJ'. I haven't forgotten since.

I wanted to explore some of New York's sights the day before so ventured out into the city after waking stupidly early in my airport hotel. I visited the Natural History Museum, Strawberry Fields, and the sight of John Lennon's assassination. Having gorged on *YouTube* clips of US chat show hosts; Fallon, Kimmel, Leno and Letterman, I stepped into the Ed Sullivan Theater, unsuccessfully entering the show ballot.

I was in Times Square soaking it all up. One of the most amazing things to do in New York is take a minute and stand still whilst everything moves around - a life-affirming moment. I made it to Madison Square Garden, where there was a basketball game scheduled - the Knicks against the Bulls, no tickets available. I was disappointed but thought I'd head back to the hotel but first pick my tickets up. The lady who directed me got my tickets and said, 'Wow, these are great seats'. It was all sinking in.

After spending $100 in taxi journeys, I thought I'd try a bus back to Ridgefield Park, New Jersey, where my hotel was. No buses went that way, but on my way out of Grand Central, a man approached me, asked, 'Do you need a taxi?' I said yes and got in. From that moment, things began to go wrong, very quickly. He didn't have any idea where he was going. I should have known he was clueless when we finally got on the freeway and went past my hotel at least three times. We finally arrived at the hotel and he said words I will never, ever forget, 'That'll be $600 please.'

I was astounded. Lost. Shocked. Scared. I'd saved $900 for the trip, $200 had disappeared already on taxis and food etc. As I hadn't yet checked in to the hotel I had all my cash in my wallet. As I counted out the dollars, $50 by $50, I can still feel the sense of dread he'd demand my Springsteen ticket too. I grabbed my belongings, never relinquishing my ticket, and ran into the hotel. I reported the incident, but nothing came of it.

There I was in my hotel room, lost, broken, bereft at the loss of most of my money, my faith in people absolutely shot. I phoned Mum and Dad. They saved me, in more ways than one. Later that night, the girl I'd been seeing prior to going to New York texted and said, 'Hope you are having an amazing time'. I texted back, 'Long story, are you OK to talk?' Over the course of the next two and a half hours we talked and talked on the phone. By the end of it, I had a girlfriend.

My parents forwarded me enough money to get to the gig the next day and enough to cover any merchandise I wanted to get. The next day I changed my flight for April 10th. as far as I was concerned I wanted out of New York as quickly as possible.

It was the longest wait that day as I sat in my room, watching the clock tick by. Then the time finally arrived for me to see The Boss. I said to the same receptionist who saw me the day before in a much different state, 'I've got a date with The Boss', a massive grin on my face. I got into a proper taxi and was on my way.

I made it to Madison Square Garden and Sirius FM we're setting up. I just sat there and took it all in. I wasn't in the arena, but after the emotional trauma of the day before this was a most welcome distraction. The doors opened, and I was on my way - I took my seat and was in awe, finally there. I spoke with a couple of people, answering some odd Bruce trivia. I got talking to two lovely women who took pity on me, buying me a beer, peanuts and a hot dog. They also give me $100 for my trip home later that night. To this day I don't know whom they were, but if by a small chance they're reading this - thank you so much for everything.

The moment arrived, the lights went up and 'New York, New York' by Frank Sinatra boomed out. I screamed. It was an out of body experience. There they were - Max, Stevie, Garry, Roy. It seemed an age before Bruce took to the stage. When he did, it was the most amazing moment. After everything, I was seeing him live. I heard the immortal 1-2-3-4-5 of 'Badlands' and for the next five minutes shouted every word and played, unapologetically and with a massive smile on my face, serious air guitar. The rest of the gig was amazing; from the powerful guitar-playing of Nils Lofgren during 'Because the Night', the emotion of 'Tenth Avenue Freeze-Out', to 'Shackled and Drawn' and the rarity of 'Thundercrack'. I've never been religious, but there was a point during 'Born to Run', probably the closest to a religious awakening I'd ever had. As the gig ended

I just sat and contemplated what had gone before and texted Dad, simply, 'Words cannot describe what I've just experienced'.

It's a relief to say the rest of the trip occurred without any other dramas. It was the most amazing time of my life, one I won't ever forget. The trip has gone into folklore with my family. Whenever a taxi is involved, you can guarantee a pun about a yellow cab somewhere. I don't have any regrets though.

As a side-note, the girlfriend mentioned is now my wife of two and a half years, and we also have a little baby boy, 11 months at the time of writing. Not all bad things have to end badly. Bruce taught me that.

PALACE OF AUBURN HILLS

12 APRIL 2012 DETROIT, MICHIGAN

I WAS THERE: ROXANA HILL

I travelled from a town in Western Michigan called Plainwell to Auburn Hills, approximately 175 miles. However, what brought me to Michigan initially was my infatuation with a man I met in Auburn Hills, MI, about two years prior. The reason I fell for him was because of his striking similarity to The Boss!

I moved from Dallas, Texas to Auburn Hills, MI to attend law school in 2010. A year later I met Scott Walri, who reminded me so much of Bruce, especially when he smiled. He had a certain likeness to Bruce, and I became infatuated with him.

I met Scott at church when he sat next to me. I quickly became good friends with him, and later, a close romantic relationship followed. All because he looked like Bruce!

In January 2011 I moved back home to Dallas but that October

I got a job in Western Michigan (Kalamazoo) for a worldwide logistics company and relocated from Texas, so I could be close to my hot Bruce lookalike. He was about 30 years older but a very attractive older man. I guess you can say his likeness to Bruce is what brought me to Michigan, even before the concert. I wasn't even a fan of the real Bruce Springsteen until after I met his doppelganger. Then I started listening to more of Bruce's music and became a huge fan.

I remember he was drinking beer from a plastic cup during one of his songs and came close to the floor area. He guzzled the entire cup in one gulp while rockin' as everyone cheered and yelled. Then when done, he tossed the cup to the floor area, a few feet away. I jumped as high as I could to reach it but someone else got it.

The song that particularly stood out to me was 'Death to my Hometown'. I loved the Celtic music. I was in the floor area near the stage. Several fans around me jumped up and down to that song, everyone really got into it, and it was an amazing experience.

Dear Bruce Springsteen fan,

We just wanted to make you aware of the general admission seating policy for your below event.

Bruce Springsteen
The Palace-Auburn Hills
Thursday April 12, 2012 7:30PM

What do I need to do?

The general admission (GA) floor seating for this event is designed with a forward and rear barricade system. The forward barricade allows randomly chosen patrons with 'GA' tickets to enter the area of the floor closest to the stage. GA patrons are chosen randomly via the numbered wristband lottery procedure described below.

The 'lottery' allows holders of general admission tickets a random chance to enter the forward barricade area on the floor, closest to the stage. This is entirely optional and can be disregarded by GA ticket holders who do not wish to enter the lottery for a chance to be placed in the forward barricade.

1) On the day of the show, sequentially numbered wristbands will be distributed beginning at 5 Hours prior to Doors. This will take place at gate designated for GA entrance Lottery. Wristbands will be distributed until 2 Hours prior to Doors. (No additional lottery/floor wristbands will be distributed until after doors are open)

2) Patrons must be present and in possession of their GA ticket to receive wristband. Only one wristband per patron will be issued.

3) After the patron's ticket has been verified as a GA ticket. A wristband will be issued and affixed to the patron's wrist.

4) Anyone who receives a numbered wristband prior to doors has an equal chance to be first in line to enter the Front Area. A wristband does not guarantee a place in the Front Area.

5) Patrons who have received a wristband may leave the premises. They must return 1 hour and 30 minutes before Doors.

6) Patrons who received a wristband and are present for the drawing must be ready to enter the venue. This means they should not be carrying any prohibited items with them. e.g. backpacks/ large bags, cameras, recording devices etc. If there are any questions regarding prohibited items, please check with venue staff prior to the drawing.

7) A starting number will be randomly picked 1 hour and 30 minutes prior to doors. A patron will draw the starting number. This number will be announced at gate designated for GA entrance Lottery.

8) The patron wearing the wristband that matches the starting number will be first in line. All participants are requested to remain in sequential order, as venue entry and Security screening will begin immediately following drawing. Patrons will be directed by

tour and venue staff through this process.

9) All patrons with GA tickets and a wristband who wish to enter according to the lottery need to remain present to be processed and escorted into the venue. Failure to be present for drawing, or not remaining throughout the lottery entry process will result in forfeiture of lottery position.

10) Once inside the venue, a second wristband will be issued to identify those who are within the winning range. This is required to enter the Front GA Area.

If you need anything else, we're always here for you – just hit reply and ask us or visit Ticketmaster.com! You can also find this information on Bruce Springsteen's website at http://www.brucespringsteen.net/news/2012/galotteryprocedures

Thanks for being a fan!

TIMES UNION CENTER

16 APRIL 2012 ALBANY, NEW YORK

I WAS THERE: JANE ARNONE

I almost didn't go to this show. It was two days after my mother's funeral. But I was talked into going by my brother, another lifelong Bruce fan, who convinced me that if anyone could make me feel better, it was Bruce.

I had general admission tickets (hard to get on that tour), grabbed my 13-year-old daughter Molly and made the three-hour trip to Albany, in time to get wristbands and participate in the lottery. We ended up 50th in, front row, toting a sign Molly made on the trip: 'Janey Don't You Lose Heart', For My Mom Jane, R.I.P. 7/10/22 - 4/11/12.' 'Janey Don't You Lose Heart' has always been my go-to song during hard times, and I was hoping to hold the sign high enough that Bruce might see it and play 'Janey' for Molly, my Mom (also Jane) and me. He did see it, and played an acoustic version dedicated to Molly. You could have heard a pin drop when he slowly launched in. It could not have been more filled with love, sympathy and compassion for the loss of our Janey. We appreciate it so much. I wish I could have thanked him personally.

People ask me how I could still connect with Bruce's music as passionately in my 50s as I did at 15, and there's an easy answer: his music, like 40 years of life, has woven in and out of so many places that it always speaks to me with a new, relevant voice. My question back to anyone who asks

is always, 'How can you NOT connect with Bruce Springsteen's music?'

Later this same show, Bruce pulled up Molly for 'Dancing in The Dark.' This is a photo from that moment. I'm the woman in the front row (in the Light of Day 12 shirt) looking on in amazement.

ESTADI OLIMPIC

17 MAY 2012 BARCELONA, SPAIN

I WAS THERE: MIKE SCULLY

Besides being a Bruce fan, my wife Julie's also a travel fan,

which I am not. In 2012, she cleverly talked me into a trip to
Barcelona by getting us tickets to Bruce's two shows there. I've
seen approximately 150 Bruce and the E Street Band concerts
since 1973, but I'd never seen one of the legendary overseas
shows, and she knew it. Next thing I knew, we were on a plane
to Spain.

The first thing we noticed was that European Bruce crowds
are younger than American ones. The level of excitement is
unmatched because when Bruce plays there, it is an EVENT.
They don't get a first-tour leg of multiple nights in arenas, then
a second leg of stadium shows like in the US. This is it for them
and they are going to make the most of every moment.

They don't just sing the lyrics, they sing the tune. They're
so excited they can't wait for the lyrics. When the band played
'Talk To Me', the Southside Johnny favourite, the whole stadium
was singing from the opening note. They jump up and down in
place. If you don't time it right and jump with them, you get hit
in the face with their backpacks, so you better get in sync.

Bruce always makes it a point to try to address the overseas
crowds in their language, and that night, he spoke in fluent
Catalonian. I don't know everything he said, but it was much
more than a 'How ya doin', Barcelona?' The people loved it. It
was the Wrecking Ball tour, so he was featuring songs from that
album, including a rousing, angry 'Death To My Hometown'
and an emotional 'Jack Of All Trades,' but he also dropped in
tour debuts like 'You Can Look (But You Better Not Touch)' and
'Hungry Heart.' He also played 'The River' so maybe he was
subconsciously getting an urge to break those songs out again on
a later tour?

My favourite moment of the night was when he took a sign
from someone in the crowd that contained the very specific
request, 'Prove It All Night with 1978 Intro'. He showed it to
the band. Julie and I saw a few confused looks between the
musicians onstage, something you rarely see at an E Street
show. There were some quick consultations between Nils, Roy,

Steve and the rest of the musicians. I always loved the long instrumental intro the band did in the late Seventies, early Eighties tours, but it had gone away over the years. Was it really going to happen right now in Barcelona in 2012? They jumped into the song and slowly the intro came together, Bruce and Steve matching each other on guitars that shrieked into the beautiful night sky.

Just like it did all those years ago, it worked the crowd into rock'n'roll frenzy before a word had been sung. Bruce and the band nailed it. And since that night, this version periodically pops up in E Street shows, so I've always been grateful to that fan in Barcelona who held up that sign with that incredibly specific request. And to my amazing wife Julie, who tricked me into a musical experience I will never forget.

STADIUM OF LIGHT

21 JUNE 2012 SUNDERLAND, UK

I WAS THERE: MICK STOKES

I went with my brother-in-law. We got a non-drinker to drive us up to Sunderland from Liverpool where we stayed overnight. During the show between songs Bruce was getting people to pass up their signs and banners where he put them all face-down on the stage and turned them over one by one and played and sung them. During 'Working on the Highway', he forgot the words and kept calling Steve's name to take over, but Steve just said no and laughed at him as he stopped dead and ran the words over and over until he remembered them.

The show was approximately four hours, with no break. My tickets were a surprise present for me and it was the greatest outdoor gig I've ever been to. To sing 'Johnny 99' was a big deal for me, being my joint No.1 Bruce song. He opened with 'Badlands', my brother-in-law's favourite. When Bruce finished that, he sat down and said, 'I can go now'.

ETIHAD STADIUM

22 JUNE 2012 MANCHESTER, UK

I WAS THERE: RACHEL FISHER-IVES

I saw Bruce at The Etihad Stadium in June 2012 and wondered why everyone was booing him. I didn't realise they were shouting, 'Bruuuce'!

It was a cold, very wet day. Certainly not the best conditions for an outdoor concert, but it was still a fabulous experience, as I've been a fan of Bruce since the Eighties and had never managed to see him live. My partner, Russell has been a fan since the Seventies, and I

Rachel Fisher-Ives and partner Russell

managed to get these tickets as a birthday present for him.

I was 42, and Russell 47 at the time, and we'd travelled across the Pennines from Halifax, West Yorkshire. It wasn't a pleasant journey because of the heavy rain, and by the time we got there, there were no seats left under cover, so we sat in the rain!

'Born to Run' is one of my all-time favourite songs; so it was a bit of a dream come true to hear it performed live. One thing that really stood out to me was Bruce being under cover and holding his hand out to feel if it was raining. When he felt it was, he came out and joined us in the rain.

SYNOT TIP ARENA

11 JULY 2012 PRAGUE, CZECH REPUBIC

I WAS THERE: ODED REGEV

Like most of the world, I first heard of Bruce in the Eighties. I was
born not in the USA, but in Haifa, Israel. Like the whole world,
Israeli radio blasted the hits of *Born in the U.S.A.* and *The River*. I also
lived in London from 1981-86. My big brother Amit was a big fan
and I remember, among others, a *Born in the U.S.A.* cassette, his Live
75-85 CD's and the *Tunnel of Love*. The first albums I bought were
Human Touch and *Lucky Town* in 1992. It was 2002's *The Rising* which
made me a huge fan though. I have a thing for artists who remain
creative after their so-called peak.

Between 1998 and 2006 I worked in a CD shop, Zlil, in the Haifa
mall, not far from the beach. Me and the manager Dudi (David)
Levi became great friends and enjoyed spreading our love of music
when people still came to shops to buy physical CDs and listen to the
recommendations of their workers.

Amihay Borenstein was a regular customer. When Springsteen
released 2003's *Essential* CD (a triple CD, including a third CD of
unreleased music) I recommended it to Amihay, 18 by then. He
declined, stating Springsteen was too bombastic. I insisted and told
him if he didn't like the CD, he could return it.

Fast forward to 2012, Springsteen had become Amihay's and my
favourite artist. When he decided to fly to Prague to see The Boss
for the first time, I knew it was time for my first show. I was nervous
about taking time off from a job I started barely a month before,
but knew it was now or never. The stunning 2009 Hyde Park DVD
(*London Calling*) was played regularly in my home and convinced me I
had to see him live, but when Clarence Clemons died, I thought my
dream was over. Thankfully the excellent *Wrecking Ball* CD and tour
proved me wrong.

We bought Golden Ring tickets for a ridiculously-cheap price and
waited in the glorious sunshine for our dream to come true. This is

Springsteen of course, so we had no idea what he would open with. The moment he walked on stage and opened with 'The Ghost of Tom Joad' (this was his first visit to Prague since that album's tour in the Nineties), we were hooked. When the harmonica sounds of *The River* were played, I truly realized I was living the dream (Amihay's peak moment, leaving him in joyful tears, was 'Land of Hope and Dreams'). I was seeing the greatest live act in the world. My numerous sign requests were not seen, but in three and a half hours I got everything I wanted, and then some.

When the concert ended, we knew only one thing for certain: we were going to see The Boss again. Amihay's dream of getting Bruce to sign his collection would have to wait, as Bruce had to hurry from his hotel the next day to his Vienna concert. Ironically, when we flew back, we discovered that virtually every fan who had not made any special effort to meet Bruce face-to-face had seen him, whether outside or in the gym. The Prague experience also included an unforgettable Damian Rice show, ending with him walking with fans to Karl Bridge and continuing the concert.

When we returned to Israel with a lot of others who saw the Prague show, we realized we were far from alone in our love for Bruce in the Promised Land. The dream of Bruce coming to the Holy Land remains fantasy, but we discovered the 'Bruce Springsteen Israel' *Facebook* page, with plenty of other fans with the Bruce bug. By 2013 we were much more prepared for the next European tour and found other fellow Bruce fans for the trip. The Prague 2012 show, we later discovered, had been many Israeli fans' first. Now I think about it, at least in the Golden Ring, other than Israel, I remember lots of Europeans, especially British and Italian.

A year on and me and Aviv Ben Israel decided to meet for the first time at Wembley at 6am (some fans arrived days before), amid typical English weather where 'just a passing shower' (as the PA announced) turned into a massive storm. But by the time we entered the stadium, the sky was clear. We were inside the Mecca of English football, waiting for Bruce. It was a day after my 39th birthday, the day I had flown in. A perfect birthday present.

While we waited, we wondered what the set-list would be and if we would get a full classic album in the middle of the concert, as happened a few times that summer. We got *Darkness of the Edge of Town* and an unforgettable show, including gems like 'Lost in The Flood.' Incredibly though, the Coventry concert five days later would be even better.

Amihay is religious, so he missed the Saturday concert, but joined us bright and early at 6am that Coventry morning. When Aviv and me woke an hour earlier at a nearby Birmingham hostel, Aviv told me the tragic news that former *Sopranos* star James Galdolfini had passed away. How would this affect co-star and close friend Steve Van Zandt? Bruce dedicated the *Born to Run* album to him later that day in arguably my favourite Bruce concert.

When Bruce announced he would play that whole album, it was as if my favourite team had won a trophy. I'd get to hear 'Backstreets' and 'Jungleland' live! There were so many highlights that day: we literally discovered Bruce was flesh and blood as we touched his sweaty hand during 'Hungry Heart'. I met more fellow Israeli Springsteen fans for the first time (Arnon Reuveni and Sigalit Shalom), but the highlight was the now-legendary man-hug moment. Bruce saw a sign of a young man looking for a man-hug after his girl broke up with him. He gave him that hug. How many stars would do that? This was much more than just great music.

The whole week and a half that summer will probably always remain the highlight of my live concert experiences: Springsteen playing two three and a half hour shows, including two of his best albums and before and after those concerts - The *Thriller* musical in London, Neil Young and Pet Shop Boys at the O2 in London, Rod Stewart in Birmingham, The Killers at Wembley, and Bon Jovi in Prague. There was one more thing I had to complete.

Glasgow was sandwiched between Wembley and Coventry in 2013, and it was too complicated to get there. But I was determined to go, bringing with me Mor Perry, who had never seen Springsteen before (she would be at Wembley too). Needless to say, she became hooked to Bruce that day.

We expected cold Northern weather, but instead had one of the warmest days in Scotland. It was so hot I thought Bruce had come to Israel after all. People were cooking on the grass outside Hampden Park, home of legendary football matches and concerts. When you entered the stadium, you could feel the history.

One of the nice people we met outside held a 'Waiting on a Sunny Day' sign, a song Bruce sings virtually every concert while bringing a kid to help him along. She was worried Bruce would open with that and Bruce would not have time to see her sign, but I promised her he never does. He did... oops.

At this stage I was captivated even listening to the sound-checks when we were still outside, usually hinting at tour premieres that day or in upcoming concerts. That day was no different. Glasgow was unforgettable, even though I learnt that the promise of a 10-minute walk to the centre of town after the concert could be closer to an hour.

Coventry isn't the most luxurious place on the planet, but once again it produced my favourite concert of the tour. I met another Israeli fan, Alon Yaa'cobi, who had gone through hell and back to finally have his dream of seeing Springsteen for the first time come true and wrote a brilliant book about his experience. He would join me at Wembley again.

Before Coventry he came early so we could see the concert together. At Wembley he would arrive even earlier than me. That's how we Tramps get hooked on getting close to the band. A magical night which included a personal favourite, 'Drive All Night', then an encore including a tour premiere cover of 'Travellin' Band', which has since become one my favourites, and a cover of 'Seven Times To Rock', taking me back to Prague 2012 where I heard it for the first time.

My most recent Springsteen concert was Wembley. I arrived late that day, having been to Coldplay's Head Full of Dreams concert in Manchester the day before. Set-list wise it was probably the best of my 2016 trilogy and is the concert I listen to most.

There's nothing like an E Street Band tour with the wonderful experience of meeting fellow fans from across the world - from young kids to fans aged 90, visiting new places, guessing the set-lists (or following them online when you're not there). Aviv was the official set-list follower of the Israeli group. It's also incredibly rewarding hearing fellow fans have their dreams come true. Amihay had driven the Israeli group mad with his obsession of hearing 'Mary's Place' from the excellent *The Rising* album live.

If heaven forbid, Bruce decides to quit tomorrow, he has still left us with tons of amazing music and unbelievable concert memories. If he decides to stay on Broadway or just appear live in a different format near his US home, nobody can begrudge him. That said, while I know the dream of him appearing in Israel grows further away every year. It would be an unbelievable experience for him and the band as well as us. At this stage, how many special places are left for Bruce and the band to conquer for the first time? Speaking for the European fans and all those who want to see him and the band, all I can do is quote what someone told Bruce back in 2001: 'Bruce, we need you!'

The 2012 Springsteen Hyde Park concert in London, England closed to boos and whistles from the audience after the organisers ended the concert to comply with their licence, which allowed them to run the concert until 10.30pm.

Licences are granted until certain times to protect residents in the area from noise late at night.

Springsteen was joined on stage by Sir Paul McCartney to play Beatles classics 'I Saw Her Standing There' and 'Twist and Shout' and could be seen trying to talk to the crowd without any amplification as they appeared ready to launch into another number when the power was switched off.

Steve Van Zandt vented his fury at a 'police state' and London's mayor, Boris Johnson, criticised 'an excessively efficacious decision', saying the band should have been allowed to jam in the name of the Lord.' He added, 'I'm sorry but I have to be honest I'm pissed ... It didn't ruin the great night. But when I'm jamming with McCartney, don't bug me!'

Actor and comedian Stephen Merchant said on Twitter, 'Ashamed to be British right now'. Springsteen and McCartney playing 'Twist & Shout' in Hyde Park and council pulled the plug cos of curfew.' And journalist Richard James said, 'Springsteen and McCartney: Only in Britain could a local council pull the plug on the greatest artists of the last 50 years giving it all.'

HYDE PARK

14 JULY 2012 LONDON, UK

I WAS THERE: LYN WARD

After following Bruce since the release of *Born to Run* in 1975, I finally got to see him live at the infamous Hard Rock Calling event on 14 July 2012, in Hyde Park London. It was made famous by the curfew and the organisers pulling the PA system while Bruce and the E Street Band, who had been joined by Paul McCartney, kept playing on stage. The crowd kept pleading for the organisers to let us all hear and let the party continue, but to everyone's regret we had to leave not knowing what else we might have enjoyed. Such a shame, but I gather the penalties for the organisers letting Bruce continue were substantial. They should have had a whip-round - there were enough of us there.

I WAS THERE: GREG ANDREWS

Walking on stage to start his set in the late Saturday evening sun, Bruce blew us all away immediately with a majestic 'Thunder Road' - starting and finishing on harmonica, his vocal accompanied only by Roy Bittan on piano and 80,000-odd of us singing along. Arguably the greatest song ever written, delivered beautifully.

At the end of the show the already-poor sound system seemed to drop to a fade before it was clear the sound had been cut. For Springsteen to be cut-off like that was a shameful embarrassment for every Londoner.

I WAS THERE: JAMIE RICHARDS

I'll make it clear that I was not always a Bruce Springsteen fan; I'm a bit of a latecomer in fact. The reason mostly being that when he first became known to me was during his radio bashing days of the mid-eighties, the yuppie pleasing bombast of his 'Born in the U.S.A.' period, and back then I was a mere heavy metal teenager with a penchant for Saxon and AC/DC, and about to be engulfed by the ferocity and excitement of the Metallica-led thrash invasion. To me he sucked big time. Over the years though I've warmed to his music, not that album you understand, but there's a lot more to the man than obnoxious, big production radio hits. His appetite and enthusiasm are unquestionable, and tonight he serves up a relentless three and a quarter hour set, during which the closest he comes to leaving the stage is when he rounds the drum kit to put his face in a bowl of water before coming straight back to us.

Opening the set in typically 'bare' fashion, he simply walks on and takes a harmonica from his pocket and introduces 'a love letter that I wrote the very first time I came to London in 1974', which is obviously the mighty anthem 'Thunder Road' and performs it with just the accompaniment of a pianist. In front of 80,000 that's a ballsy start, even for the man they call The Boss. 'Badlands' kicks off the party proper, and the park is not just rocking but positively bursting at the seams, with decent foot space at a premium. New album 'Wrecking Ball' is well represented tonight, and Tom Morello makes the first of many appearances on 'Death to my Hometown'. He's a personable performer is Springsteen, committed to his craft to the point that he insists on interaction with his audience. He takes a sign from a punter at the front requesting an obscure song, 'Take 'Em As They Come', and duly plays it, and pulls a youngster from the crowd to help him with the chorus on 'Waiting on a Sunny Day'. Unfortunately for me, I seem to be surrounded by the 'Born in the U.S.A.' crew, more interested in 20-minute trips to the bar and the bogs and taking pictures of each other and new 'friends for life'.

Springsteen continues in fine fashion, even though it's increasingly obvious that the sound is way too quiet for this size venue. Where Soundgarden deafened 20,000 assembled stage front the previous night Springsteen is blowing in the wind to 80,000, spread way to the back of this place...and it's un-cool really. I stick with it though, and a fine version of 'Because the Night' makes it worth it, followed by a rock'n'rolled up, extended version of 'Johnny 99'. Morello returns and stays for some time, finally being let loose with a signature solo on 'Land of Hope and Dreams'. After the briefest of breaks, Springsteen leads his troops back out for more, and before long the hit factory the 'one gig a year' segments of the massive crowd have been waiting for duly comes their way: 'Born in the U.S.A.', 'Born to Run', 'Glory Days' and 'Dancing in the Dark' (complete with dark-haired Courteney Cox stand-in, selected from the crowd for a dance with the man himself). The parties around me erupt into bouts of drunken shout-along 'singing' that almost drown out the band, and surely leave them dreaming of those halcyon days of filofaxes and their first BMW - they are in rapture; and then they send someone for more pints.

A grand finale is coming though, and just when they thought it was all over a certain Mr McCartney enters stage left, Sir Paul I believe we call him now, and accompanies the band on a run through of old Beatles classics 'Saw Her Standing There' and 'Twist and Shout'. Whatever your stand-point, that's a pretty impressive ending; although it wasn't quite finished - literally, because amid all the excitement, Springsteen and Macca over-ran the strict curfew, and at 10.40pm sharp the sound disappeared - silence! Seriously, Bruce Springsteen and Sir Paul McCartney on a stage in a park in London, just finishing off the last few bars of a couple of Beatles songs in front of 80,00 paying punters, and some faceless employee of the organisers just pulled the plug on them, simple as that. No 'Thank you, goodnight,' no, just silence.

I made a sharp dash for the exit through the assembled, by now trying to get drunken chants of 'turn-it-up' going. For pity sake, don't they understand that rules are indeed rules? I'm sure someone took down a memo.

Bruce Springsteen and Steve Van Zandt made a surprise appearance at a memorial concert in Oslo's City Square, on July 22 2012 to mark the anniversary of the Norwegian 2011 terror attacks, in which 77 people died. The event, which also featured a number of local artists, saw Springsteen and Van Zandt playing the protest song, 'We Shall Overcome'. Springsteen told the 60,000 strong audience, 'Steve and I are honored to be included here tonight. For all of us who love democracy and tolerance, it's an international tragedy.'

ULLEVI STADION

27 JULY 2012 GOTHENBURG, SWEDEN

I WAS THERE: NICLAS ERIKSSON

I'm 20-years-old and I've been to eight shows, all of them in Sweden. My first live-experience of Springsteen was in 2012, at Ullevi, Gothenburg. I was very excited and looked forward to the concert, but my expectations were that the average age would be 50-70, and it would be boring. But hell no, it was 15-70, everybody sang, everybody knew every word, and everybody had the time of their life. We became one, the audience became a family; we sang, danced and jumped together. That was the start of my long admiration for Bruce and the E Street Band. The heart, the spirit, the togetherness, the power, the love and the faith in the lyrics, the music, the feeling. Words can't describe a Springsteen concert.

On July 31, 2012 on the final show in Europe on his Wrecking Ball tour, Springsteen played his longest-ever show when he played a 33-song show, which lasted four hours six minutes at Helsinki's Olympiastadion, Finland. Earlier in the day, prior to the show proper, Bruce performed a five-song acoustic set for early arrivals.

GILLETTE STADIUM

18 AUGUST 2012 FOXBORO, MASSACHUSETTS

I WAS THERE: SCOTT WALMSLEY

I'll never forget the first time I heard 'Jungleland' live. It was about two hours into a typically energetic Boston Garden set when things

got quiet. Then Soozie's violin and Roy's piano promised that
something special was about to go down. Close to 20,000 members
of The E Street family were about to embark on a twelve-minute
odyssey down Flamingo Lane. We were going to ride with the
Magic Rat in his sleek machine like some lost outtake from *Midnight
Cowboy*. We were going to drink warm beer in the soft summer rain.
We were all going to meet beneath that giant Exxon sign (or, being
in Beantown, maybe we could make it a Citgo sign for the night).
20,000 disciples were waiting for our fearless leader to tell us where
he was going to transport us next. We dodged cops, we flashed
guitars like switch-blades, and we hustled for the record machine. We
dressed in the latest rage, but we also struggled in dark corners. We
were on a ride like no other.

'Down in Jungleland…'

It's a truly unique and communal experience to sing those
three words. Look to your right: three guys in their mid-50s,
salt-and-pepper hair, arm-in-arm, swaying back and forth. Look
to your left: a young girl, maybe 14, with Taylor Swift lip-stick
and skinny jeans, singing every word like it was the latest Pitbull
hit. Look in front at the preppy college kid in the Abercrombie
shirt and the Northeastern hat, taking it all in. For three words,
we are all one. Singing at the top of our lungs so the entire world
will know exactly where this epic saga is taking place: *'Down in
Jungleland. Jungleland is not a place for the meek of heart. It is dark, and
it is formidable, and it is daunting'*. But more than anything it is alive.
And we couldn't possibly have felt more alive.

Cue the Big Man… Enter Clarence. Larger than life, even
from 50 rows away. I've listened to the sax solo from 'Jungleland'
countless times. I've listened to it in my '83 Ford Escort with a
bungee cord holding the door closed. I've listened to it while
mowing my lawn in 95-degree heat. I've listened to it in the
shower. But until that moment I'd never heard it live. Surreal.
I was taken somewhere I didn't know I could go. It filled the

entire arena until there was no space left to even breathe. 20,000 people in hushed reverence, all in awe of the Big Man. When he finished and stepped back into the shadows, I felt exhausted, like I somehow had a part in what just occurred. In a way I did; I think we all did. I'd like to think the audience was some kind of medium between Clarence and the Gods of Music.

Cue the Boss... As the last note of the saxophone rings through the arena, the Big Man fades into the canvas that is the E Street Band. As Bruce steps up to the mic., we all know our adventure with the Magic Rat is coming to a close. But even after we watch the Rat get gunned down by his own dreams, and after the girl shuts off that bedroom light, one more thrill awaits. That cry. That furious wail that comes from the most remote depths of Bruce Springsteen. It's the culmination of this 12-minute movie we've all just watched—no, acted—in. Everything we've seen and witnessed, in the darkest depths of the city, comes forth in the most guttural way. It's a cry that carries away everyone in that arena. Where you go is up to you. Maybe you just want to drink beer on the hood of a Dodge. Maybe you want to race across that Jersey state line straight into the heart of darkness. Or maybe you want to go beneath the city, where the unspeakable awaits. But that's Jungleland, right? Choose your path.

Fast-forward to Gillette Stadium, Foxboro, Massachusetts, on August 18, 2012. The first time I heard 'Jungleland' live since the tragic passing of Clarence Anicholas Clemons, Jr. From all accounts, this was only the second time the band had played this song post-Big Man. Many heads were turning as Soozie and Roy started their two-person symphony. Really? Could we be this lucky? We knew Jake Clemons had chops, but was he ready for this? His Uncle's signature piece? Four minutes into the song we all found out. Jake delivered a gorgeous, soaring solo that would have brought out Clarence's huge and beautiful smile. Perhaps the best part was watching The Boss during the performance. He was so proud.

I WAS THERE: DEBBIE JOHNSON

The start of the Wrecking Ball tour, the first tour without Clarence. At Gillette Stadium with an estimated 70,000 plus people, when he showed that montage and the crowd went crazy, and yet everyone could see how hard it was for him. For once, it felt like we were carrying him through. Wrecking Ball ended its very last night at the Mohegan Sun in CT. I was there. Bruce and the E Street Band were outstanding. At the very end he sat alone at a small piano, under a soft spotlight and he quietly, humbly, very heartfelt started in earnest to thank his fans for this tour, and then he went slowly into 'Dream Baby Dream'.

Everywhere, fans were sobbing. We all felt his sincerity, his gratitude. It was a very touching moment that I'll never forget.

METLIFE STADIUM

19 SEPTEMBER 2012 EAST RUTHERFORD, NEW JERSEY

I WAS THERE: DENISE DILLON

I'll preface this by saying I'm well north of over 100 shows. I've sat everywhere - from the nosebleeds, to front and center in the pit and everywhere in between.

But this show was the first pit experience for my daughter, aptly named Caroline Asbury. She was my first child so of course she was named after Bruce's first album, *Greetings from Asbury Park, N.J.* I'd go on to name my son something Bruce related, as well as my two dogs, but that's a story for another day.

On this warm Indian

Denise Dillon and aptly named Caroline Asbury

summer night, I had the most heart-warming experience with my then-10-year old daughter; I can still shed a tear when I hear anything live from this show on satellite radio.

We arrived early in the day to stand on the pit line, anxiously waiting for our numbers, and then for our numbers to be called. Whatever our number was it was pretty close, within 50 or so of the number to be selected as the first to line up. Caroline stood on that line for a good six hours with me, getting smiles and winks from fellow fans. Thinking how cool it was that her mom let her cut school to do this. This was her third or fourth show by then and she was ready for the big leagues, the pit and all it entailed. Again, it all paid off, as we were stage left against the barricades.

I had hopes of her being hoisted up on stage for the chorus of 'Waiting on a Sunny Day', but she was a bit to0 shy. No matter how much I encouraged her, or how hard fellow fans tried to.

Caroline and I shared the most amazing moment together during the show - it was almost as if the 70k people there with us had just vanished. It was during 'Mansion on the Hill', a song I'd heard countless times before; a bathroom break or beer-run song in the past that was filling my ears for as it was the first time. For it was Caroline's first time hearing this song. Period.

She and I both listened intensely to the lyrics - the poetry of this song sung by Bruce and Patti. We were both moved beyond words. I cried. She cried. It was a moment shared between us that I will never forget.

'Mansion on the Hill' is now one of my top five Bruce songs because of this warm Indian summer night spent in the swamps of Jersey, sharing a common love for a magnificent poet.

METLIFE STADIUM

22 SEPTEMBER 2012 EAST RUTHERFORD, NEW JERSEY

I WAS THERE: AARON GOLDMAN

I've been following Bruce since I first discovered his music when I was 18. I've seen him up and down the East Coast, in more cities and venues than I could count. But the show that stands out most was at MetLife Stadium, New Jersey, the last of a three-night stand. My wife and I got there the night before and parked our car outside the stadium and listened to the encores before driving to our hotel. Diehards will insist that his shows in Philly and/or Europe are the best but make no mistake: Jersey shows are special.

Mr and Mrs Goldman in New Jersey

On the day of the show we got there early because there was a special tailgate for Richard Nappi, a Lieutenant in the New York City Fire Department and avid Bruce fan who died in a fire earlier that year. Friends and family had t-shirts and beer koozies made up with his face on it and encouraged people to bring food and meet each other. A great time and a fitting tribute to a great man.

We went in an hour or so before the show and took our seats. A bit disappointed to be nearly as far away as humanly possible in the gargantuan football stadium, we were nonetheless excited to see Bruce, as always. But we were immediately surprised to see that the entire floor, normally long since filled with fans that lined up for hours to get wristbands and secure their spot, was completely empty. No one could figure out what was going on until finally word began spreading that there was a looming lightning storm, and the venue was making all of the people with wristbands wait in the tunnels until they got the all-clear from their weather service.

'Oh shit, what if they cancel the show?' we said to ourselves.

It's getting close to showtime and there is no sign of progress. Then, an usher comes and tells us that unless our seats are under cover, we vacate and move into the concession area. We were literally in the first unprotected row, so basically if we leaned back a little we would be covered, but they were unrelenting and made us move. We sit in the concession area for what feels like an eternity. It's now an hour past showtime. 'No way this show is happening', I said, as it is suddenly feeling like we wasted a whole lot of time, effort and money on a trip to Jersey with nothing to show for it. At best, we figure he will come out and eventually play a shortened performance.

Then, finally, an announcement comes on saying that the show will begin at 11, usually about the time the show is ending. The very official sounding announcement goes on to say it will be a 'full length show.' We stare at each other in disbelief. 'So, Bruce is going to play until two in the morning?'

It then occurs to us that the following day is Bruce's birthday, and we realize we are going to be spending Bruce Springsteen's birthday with him, at his show. In his home state. Holy shit.

Hours later, after we are finally let back to our seats and the people waiting forever in the tunnels are permitted on to the floor, the house music comes on signalling the band's entrance. For weeks they had been coming on to 'Summer Winds' by Frank Sinatra, which was appropriately replaced that night with Wilson Pickett's 'In the Midnight Hour.' The band members made their way to the stage one by one, with Bruce, as always coming on last. 'Will he acknowledge his birthday?' we wondered.

As he walked up the steps on to the stage he took the unusual step of walking all the way out onto the catwalk into the crowd and put his arms up to feel that the rain had stopped. Walking back to the mic he proclaimed, 'I think I just invited 55,000 people to my birthday party.'

Ploughing through classics like 'Out in the Street' and rarities like 'Cynthia' and 'Janey Don't You Lose Heart,' Bruce and the band were on fire. At midnight, the crowd sang Happy Birthday, and the band broke into their own rendition of 'In the Midnight Hour.' It was clear that they were just getting started. Jersey favourite Gary U.S. Bonds joined him for 'Jole Blon' and 'This Little Girl'. Bruce dedicated 'Into the Fire' from *The Rising* to Lt. Nappi and his family, who were in attendance.

In the encore, Bruce completely let loose. 'Seven Night to Rock,' 'Thunder Road', and of course 'Born to Run.' He referenced his birthday over and over and was having more fun than anybody in the stands. During 'Glory Days', in between 'Oh yeahs' and 'Alrights', he yells 'Hey Steve!' Steve replies 'Yeah, baby?' and Bruce responds, 'Did I mention it's my birthday?' He brought the house down but wasn't done yet.

After all that, approaching 2am, a birthday cake was brought out. Ever mindful of his fan-base, Bruce cuts pieces of cake and begins handing them out to fans in the front rows, sure to give the first piece to Obie Dziedzic, his original fan dating back to the late Sixties when he was playing for audiences in the single digits. Some 45 years later, in front of nearly 60,000 people, Obie was still there, front and center.

Finally, Bruce brings his mother and siblings onstage, and closes the show with an epic 'Twist and Shout', featuring his mother on background vocals.

He ends the night during the final chorus with 'Thank you for your patience tonight. Thank you for being here. And by the way, it's my birthday!'

Bruce has a way of making every show special, and every person in the audience feels as though they are in on a special occasion, an event that is only happening that night, and if you aren't there you can't simply go the next night in the next city and feel like you saw the same thing. That was never truer than on this night, and we were grateful that Bruce partied with us on his birthday, if only for the first few hours.

I WAS THERE: SUSAN STORRAR

It's 10.30pm. We've been waiting hours. Is he coming on? Or are we going home, deflated and defeated?

It's the MetLife Stadium. East Rutherford, New Jersey. Hopes are high. We're all expecting that extra sparkle on his home turf. Trouble is, the bloody weather. Earlier in the afternoon word came that a storm was forecast. Apparently if lightning is due to strike within three miles, the gig can't happen.

It's already been an eventful trip. 100 European fans, staying at The Berkeley in Asbury Park, on a Bruce pilgrimage. We've been to Freehold, seen the fire engine with 'Born to Run' on the side, and managed to get into the local press; such is the extremity of our adoration. We'd seen the previous two nights, so I guess it's a bit greedy to be disappointed if tonight is called off. But it's September 22nd. Bruce is 63 tomorrow, and it is his home turf. It's got to be special.

They let us in as normal. We had seats but didn't realise until we got here that we were in the posh bit – an indoor bar and restaurant in our section and a couple of rows back from our seats. Great view. It was eerily quiet when we came in. Nobody in the pit or on the pitch. Just the seats, never seen that before. We didn't know until later that the pit queue was standing in a tunnel somewhere, away from the threat of lightning, until now – some really sore feet the next day!

Eventually the rain did come and they decided to evacuate – except for us. We were told to just sit in the bar and wait. It was crowded but the atmosphere was electric. The bar was great and they even had vegetarian sushi! As ever, conversation turned to 'Have you seen him before…how many times…where?' I've never counted, but I have kept all my tickets. I fear the competitiveness. I'm saving the counting for my old age when I intend to go down memory lane, big time. But I get talking to a man who's sitting there on his own reading a book. Turns out this is his 180th show. He's a psychiatrist in the UK, and his colleagues doubt his sanity. I just think he's very, very lucky.

I've seen a good amount of shows, but why is it that you can just never retain them in your memory? They become a pale imitation of the real thing. It's all about the moment, when he's in front of you, and you just can't be sure what's coming, but you know it's going to be great.

It's 10.30, the rain's eased off (just one lightning strike) and we've almost given up when a woman comes over the PA and explains that not only will the show go ahead, but Bruce will play a full show, despite the late hour. The thrill is tangible in the air, everyone's smiling and all rush to their seats. We're ready.

The crowd is back on the pitch. Finally, people are let into the pit, and within moments the band is on the stage, and the show's on. The band's tight and hyped up by the wait and Bruce is like a small boy, delighting in the change in routine and of course the imminent celebrations. We're riveted.

We've already had so many treats. On previous nights, we had a solo pre-show performance, a world premiere ('Living on The Edge of the World'), several tour premiers, and appearances from Vinny Lopez and Gary U.S. Bonds. Expectations are high and he doesn't disappoint. By the end of the night the trip has embraced 65 songs. Tonight of course we get 'Who'll Stop the Rain?' but the highlights for me are 'Cynthia' and 'Janey Don't You Lose Heart', one of my favourites and so rarely played. This ends around midnight and at this point Bruce becomes ecstatic. 'Do you know it's my birthday?' he says, jumping up and down with the child's grin on his face. We sing 'Happy Birthday', not as well as we should. The songs go on, Gary comes back for another guest slot and Bruce keeps reminding us. Eventually, in the home straight his family appears onstage and a huge guitar-shaped birthday cake is wheeled out, much to his delight. He struggles to blow out the candles - he explains he's 'sixty-fucking-three.' I wonder what he wished for. He gives the first slice to Obie, his first fan, at the front of the pit as ever. She must have loved that. We sing 'Happy Birthday' again, this time under Steve's leadership, and we do a better job. Then it's full throttle into the final run, family joining in.

It's 2.15am. He's calling it a night. We file out into the early hours, too hyped to sleep, knowing we've just shared a very personal moment with Bruce and had one of the most fun-filled nights of our lives.

XCEL ENERGY CENTER

12 NOVEMBER 2012 ST. PAUL, MINNESOTA

I WAS THERE: ALEX JOHNSON

I am a 26-year-old college football coach from Minnesota. I've been a Bruce fan since I was in middle school; I've seen him live 11 times. I was the one who got my Dad (who graduated high school in 1978, PRIME Bruce era, can't believe it) into Bruce. At different times in my life, Bruce has been many things: a counsellor, a confidant, a brother, an escape, and a preacher to name a few. The thing that means the most to me is the communal experience that a Springsteen show provides for all of us in attendance. I've got a couple of quick stories that illustrate my personal experiences.

The wait between the wristband lottery and the start of the show is an extremely interesting time. It feels agonizingly long because all you want is to see Bruce stroll on stage and greet you with his trademark 'good evening' before counting the band into the first song. However, in my experience, you often meet some of the most interesting people in that time period. At a show in Pittsburgh, I met two guys who had driven down from Toronto for the show. Both had seen Bruce over a hundred times, and we spent hours swapping set-list stories, tales of getting into the pit, and other artists we loved to see live.

At a show at Giants Stadium, my Dad and I got to know a newlywed couple. The wife was the Bruce fan; her husband was along for the ride. This was a pretty accurate comparison to the dynamic between my Dad and me. She and I both had a few specific songs that we wanted to hear that night, which is common, but there was one song on both of our lists: 'I'm Goin' Down'. When Bruce started to hammer the first chords of that song, she whipped around and grabbed my hand like I was her old friend she hadn't seen in years. The two of us shared that moment that was only made possible by the man behind the mic. It was the culmination of our totally separate lifetimes of experience, combined with the emotion tied to the music, but it connected us at that moment. Two people who just met a few hours before, and I'm still telling that story 10 years later. I bet she is too.

My other story is along that same line, about a shared experience between strangers. At one of the hometown Minnesota shows I've attended, I ended up on the floor standing next to a middle-aged guy who had brought his entire family. The youngest kid had to be six or seven at most. We chatted a bit before the show, I mentioned how cool it was that his kids were sharing this experience, but that was it. Right near the end of the main set, Roy Bittan launched into the first line of 'Jungleland' on the piano. I hadn't mentioned that song to the man next to me, and vice versa. But at that moment, we looked at each other in mutual understanding of how cool the moment was. I'm not huge on physical contact with strangers, but at that moment I said, 'Fuck it, this guy is my friend and I'm glad he's here with me' and threw my arm around him. At that moment when Bruce steps back from the mic at the end of the first verse, we both threw a fist in the air and screamed: 'Down in Jungleland!' I haven't seen that guy since then. I don't even remember seeing him after the show. But for a few minutes on the beer-soaked floor of the Xcel Energy Center, our lives collided, and we shared a moment of mutual understanding where we understood each other perfectly, even though we didn't know each other at all.

This is what Bruce does. The personal nature and deeply relatable themes of his music lend themselves to being important to people's lives. When we all bring those individual experiences and feelings into the same building, and our guy Bruce is up there matching our intensity with his wildly passionate performance style, these moments pop up all the time. This is what brings me back time and time again to see Bruce live. This is how he's been able to pack arenas and stadiums for 40 years. Bruce Springsteen's music is just the context in which all of this is possible. He gives us a forum to find what is becoming rarer by the day in this fake news social media internet-troll world: human connection. For that, I will be eternally grateful.

GLENDALE ARENA

6 DECEMBER 2012, GLENDALE, ARIZONA

I WAS THERE: SANDY TRAPP

The last US date of Wrecking Ball tour. My husband and I flew to Scottsdale; rented a convertible, hung at the pool at the resort we stayed at and promptly spotted one of his backup singers. Jim was right - the band WAS staying here! I was inspired to make a sign request: 'Dear Santa, My Wish is to hear 'The Wish' but we weren't close enough to the stage for him to see it. Hearing 'Incident on 57th Street' with Bruce at the piano was everything.

Post-show, we headed to a little lobby bar at the resort, and ran smack into Jake Clemons, who was so sweet! The entire band except Stevie and Bruce were in that bar, eating and drinking. We kept a respectful distance but ended up chatting with everyone through the course of the next few hours. Everybody signed my sign! I never did fall asleep that night.

The adrenaline rush when a tour is announced: plotting out ticket strategies, possible road trip cities, watching the set list for the first few shows. Counting down the days. Day of show: pre-game drinks to talk about what songs we will/won't hear. Deciding on a 'pee song.' Excitement!

The only good part about a Springsteen show ending: heading straight to a bar to do a serious recap with friends, review the set-list and try to come down from the high that will ultimately last for days. There is nothing like it!

I think I've seen 19 shows. Feels like more. Whenever somebody asks me how many I've seen, the answer is simple: not nearly enough.

2013

ALLPHONES ARENA

18, 20, 22 MARCH 2013 SYDNEY, AUSTRALIA

I WAS THERE: LYNETTE GIGLIO

I have seen Bruce 20 times. April 2012, there was no sign of Bruce coming to Australia, it looked like another World Tour in which Australia was going to be forgotten. With much encouragement from friends and a shrug from hubby I was going to make part of

my bucket list come true, the full version involved a six-month tour crawl. I was going to New Jersey. Even at this late stage I managed to secure tickets to all three shows at Metlife, even pit ones. Hotel booked, air ticket booked - check. My husband arranged for a car to collect me from the airport and take me to the hotel, I think he was a bit worried I would get lost somewhere between JFK airport and Rutherford, a possibility as it would be only the second time I had been out of Australia and the first time on my own. I was thrilled and everyone I told, friends, family, kids teachers, were just as thrilled, I think they knew how much this meant to me.

Why Metlife? Four reasons: one - New Jersey is Bruce's home state; two - first time playing this arena; three - The Eve of Bruce's

birthday and four it would give me the opportunity to venture down
to Freehold and Asbury Park. All the places I had heard about
in songs, images Bruce had painted in my mind. Excitement was
building the daily countdown reached three weeks to go, then I
noticed something wasn't right. I was bleeding before my period was
due. I decided to visit the doctor to ensure any minor problem could
be handled before I was due to fly out. He did a blood test and pap
smear to rule out that I wasn't pregnant, wasn't having a miscarriage.
As an afterthought he said cancer, which wasn't likely.

The next day we received a phone call saying he needed to see us
right away. I knew what he was going to say without having to hear it
said. My husband, ever optimistic, said it didn't mean anything bad.
The blood tests came back clear but the pap smear came back with
a cancer diagnosis. Showing great clarity of mind considering I was
in shock and we were still in the doctor's room, my only comment
was 'Crap.' After a few minutes of what this meant sinking in, I was
a bit teary but trying to hold it together. My husband asked if I was
upset at the diagnosis or the fact I would be missing out on Bruce.
My response was 'Bruce.' It was something I had always wanted to
do, and just as I was set to realize my dream it was crushed. To get so
close was devastating and dare I say it - not fair.

Further tests revealed that I was an exciting case to many of the
oncologists and pathologists at the hospital. My cancer was rare,
aggressive, high-grade and malignant. All the things you don't want
to hear in one sentence. One of the pathologists said he hadn't
seen this in his 30 years in pathology. The largest case study they
could find was five people (upon asking how the group had faired,
the doctor said two good, three not good prognosis). After many
specialist consults it was decided my treatment plan was to be a
radical hysterectomy, heavy aggressive chemotherapy and possibly
radiotherapy. So mid-September saw the surgery complete, at home
recovering lying in bed watching the live set-list feeds appear from
my fellow Tramps for my three Metlife shows, reading the posts,
watching YouTube videos and crying, realizing what I was missing.
This was a low couple of weeks.

The end of October saw me start chemotherapy, six cycles. One cycle held every three weeks. Each weekly cycle ran over three consecutive days. I had a heavy dose of the same drugs used for treating lung cancer. The first two cycles were not too bad; yes, I had nausea and was tired but otherwise okay. The fourth cycle saw me starting to lose my hair, which was a bad week. It wasn't so much the hair going, as it will grow back, it was more that I went from appearing normal to someone who looked sick.

When I looked in the mirror I was no longer me, I was now a 'sick' person. This is how I would be seen by the outside world as well. Cycles five and six were hard. The treatment had a cumulative effect, so it really affected me. For these last two cycles the nausea was horrendous, vomiting was an added extra, the aches and pains were catching up with me. Also, pills that had to be taken daily numerous, blood tests every cycle. Ensuring I was careful of people who were sick, as my immune system was non-existent. The good news during this period was it had been decided that I did not need radiotherapy.

Analysis of the tumour deemed it to be Small Cell Uterine Carcinoma, and it had tunnelled its way halfway through my uterus wall in three months. If I had not acted in another three months, it would have made it all the way though and my prognosis would have been totally different. I would become another of the three 'not good' patients. To all the ladies out there, please see a doctor if you notice something not right with your body. Many of my friends had not had pap smears for years. They all went and had them done.

During this time, I decided to write a letter to Bruce's management and faxed it off. I didn't want special treatment, tickets to a show, my request was simple – please give Australia some tour dates. Hoping but not expecting anything to be achieved I was ecstatic to see Australian dates announced. Was it my request or just fate? Probably just a second chance if I could grab it. Hoping for more luck I joined the masses clamouring for tickets. After one brief moment of good fortune I managed to get in the pit for the first Sydney show and in the stands for the other two. My eldest son, just turned 13, said he would come with me, as my husband had been to the two previous tours and declared he was a 'bit over the Bruce thing.'

Fast forward to March 2013. I arrived at the Arena early to discover there was the pit numbering system in place. Sent out an SOS to a friend to collect and deliver my son to me, spoke to his school and arranged to have him granted leave so he could get his number. A lady in the office was a fan also, so she totally got why it was important. We managed to get 53 and 57. I was on cloud nine; surely this would give me a close stage experience. We ended up front row at Soozie's side of the stage. My son had made a sign requesting 'Outlaw Pete', his second favourite song after 'Born to Run', which is a concert staple, so he opted for his second song. On the bottom of his sign and the back, he wrote, 'Can you have a photo with my Mum? She has cancer'.

Halfway through the show, Bruce took his sign, ruffled his hair and nodded. The stars were aligning, I was stunned, I probably would have fit in with any hysterical Justin Bieber or One Direction fan. We were now jumping along with the rest of the pit hands up pumping the air, in my case smiling like there was no tomorrow. We arrived at 'Tenth Avenue Freezeout' and I'm thinking no, this is way too quick and wondering if I would manage to get my photo.

Bruce leans into his laid-back pose, which I marvel at every time he - one, gets down there and two, makes it back up. He starts heading over to our side of the stage. He kneels in front of me, takes my hand and sings me a verse. I'm singing/screaming right back; I can guarantee I looked rather insane, although no footage appears to be in evidence! Given I still had no hair left, picture Britney Spears during her bad period and a bandana, which I'm sure most people who saw me assumed was a tribute to an absent Steve. Bruce bends down and I get a kiss on the cheek. He stands up, ruffles my son's hair again and is gone. I did manage to say thank you to him, I had enough presence of mind to remember my manners, but not enough to give him my letter for Patti, which I had printed off in the hope I would be able to pass it along. I am left standing there, hugging my son and speechless.

Fast forward five days to the last Sydney show. I decided to get there early and see if my luck would surface one last time. I was with around 10 other fans waiting for Bruce to arrive. I had made a sign, again remembering my manners, thanking Bruce for my kiss but stating it had washed off in the shower, could he stop for a photo. After around 90 minutes the skies opened up and it poured for around 15 minutes. We were all hoping he wouldn't drive up at that moment. The rain stopped and 15 minutes later his car approached, I held out my sign and was rewarded with him stopping. I managed to get a photo, he signed my ticket, took the letter I had written to Patti eight months earlier and had planned to take to the New Jersey shows. Bruce asked where my mate was. I told him he wasn't here tonight, thrilled he remembered us from the Monday show. When I rang home to tell him that Bruce wanted to know where he was he was a bit put out that he had opted out of the show that night. Then once again he was gone, another brief encounter that leaves you feeling like the world is perfect and you can accomplish anything.

So, we fast forward to 4 August 2013. I've just seen the movie *Springsteen and I*. My thoughts on the three words I would have submitted if I had been well enough at the time are…

Sanity – during the initial uncertainty of my cancer worries he was what helped keep my thoughts quiet and to stop my mind from racing down dark avenues, especially lying in bed late at night in the dark when there were no daily distractions to help keep your focus elsewhere.

Important – the song 'Stolen Car' has become how I can best sum up my fears of the past year that I didn't share with others and how I was hoping I would be okay, if not, that I would get at least eight years to see the boys through school. The latter thought is still what I aim for. Whenever I have needed music to help me recharge my spirits, to cheer me up, to commiserate with me or just for the pure joy of dancing around the house he has a song that gives me what I need.

Friendship – his music has been with me for 30 years ever since I bought *The River*. Ironically, the reason I bought it was not hearing the title track, this was the song that made me listen and wonder what else was there, but hearing 'Stolen Car' and just falling completely in love with his song-writing. Bruce's music and his words have always been able to help me celebrate when I was happy, comfort me when I was sad and over the past year help me fight this disease. It has brought me many new friends and kindred souls. I have my blood family and my Tramp family, that make me laugh, make me cry and provide me with, thanks to the global location of everyone, a voice coming down the line 24/7. To all my fellow Tramps, I say thanks for all you've given me this past year.

'And I'm driving a stolen car
On a pitch-black night
And I'm telling myself I'm gonna be alright
But I ride by night and I travel in fear
That in this darkness I will disappear'

What would I say to Bruce, remembering we should all use our manners? Sanity, Important, Friendship - thank you.

Bruce's music continues to be my mainstay and now we're 36 years into a one-sided conversation. I received my five-year clearance at the end of 2016 and am now considered cured. I travelled to Los Angeles to see two River '16 tour shows and got to hear 'Stolen Car' live. I also managed to get my bookend song in Brisbane in 2017. Better Days, indeed it is.

ENTERTAINMENT CENTRE

14 MARCH 2013 BRISBANE AUSTRALIA

I WAS THERE: NADA SMITH

I've been a Bruce Springsteen fan since I was 16 years old - my school friends and I were in a record shop one day after school and decided to pick an album out and whichever one we chose we would start to follow that artist. I picked out *Born to Run*. I went home and listened to it. The first sound of 'Thunder Road' - I was hooked. He has been beside me ever since that day. Then of course along came

'Dancing in the Dark' and I, like every other girl, wanted to be the one to dance with Bruce. I talked about it constantly.

Fast forward many years and many concerts, my dream came true one magical night in Australia, 2013.

Bruce had not been to Australia for 1o years, since the 2003 tour. I had been with my family to see him in New Jersey in 2009 - thinking that might be the last time I would see him. When he announced the 2013 tour I was so excited and knew this would be my last chance. The dance was going to happen, I just knew it.

Bruce's first concert was to be in Brisbane - we got tickets. We live in Adelaide, about 1,000 miles away. My eldest child had become a convert and was excited to help me achieve my dream. I knew I needed a sign, but what could it say that would get Bruce's attention? What lyric? What words? We had many months to think about it I had come up with a few song lyrics but couldn't really settle on anything.

We bought the cardboard and the paint. It wasn't until the night before we left for Brisbane that Georgia said, this is what we are painting – 'Bruce, please dance with my Mum'. I was happy with that.

Off we went. We got to the hotel and met a man called Jamie. Little did we know this man with a Bruce tattoo on his calf would be

pivotal to my story. He told us about getting there early to do 'roll-call'. We had never heard of this. When we got there, we saw we had to get a 'number' and wait in line in order to be able to get in early and secure a good spot. No. 72 and 73. At 6pm we were let in and managed to get smack-bang in the middle of the stage.

I was so excited to be seeing Bruce again.

Bruce shows Georgia's sign to the crowd

It was so surreal. Bruce walked out at the start of the concert, sang a few songs, then looked over and saw Georgia's sign. He smiled and winked at Georgia. OMG, was this going to happen?

This was the concert, if you read his autobiography, you will recall that he mentions how this was the first time he would be performing live after his awful neck problems (He was not to perform for three months, and this was the first concert back from that). We could see in his eyes his happiness at seeing the crowd welcoming him back - there was lots of love in the room.

After what was an amazing concert it was time for 'Dancing in the Dark'. The song started - it seemed to go on forever. It was getting close to the end - Bruce when are you coming to get me?

Then he walked over and took Georgia's sign. Showed it to all the crowd, who screamed with excitement, then Bruce held out his hand and invited me up on stage. We danced! It was amazing. I was able to say thank you to him - which is what I had wanted to do, and I gave him the biggest hug, something I also wanted to do. I had dreamt about it for a long time.

It was a good, good, night. The thing about Bruce is, he's so

Nada Smith enjoying a dance with Bruce

humble and so grateful for his fans. I honestly felt he was so happy to be dancing with me, so happy I chose him - not the other way around. His concerts to me are like a religious experience. He is the ultimate rock God to me and I was privileged to be able to share 45 seconds of his time one amazing night in 2013.

ROD LAVER ARENA

24 MARCH 2013 MELBOURNE, AUSTRALIA

I WAS THERE: NATASHA WARRINGTON

I've loved Springsteen since I was eight years old after seeing him singing 'Dancing in the Dark' on *Top of the Pops*. I was born in England and came to Australia when I was 10. Fast forward to 2013, the first anniversary of my Dad dying, I was praying to get on that stage and so many things happened that night to make me believe my Dad was there. I did get up on stage that very night, and was a crazy, happy (slightly psycho) chick on stage. My dreams came true.

I was turning 37 three days later. Bruce played 'We Are Alive' that night, a song that makes me think of Dad. He also said, 'This is for all your ghosts out there'.

WEMBLEY STADIUM

15 JUNE 2013 LONDON, UK

I WAS THERE: SADIE BLANKLEY

It was a privilege to be at Wembley on 15 June 2013. To share in the vastness of the venue, the phenomenal range of songs and the skill of the band. To witness the perfection of a complete and uninterrupted performance of the whole *Darkness on the Edge of Town* album. That's the one where it all began for me in 1978, with melodies and lyrics which have been constant companions ever since.

But I won't be back again for the live circuit, it's too frustrating trying to see when you're standing in the thronging crowd, however

good-natured the atmosphere, and Springsteen and his music aren't made to be coolly observed from a distant seat – be close and be part of it or not there at all. Trying to revisit life's experiences can only end in disappointment and there comes a time when memories must be laid to rest and left in peace.

Knowing this in my heart, I wept through the final encore - after more than three hours on stage with the E Street Band, the man alone with guitar and harmonica and a sublime acoustic rendition of 'Thunder Road', surely a farewell performance just for me.

I did go again to Wembley to see Bruce when he toured in 2016. The whole experience could not have been more perfect. I got to stand up front, with a great view and room to leap around. The weather was warm and sunny, but we got into the shade of the stadium just when it began to get scorching. The crowd was orderly and lively. I made new friends. The venue staff got us in and out without a problem and I was grateful to be in a hotel room within 15 minutes of the last encore while thousands of others were still descending on the tube station.

And the concert lived up to every expectation. Three and a half hours of non-stop energy from a pro that gives his all to every performance. Bruce's music has been the soundtrack to my adult life. His back catalogue is unrivalled and spans a vast spectrum of genres. His songs tell stories of life, loss, love, joy, history, war, politics and faith. The East Street Band have been his soul-mates since the early Seventies, and with millions of other fans I mourn the passing of those who didn't make it this far.

STADE DE GENEVE

29 JUNE 2013 PARIS, FRANCE

I WAS THERE: EELCO KLOMP

The first 29 years of my life was spent waiting for a moment that just didn't come - until one day in 2002 when the angels ride that road down from heaven on their Harleys. I met the love of my life (Jetske),

*Eelco and Jetske Klomp celebrated
their wedding anniversary seeing Bruce*

who I still love with all the madness in my soul.

It still feels like we are made for each other. I think when Bruce Springsteen wrote the line, '*We liked the same music, we liked the same bands, we like the same clothes*', he had us in mind.

On 12 December 2005 we got married and Bruce had to be part of it. Our marriage theme was 'If I Should Fall Behind'. We put a line from that on our wedding card, with the live in NYC version played in the Town Hall where we married, my brother playing it for us on guitar in the church. That was a very special moment. Although the church was filled with family and friends, I had the feeling there was just three people there - my brother, my wife and I.

We were on holiday and noticed on a Dutch message board a Tramp offering a free Springsteen ticket for a Paris show. He had a spare ticket and he would rather give it away for free then selling it to not a real/big Springsteen fan. I told my wife about this. That year we had already seen Bruce in Hannover, Milan and Nijmegen, but if you have ever have been to a Springsteen show you only want one thing: more shows. We talked about it and browsed the Internet and found another ticket for the Paris show.

What to do? We only had a few days left of our holiday and this could turn out to be the best end of a holiday ever. We just did it, we bought the ticket, got the other ticket for free and booked a hotel just on the other side of the street of the Stade de France stadium.

The next day we left early from the north of the Netherlands to Paris. After a six-hour drive we arrived at the venue and took a walk around the stadium. We didn't have front of stage tickets, so were not in a hurry to enter the stadium. I thought to myself, what if Bruce does a pre-show? If that would happen we'd never forgive ourselves. We went in, got as far to the podium as possible. What happened next was amazing. Bruce played acoustic versions of 'This Hard Land', 'Burning Love' and 'Growin' Up.' A private mini-concert in front of just a few hundred fans. Wow. We could now remove this from our bucket-list.

A few hours later Bruce came back on stage with the E Street Band and we saw a great show, including a performance of the full *Born in the U.S.A.* album. The next day we drove back home and ready for the working life with a big smile on our faces!

One of our wishes was to make a 'Bruce pilgrimage' to New Jersey and see Bruce play in New Jersey or New York. When he announced the Springsteen on Broadway shows we tried to become a verified fan, get a code and get tickets. Unfortunately, no luck, but we got our next chance when more shows were added. Faith was rewarded and my brother and I both got a code, getting tickets for the same date.

Guess which day we went - 12 December 2017, our wedding anniversary. Our wishes came true and we'd celebrate our wedding with my brother and my other best friend, Bruce Springsteen.

We had the best wedding anniversary we could dream of. We

made a helicopter flight and had a great aerial view of the New York City skyline and all the Big Apple's iconic attractions. We went early to the Walter Kerr theatre and waited to see when Bruce arrived. A few days earlier we had a bought the iconic *Greetings from Asbury Park, N.J.* postcard at the famous Stone Pony venue. When Bruce arrived with Patti, he signed some autographs at the opposite side of the room, then came to our side to sign more autographs, but skipped us. He then came back, grabbed our postcard, signed it and went into the theatre. An hour later we saw a great Springsteen on Broadway show. This day could not really have been any better.

Eelco Klomp's Bruce-related website, www.mybosstime.com encourages fans to help create spreadsheets of set-lists of songs played live to create personal Springsteen statistics. Its database includes setlists from 1974 onwards, with the site in 10 languages, involving users across the world.

WERCHTER GROUNDS

13 JULY 2013 WERCHTER, BELGIUM

I WAS THERE: LORAINE VERLEYE

I was 14 when I saw Bruce Springsteen in Belgium during the TW Classic. I don't remember when I heard him first, but I'm pretty sure it wasn't from my parents. My family listened to The Beatles, Depeche Mode, Simple Minds, AC/DC, Iron Maiden and others, but there were no Springsteen CDs in my house. Fortunately, I bought them to complete the collection.

When I saw Bruce was coming to my country (finally), I asked my parents to attend. Fortunately, they said yes. I was so happy to see Paul McCartney in Warsaw and Bruce Springsteen the same year. And I hoped Paul would come to TW Classic with Bruce to sing two or three songs together. I couldn't stop watching their show at Hard Rock Calling, London.

I don't like going to festivals or concerts. I hate it when there are too many people around me. But it was amazing. He is The Boss and I wanted to see him. The best thing about him is that he cares about his fans and we can decide the songs he and the band play.

There's always one song which makes me cry. One harmonica note … yes, 'The River'. I don't know why, but it is. After the show I was so sad but so happy. And now, my mum can listen to his music without saying anything.

Bruce came back in 2016, but unfortunately, I couldn't attend the show. So please, come back to Europe, and why not sing, 'I Saw Her Standing There' with Paul McCartney. Maybe one day, I will attend

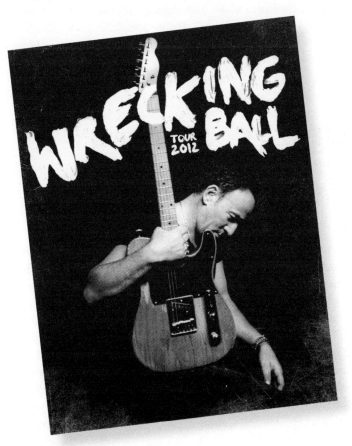

Bruce's show with my children.

THOMOND PARK

16 JULY 2013 LIMERICK, IRELAND

I WAS THERE: JIM CARROLL

Bruce Springsteen saved my life. That's probably a bit of an exaggeration, but it makes for a great opening line. He's been a part of my musical life for as long as I've had a musical life, albums like *Nebraska, The River, Darkness on the Edge of Town* and *Born to Run* sound-tracking my teenage years as I stumbled on them one by one.

My favourite tune is 'Born to Run.' I could be a nerd and go for some deep cut, yet this is the one for me. It's an evergreen banger, a track which never loses its edge, its thrill, its energy, its power, its gumption, its appeal. My wife Lisa and I chose it for the first dance at our wedding, so there's that magic moment as well.

The songs and albums shaped Springsteen for me, but the live show illuminated the experience. I've seen him a bunch of times at this stage. Every time I think I've seen him at his best, he comes back and confounds you by taking it up a notch. That 2013 show in Limerick's Thomond Park was the latest case of something else.

I WAS THERE: JACKIE O'MALLEY

We were heading back to the car after seeing Bruce in Limerick. We were going back over every second of the gig. One by one these huge black limos were passing and my friend Jen said that the band all travel separately after the gigs in order to chill out. We stood and watched this cortège pass by, no idea really who was in any of them because of the tinted windows. The fourth one stopped and the man himself rolled down the windows and asked if we had been at the show, what we thought of it, how far we had travelled and for a couple of words as Gaeilge. I didn't have the wit to ask for a selfie, maybe next time!

MILLENNIUM STADIUM

23 JULY 2013 CARDIFF, UK

I WAS THERE: ROB & JEAN PARSONS

A last-minute decision to see Bruce on the Wrecking Ball tour
came about as we had seen him at Wembley in June but left slightly
disappointed - not by the band or set-list (one of the best I'd ever
seen, including Rob's favourite album in full - *Darkness on the Edge of
Town*), but we had seats way up in the Gods and the sound was awful.
A late ticket-drop occurred for the Cardiff show so we snapped up a
couple of tickets not realising Rob only had one day of holiday left at
work. This resulted in a journey from Cornwall to Cardiff to see the
concert and a drive straight back home, arriving at 3am to start work
at 5am. However, it was more than worth it.

   We arrived in Cardiff expecting a usual stadium show - i.e. far
away from the stage and not the best sound. Upon entering the
stadium, we noticed that the roof was shut and the stadium had been
divided in half, resulting in us having seats with a great view. These
facts combined to make this concert the best we've ever attended
- not because the set-list was particularly good or the band played
exceptionally well, but the atmosphere was nothing like we'd ever
witnessed before or since.

   The sound from the crowd was unbelievable, a 'wall of sound'
contained within an arena-sized venue, off the scale. The 'Badlands
chant' reverberated around the crowd like a tidal wave, even Bruce
stopping and staring and encouraging it to be kept going for as long as
possible. It still sends tingles down my spine when I think about it. It was
also one of those 'make it up as you go along' set-lists, with three signs
on the trot plucked from the crowd and the requests played, including
the obscure 'TV Movie' included on the *Tracks* boxset. This had band
members slightly flummoxed for a moment, but they nailed it, although
Bruce said that was the first and last time it will ever be performed. He
came on at the end and performed two acoustic songs, 'Janey Don't Lose
Your Heart' and 'Thunder Road', rounding off the best night ever.

NOWLAN PARK

27 & 28 JULY 2013 KILKENNY, IRELAND

I WAS THERE: RO YOURELL

I've been a fan of The Boss all my life, since being introduced to him by my parents' tape deck on winding summer car journeys. I first started singing and playing guitar at the height of Brit-Pop, and although Oasis, Blur and Supergrass featured heavily in my repertoire, it was still Bruce's words that resonated most strongly with me. I performed 'Growing Up' for my Leaving Cert Music practical. It was the sense of yearning, of longing in his lyrics that I identified with as a teenager.

Fast forward 15 years to July 2013 and I'm standing on his stage, in Nowlan Park, Kilkenny, with my band Delorentos. In a few hours, he will confound the passage of time, for the umpteenth time, to rock the capacity stadium to its core. Even the sceptics and those who are only there because it's the event of the summer, will be swept up by the energy, passion and giddy enthusiasm that he brings to every performance.

Needless to say, I'm feeling pretty inspired and catching a glimpse of his microphone stand, rooted to the centre of the enormous stage, I briefly consider whether I could emulate some of his remarkable pole-dancing technique, but decide against it (more yoga required). It's an amazing experience. The day is warm, but the audience are warmer still and give us a generous, buzzy response.

I didn't get to meet the man himself. Had I, I would have said 'Thank you, for showing me that giving really is the best way to receive and that it's not just what you say, but how you say it, that matters.'

PARQUE DOS ATLETAS

21 SEPTEMBER 2013 RIO DE JANEIRO, BRAZIL

I WAS THERE: MARIA ESTRELLA

This was my first and only Bruce concert, where he played all *Born in the U.S.A.* At the first part of the concert I was at a place more distant from the stage, with my husband. But in the last five songs, we went further to the stage, where we met my son and felt the power of being near Bruce. Fantastic! Since then, I wish for a new show in Brazil, but that has never happened, as yet.

2014

The High Hopes Tour featured special guest Rage Against the Machine guitarist Tom Morello. The tour was seen as a continuation of the previous tour and was in support of his 18th studio album, *High Hopes*, released in January 2014.

Guitarist Steven Van Zandt was forced to miss almost the entire North American leg due to the filming of his television series, *Lilyhammer*, while Patti Scialfa appeared on a

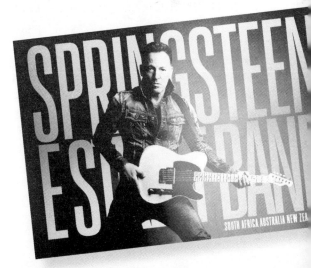

few North American dates. 182 songs were performed on the High Hopes tour and Springsteen announced at the tour's conclusion the band would be taking a break for the remainder of the year.

Springsteen paid tribute to Joey Ramone during a surprise appearance at the Light of Day charity gig - which raises funds for research into Parkinson's disease. He performed the Ramones classic, 'Do You Remember Rock'n'Roll Radio?' with Jesse Malin.

PARAMOUNT THEATRE

19 JANUARY 2014 ASBURY PARK, NEW JERSEY

I WAS THERE: MIKE PETERS

I first met Bruce in the Eighties backstage at a little club called The Ritz, where Little Steven was playing. I was invited to the dressing room to meet Little Steven and Bruce was there. He came over to me and said in his New Jersey accent, 'Hey, The Alarm, yeah! I was fixing my car and listening to 'Rain In The Summertime'. That's a great song!'

When I turned up for the sound check for the Light of Day Benefit Concert I saw a whole stack of iconic Fender Telecasters and immediately knew whose those were. I knew he was going to play. I was in the dressing room and Bruce walked in and said, 'Hi Mike, it's great to have you here. Looking forward to playing with you later.' I was thinking to myself, 'Can you say that again, please'. A shiver goes down your spine and you think to yourself, I've got to show this man what I'm capable of as well. I stepped up to the mic and started singing a harmony - I think that surprised Bruce, because when I looked over he was grinning all over his face. I hope he was thinking, 'Good note!'

AAMI PARK

15 FEBRUARY 2014 MELBOURNE, AUSTRALIA

I WAS THERE: MIKE FITZGERALD

Bruce and the E Street band played for just under four hours and played the entire *Born in the U.S.A.* album, front to back. Eddie Vedder came on for the first song and played AC/DC's 'Highway to Hell'. My mate summed it up well about two and a half hours

Mike Fitzgerald, cousin Kelly and brother Tim

in, saying, 'This is a concert that just keeps on giving' The night after, he played past the 11pm curfew and got fined $35 grand, but he didn't mind.

There were people of all ages enjoying the concert, it had a great vibe. The audience were captivated by their music, and willingly so. I feel very privileged to have been at that concert, especially when he played 'My Hometown', as it had been announced that Holden, Toyota

and Ford were closing production facilities in Australia, which he mentioned before he played the song and how it had impacted on him when he was younger, with the steel mills closing etc. - you could have heard a pin drop when they played it. He's got a lot of heart, full respect to him and the E Street Band.

A photo I took that may seem insignificant (one of only three I took - I believe in enjoying concerts in the moment and being respectful of other's enjoyment), was of a couple in their Sixties, fans from way back, the husband with his arm around his wife, surrounded by people in their 20s, 30s, etc. all completely as one, fixated on the music. To me, it's an indication of Bruce and the E Street Band and the respect given back to the band.

My brother and I grew up with *Born in the U.S.A.* and didn't know he was going to play that album in its entirety. It means more to me than words can say that I got to share that concert with my brother and close friends. Such is the power of music.

ALLPHONES ARENA

19 FEBRUARY 2014 SYDNEY, AUSTRALIA

I WAS THERE: JOHN ENCARACAO

A number of my friends have a fervour for Bruce Springsteen I have never been able to understand. I have always thought of his work as prosaic and literal. His songs teeter on the edge of despair at the lack of possibilities of industrial and post-industrial America. His music, particularly his bracing, straining vocal performances, suffuse much of his output with a sense of hope.

Innately masculine, his work can walk a line between passion and bluster. Springsteen is the muscular rock god and man of the people, his empathetic tales of everyday travails and fuck-ups blasted reliably upon a road-worn Telecaster, and through a throat of steel. At the age of 64, he plays three-to four-hour shows that seem to spring from, and continues to generate in his fans, a belief in the redemptive power of rock'n'roll.

As a first-timer, I now realise, there's nothing that can really prepare you for a Bruce Springsteen concert. I cannot remember ever witnessing so much unbridled joy in a performer. Springsteen looked like he was having the time of his life, and this was contagious. He loves his music, he loves his fans, he loves his band.

Over a long show (three hours, almost to the minute) there was never once the sense of going through the motions, of anything less than full commitment.

This show opened with a stomping cover of the Easybeats' 'Friday On My Mind' (other shows on the tour have opened with AC/DC's 'Highway to Hell') and he had his Australian audience salivating at the first line. In the second song, Springsteen made use of the special track that's been constructed around the general admission standing area to do semi-regular laps of honour, singing, high-fiving, receiving hugs, giving it out and lapping it up.

After another Australian cover – The Saints' 'Just Like Fire Would' – we enter what in hindsight is a set-piece, but in the moment was totally beguiling. Eerie organ on the border of horror movie soundtrack and gospel service backed Springsteen's monologue, which began seriously but took a humorous turn as a computerised toilet seat was invoked as a manifestation of 'the spirit'.

This set up 'Spirit in the Night', from 1972, and rather than the jazzy shuffle of the original, this performance haunted like old blues in the vein of St James' Infirmary. Springsteen finished the song on the catwalk at the back of the standing area, pointed towards the stage, and launched himself, crowd-surfing on his back for a couple of minutes.

The audience delivered him on a sea of upstretched hands. It sounds like a gimmick, but there was something magical about the moment. Upon arriving back on stage, Springsteen said, 'Thanks for not killing me. It got a bit hairy there for a minute!'

At the two-hour mark, it seemed the set was over, but Springsteen barely left the stage before bouncing back with a cover of INXS's 'Don't Change', which is a great fit – simple chord progression, life-affirming lyric. While the crowd's adrenaline was peaking, he gave us 'Born to Run' and 'Dancing in the Dark'. The first suffers a false start – which Springsteen laughed off – the second featured various members of the audience being invited up to dance.

The show ended in an unexpected way with a solo version of Suicide's 'Dream Baby Dream' on harmonium that developed from solemnity to passionate invocation. In a seamless gesture, Springsteen's live harmonium became a pre-recorded synthesised string part, and Springsteen walked to centre-stage invoking the crowd to keep dreaming.

As with the whole show, the sleight-of-hand, the virtuosic showmanship is in Springsteen's innate sense of pacing, both in terms of navigating a set-list of nearly 30 tunes and in the ways in which individual songs wax and wane, hitting crests of energy and delivering the crowd to places both familiar and unfamiliar.

ROCK AND ROLL HALL OF FAME

10 APRIL 2014 CLEVELAND, OHIO

I WAS THERE: MICHAEL CAVACINI

I saw Bruce perform with the E Street Band when they were

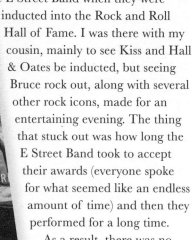

inducted into the Rock and Roll Hall of Fame. I was there with my cousin, mainly to see Kiss and Hall & Oates be inducted, but seeing Bruce rock out, along with several other rock icons, made for an entertaining evening. The thing that stuck out was how long the E Street Band took to accept their awards (everyone spoke for what seemed like an endless amount of time) and then they performed for a long time.

As a result, there was no all-star jam at the end and we didn't get out of the venue until midnight. I wasn't very pleased with them or Bruce that night. Ha!

HERSHEY PARK STADIUM

14 MAY 2014 HERSHEY, PENNSYLVANIA

I WAS THERE: ANTHONY LUCCI

I have seen Bruce Springsteen and the E Street Band live about
30 times. I first saw him at Hershey Park Stadium in 2008. What I
didn't know then was that six years later I'd be playing on the very

© David J. Bernstein

Anthony Lucci and his buddy Greg join Bruce on stage

same stage with him. That second time, I was about to graduate
from college, so had the week off. My brother Joseph, cousin Melody,
and Greg, a friend from college, all got GA tickets and arrived at
7am to get our wristbands. When the lottery was drawn about 500
people went in front of us, but we positioned ourselves center-mic
and moved up each time someone went to the bathroom. Greg and

I made a sign the night
before (we were up
until 3am) that folded
up and had blinking
lights around, reading
'Can we jam with
the E Street Band?'
We lifted the sign up
towards the end of
'Dancing in the Dark'

© David J. Bernstein

and Bruce acknowledged it. It was so large he couldn't miss it. He asked for it to be passed up and I grabbed the end of the sign. Next thing I knew someone must have given me a boost and I was on my hands and knees looking up at Bruce holding the sign to the crowd and to the band. I told him I wanted to play guitar with him, and he said, 'Let's go.'

It was the greatest two minutes of my life. My buddy Greg also grabbed one of Bruce's acoustic guitars and we finished the song with Bruce, my cousin rallying the band and the crowd on. After getting off stage, I couldn't even talk. People were grabbing us, saying, 'You touched Bruce, I need to touch you'. What I remember about being next to Bruce up there was standing that close, he's just a normal guy. But at the same time, he has one really cool job. What also was awesome is I saw him in Connecticut the week after and he went down into the pit to dance with a little girl in a wheelchair instead of bringing anyone on stage. I thought that was more awesome than him allowing me up on stage.

Anyways, I went to probably a dozen of The River 2016 shows, searching for songs like 'The Price You Pay', 'Stolen Car', 'Independence Day' and others like 'Incident on 57th Street.' No one performs like Bruce and the E Street Band. I was at the longest show in the US, in Philadelphia in 2016. I was exhausted halfway through and he kept going and going. I'm 25! He's got a lot more time on me. I don't know how he does it, but he always gives you more joy, and you always leave feeling renewed and alive.

ALLPHONES ARENA

19 FEBRUARY 2014 SYDNEY, AUSTRALIA

I WAS THERE: ILEANA ANTHONY

I grew up loving and following lots of amazing artists. I guess loving and being passionate is two different feelings. I was not always a lover of commercial radio and certainly not the disco era. I have followed Jackson Brown, The Eagles, Van Morrison and there are lots of others.

I have always loved Bruce's music - I truly found him when I was going through some tough times in my life. I was in my 50s and had been nursing both my parents through illness at home.

At the same time my eldest son Duane got diagnosed with a melanoma and it was a tough couple of years and I remember the exact day that I became a convert to Bruce. I was driving and crying about my son, so I pulled over the side of the road, and just howled.

I could not believe my load was so much and feared for my son. It was strange - I had a Bruce CD in my car and turned it up so loud with the anger. But after a few songs, and I wish I could remember them, I suddenly felt a calm come over me, and remember thinking this is so weird.

Every day when I left my parents, I played Bruce so loud that all my neighbours now know about my love for him. My parents passed not long after, three months apart, and my son had two procedures but thankfully is doing ok. Sorry about all the sad bits, but I needed to fill you in why he's become so important in my life.

Not long after, in February 2014, Bruce came to Australia but not to Perth where we live, so my hubby and I decided to fly to Sydney to see him live. There were 11 of us who decided to go – also including my son and partner, my youngest brother (a Bruce nut) and his family. We were blown away and I remember looking over at my kids and the look on their faces, like they'd been born again. That's how I felt too.

That was my first concert, then in 2015, because Bruce heard that approximately 3,000 fans flew from Perth to see him, he came back and began here. I went along with my youngest brother and again I was blown away. I kept thinking what power this man has on people. Does he even know that? Does he know what a legacy he will leave behind when he is gone? He has cured hearts and souls.

In July 2016 I was turning 60 and we decided to go to Europe, and at some point, our sons and partners decided they would meet us in Italy for my birthday. Not long before we left I got an email from my cousin's son in Italy, also a huge fan, telling me Bruce was touring Italy. And the day we were due to land, Bruce was playing in Rome at Circus Maximus, just outside the Coliseum. I sourced tickets and the day we landed, after 17 hours flying, we went to the venue around 3pm, the crowds already lining up. We jumped in line in the hot sun, waiting five hours before the start of the show.

I was so happy we did, as when I turned around to see the crowd in the stadium, it was full. I asked someone at the gates at the end how many he thought were here, and he said approximately 110,000. That was just inside - a lot of people gathered outside as well. The Italians really own him. They sing every word, even though they can't speak English. Everyone I spoke to had been to multiple shows and they passed out red love-hearts to almost everyone there. What a sea of red hearts it was.

He came on stage and I thought he looked sad and was going to cry. He started with 'New York City Serenade' with the orchestra. I couldn't stop crying. As the show progressed he seemed to come good. Even though we were tired and didn't get back to our accommodation till early morning, it would have to be the most memorable time of my life.

After that I read a book about Bruce by Peter Carlin. I am now starting to know this guy. In 2017 he came to Perth on the Born to Run tour and again my younger brother Dan and I went to all three shows, two of them in the pit. Bruce looked so happy at all three. He was smiling and joking and body-surfed right over the top of my brother and I. I thought we were going to be crushed, scary, because everyone wants to touch him.

I now wished we had gone around Australia with him at every show, but it's not always possible. Having read the *Born to Run* autobiography (the audio is also amazing), I really do understand why everyone that's a huge fan loves this guy so much. Put simply, we just get him.

I managed to get two tickets for the Broadway show, but got February 4 and could not go, so passed them on to another dedicated fan.

One thing I've noticed after each show is people's reaction outside. They all want to talk about Bruce, the three or four hour shows he put on not enough. And they all say the same things, about how he made them feel.

I'm still not surprised but amazed when I look around at every show and watch people's faces, the glow they have and the love for this special human being. Even though they are with their family or friends they're on their own journey with Bruce. Grown men just looking up at the stage in awe, so powerful and beautiful. I have not seen this with many other artists.

Bruce is the real/raw deal, his passion for his music/stories to be told going beyond singing them. He has remained true to himself and is now reaping the rewards of his dedication to working hard to be heard while staying true to his wife and family. I also think Patti is the most amazing lady to have stood by him, put up with him, and I love the way they look at each other.

'We laughed beneath the covers and count the wrinkles and the greys'

– Kingdom of Days

BB&T CENTER

29 APRIL 2014 SUNRISE, FLORIDA

I WAS THERE: JAMIE BROWNSTEIN

The 153rd show I went to changed my life. I've been following Bruce 40-plus years, and this was the show of all shows. Not only did he pick my sign and have me come dance with him, but the thing that stood out to me and most other friends that were there was how humble he was. The man I've admired forever actually bowed down to me, thanking me for my loyalty. I could go on, but this rocked my world.

That was in Fort Lauderdale, Florida, close to where I live. I was 53 at the time. But the first time I saw Bruce live was in 1975 at the Tower Theatre, Upper Darby, PA. I grew up in the suburbs of Philadelphia so that wasn't far for me. That night sealed the deal.

For my birthday my brother gave me *The Wild the Innocent & The E Street Shuffle* album. I was so annoyed he gave me this random album,

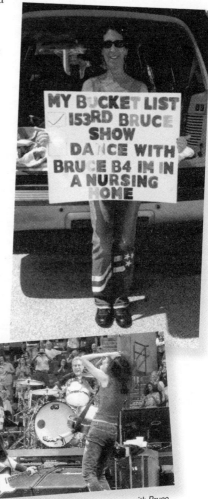

After 153 shows Jamie Brownstein gets to dance with Bruce

which I had never heard of. I threw it in the back of my closet. I went away to overnight camp that summer and from afar I could hear someone playing a song I just loved. I followed the music until I saw where it was coming from, looked at the album, saw it was 'Rosalita' and realized that was what was tossed in my closet. Had I taken a chance, four months earlier, I'd have been hooked then.

I've now been to 161 shows and can only hope he keeps doing what he loves to do. I've met hundreds of people simply because of my love for Bruce - friends I never would have had come into my world in a million years. That speaks volumes.

On November 5 2014 Springsteen participated in a charity auction as part of the 8th Annual Stand Up For Heroes charity concert in New York City - with all proceeds benefiting military service members and their families after they return home. Among the items up for bid was a day with Bruce Springsteen, including a one-hour guitar lesson, a ride in the sidecar of his motorcycle, and a lasagne dinner at his house!

Springsteen raised an additional $300,000 by auctioning off two of his guitars and entertained the audience with a five-song acoustic performance; 'Working on the Highway', 'Growing Up', 'If I Should Fall Behind (with Patti Scialfa)', 'Born in the U.S.A.' and 'Dancing In The Dark'.

2015

WONDER BAR

18 JULY 2015 ASBURY PARK, NEW JERSEY

I WAS THERE: JOE STRENO

It was a sultry summer day at the Jersey shore - like so many others. People flocked to Asbury Park to help escape the heat and humidity

Joe Grushecky & Bruce Springsteen
The Wonderbar - Asbury Park, NJ 7.18.15

back home. The beaches and boardwalk were packed - like way back in the days of old!

There were those who had also come to see Joe Grushecky And The Houserockers with special guest Eddie Manion on saxophone at the Wonder Bar. Though Grushecky and crew hail from Pittsburgh, PA, they have become sanctified by Asbury Park fans and one of Asbury's former residents - the 'real governor of New Jersey' - Mr Bruce Springsteen. Springsteen produced Grushecky's 1995 album *American Babylon*. But their connection came earlier on though the Light of Day Foundation and the first show at the Stone Pony in Asbury Park.

So the rumours begin. Joe Grushecky's coming to town? Wonder if Bruce will show up? Though the usual scenario is - Joe's coming to town - instant ticket sell out. Because when the Pittsburgh Posse is in town - Bruce is not far behind. And the residents of Asbury Park know it and are happier for the friendship of these two musicians. We all get to see Bruce and Joe play songs from both their massive songbooks. It's a homecoming for us all.

I had no idea I would be in attendance that night. It was divine providence, and a text message from my buddy Geoff Hoover. Geoff and I attended college together circa 1980 at CW Post. He and I had seen Bruce together twice before. It's also amazing that he and I live just blocks apart here in Asbury. When Geoff's son Texas declined going with his Dad, I was the next in the line of succession. Thanks Texas, and Geoff. Out of the blue, I had plans for the evening.

The plan was to meet in front of The Wonderbar at 8.50pm. Geoff would walk over from 1st and I'd walk over from 6th and meet out front. Now you have to realize, Bruce showing up, is not written in stone. You just never know if Mr Scialfa will show up. But as fate would have it - I'm telling you this WAS a magic night - as I was walking towards the back entrance of The Wonder Bar, I looked up - there was Bruce walking by himself towards the rear entrance door! Our fates were sealed! It really would be a homecoming for us all. I was smiling from ear to ear! Who wouldn't be!

My step got a little lighter as I walked to the front of The Wonder Bar to await the arrival of Mr Hoover. I texted him immediately.

While I was waiting for Geoff, this woman had come out of the bar. She was around my age and she was sporting a Ramones t-shirt. We caught eyes, and she smiled. She said, 'You know who's supposed to be 'showing up' tonight? I said, 'Yes. I just saw him walk in the back door, wearing a black and while checked shirt.' She looked at me and didn't know whether to believe me or not. 'You better not be messing with me!' she retorted. 'Me? Messing with you? No way! He IS here. Just wait and see.' With that she walked down the block a little. As she walked back, she hesitated, looked at me and said, '… you better not!' 'Or what? Your Uncle Vito is coming to visit me?' I replied in my best *Goodfellas* accent. She smiled, laughed and disappeared in the bar door again. Shortly after Geoff shows up and we're inside.

We missed the first opening band and were just in time for the second - The Billy Walton Band. Billy is also part of the other historic Asbury band, The Asbury Jukes. Though I had seen him before with the Jukes, it was a treat to see him do his solo act. That man can play! Billy and band did a really rollicking set.

In between the time he went off and Joe & Co went on, Ramones t-shirt lady and I crossed paths. I just looked at her and smiled - 'not long now!' And I was right. It wasn't long. Joe & Co took the stage shortly after 10pm. They only did one of their own original songs 'Never Enough Time' before he introduced 'the real governor of New Jersey' and Bruce strapped on his trusty beat up yellow Telecaster and took the stage - stage right of Joe. And before you knew it they tore into 'Adam Raised A Cain'. Ready! Set! Go-go-go! The crowd went nuts.

I only took a few photos during 'Adam Raised a Cain' and a very brief video. Way too many people with their phones in the air doing the same thing. Kind of annoying - but this is the modern world. I was done with that! I just wanted to enjoy the sauna and the show. Sadly, the sound was atrocious for the audience and apparently for the band via their monitors. Bruce had called out the sound guy to tweak his monitor mix and turn down his guitar several times during the night. But in spite of all that (and bleeding ears) the show was amazing! How could it not be? We had Bruce and the Pittsburgh Posse trading and playing songs like they had been doing this for years. Well - they have! They were tight! Trading vocals. Trading riffs. Having one hell of a good time! And Bruce was being Bruce. Telling stories to introduce songs. The story he told of he and Miami Steve Van Zandt living in a small Asbury Park apartment, back in the day, was one I had never heard before, and a great intro to 'Frankie Fell In Love'. 'A true story', so said Bruce.

The night was what dreams are made of. Though it might sound hyperbolic - it surely is not. The combination of Bruce and the Houserockers was tight, energetic and a force to be reckoned with. Though I'm still not in the best of health, I stood through two plus hours of amazing music from Bruce and company. Finally, towards the end of the night, Geoff and I had to take a break out onto the 5th Ave patio with all the smokers and all the fans outside of the patio fence watching the entire show through The Wonder Bar windows. Bruce had been talking to those fans on the street throughout the show, even dedicating a song to them. Geoff and I sat out on the patio, cooling down and resting our aching feet, as Bruce started 'Because the Night' and came back in somewhere before the end of 'Promised Land'. We watched the remainder of the show from the side of the bar, which was a bit less packed than in front of the stage, where we had been most of the night.

The show was amazing! How could it not be! Joe, Eddie Manion blowing the hell out of that sax all night, the Houserockers and Bruce just letting loose in a small bar in this rising beach town. As they like to say here - 'Only in Asbury Park!' Thanks again to my long-time friend and show companion - Geoff Hoover. As always, my friend, a blast. Another memorable Bruce show - that makes three. Only in Asbury Park!

2016 The River Tour 2016/Summer '17 tour was in support of Springsteen's 2015 *The Ties That Bind: The River Collection* box set and in celebration of the 35th anniversary of Springsteen's 1980 album, *The River.* The River Tour 2016 ended in September 2016, however dates in 2017 were added using the same promotional image from the original legs, and the tour was subsequently billed as Summer '17.

The River tour was the top-grossing worldwide tour of 2016 pulling in $268.3 million globally and was the highest grossing tour since 2014 for any artist topping Taylor Swift's 2015 tour, which grossed $250.1 million. Springsteen and the E Street Band also hold the biggest Boxscore for 2016, with the May 27 and 29 shows at Dublin's Croke Park taking in $19,228,100 from a 160,188 attendance for two sell-out shows.

CONSOL ENERGY CENTER

16 JANUARY 2016 PITTSBURGH, PENNSYLVANIA

I WAS THERE: JIM CURRY

It was Christmas of 2015 and the snow was gently falling outside the window of my New Jersey home. My wife Kim and I had just finished opening gifts and while I was happy we were together I felt as if something was missing, until my wife gave me a mischievous smile.

She pulled out a present from behind her back and I gazed at the Santa Clause wrapping paper looking back at me, thinking to myself, 'Could this be it'? I slowly tore away at the wrapping paper and nearly fainted at what was inside. Two tickets for the first show of The River tour 2016 gazed a hole in my head along with two plane tickets to Pittsburgh. Man, was I excited.

I counted down the days to the 15th marking an 'x' on my calendar with each passing day. Finally, the day came where Kim and I made our way to Newark Airport to our one o'clock United flight to Pittsburgh. We took in the sight of this beautiful city as we landed. The cab driver then greeted us and stowed away our luggage in the trunk. We gapped out the windows, as the cab driver went on about common tourist attractions of the city, but I turned my gaze from the window when he mentioned how celebs liked to stay at the Fairmont Pittsburgh Hotel. I made a mental note of that information as we reached our home for the next two days. We checked into the Omni William Penn Hotel, and then took a stroll down to where the show was being held. Located on 5th Avenue stood the Consol Energy Center, home to the Pittsburgh Penguins and more importantly to me, the first show of Bruce Springsteen and the E Street Band's River tour.

With jet-lag getting to us, Kim and I decided to grab some food and drinks at a hotel that was conveniently located a couple blocks away from the William Penn. We sat down at the bar/restaurant located in the lobby and as I sipped my gin and tonic, I nearly spit it out when I spotted Gary Talent and other members of the E Street Band hugging the elevator wall. My mind raced back to the conversation with the cab driver as I realized we were sat in the Fairmont Hotel. As I watched other fans hurry to the band and ask for pictures and autographs, I was tapped on the shoulder and turned around to see my now good friend Gerry, whom I had met at a previous Bruce show years and years before. He invited us to join him and his friend at their table and as we caught up with each other I watched Gerry's eyes widen. I followed his gaze and was stunned to see at the end of it was Bruce, accompanied by Patti. I watched as others approached him and when I realized that he agreed to take pictures with the other fans, Gerry and I decided that now was our chance. We walked over to Bruce in awe and politely asked if we could get a picture with him. I thanked him and then told him my wife and I flew out and how we were excited for the show tomorrow. He smiled at me and made his way with Patti to the elevator doors. After that encounter you could say that I was on a 'Bruce High.'

Saturday 16th approached. Our friends and die-hard Bruce fans Charles and Kathy arrived from Canada and joined us for a late breakfast at our hotel. We all arrived in Pittsburgh with General Admission tickets and around noon had gotten online for our wristbands, just praying that a close number would get picked for the lottery. Around five of us and a couple of hundred people gathered around for the announcement of the lottery. The least we could say was we were disappointed with the pick but exhilarated to be here. As we stood waiting to head in, I heard a low chant grow louder and louder. Fans angered with how unorganized the venue had prepared loudly screamed, 'Let us in.'

All my years going to Bruce shows I had never seen a near riot break out. Fans began to storm the venue entrance and security had no choice but to finally bend to their will. Charles, Kathy, Kim, and I made our way to the pit and were pleasantly surprised when we were only five rows of people back from the divider on Stevie's side of the stage. Now all we could do was wait impatiently.

The lights flickered off and the intro to 'Meet Me in the City' (an outtake on *The River Collection* box-set) began to play followed by the entire *River* album. After 'Wreck on the Highway', the 21st song of the set, he proceeded to play 'Badlands', 'Wrecking Ball', 'Backstreets', 'Because the Night', 'Brilliant Disguise,' 'The Rising', 'Thunder Road', and to my surprise David Bowie's 'Rebel Rebel.' A tribute to a great man who unfortunately had just passed on six days before. I have to say that cover was my absolute favourite song of the night. My favourite band was performing a song written by a great rocker. I think everyone there was absolutely amazed and heartfelt. They then played 'Bobby Jean', 'Dancing in the Dark', 'Born to Run', 'Rosalita', and the last song of the night, 'Shout.'

I was absolutely blown away by Bruce's energy and showmanship. This show had brought me back to 37 years ago when I saw my first Bruce show in my home state of New Jersey. I was on a 'Bruce High' back in 1981 and you better believe I was on a 'Bruce High' at the first show of The River tour in Pittsburgh too.

I WAS THERE: JESSE JACKSON

My first Bruce show was on The Rising tour. While I had been a fan of his music, I had never had a chance to see him perform live for various reasons. They say there are two kinds of people, those who go to a Springsteen show and say, 'Wow, that was long' and others who say, 'Oh my goodness, I want to sell everything I own and go to every show I can.' I was the second. My passion - obsession for the man, the band and the music started growing and becoming a major part of my life.

In mid-January 2016 I attended the first show of The River tour in Pittsburgh. A great deal had happened since the last time I saw

Jesse Jackson runs
the podcast Set Lusting Bruce

the band perform. I had been laid off from a job where I spent my last 10 years. It took me nine long months to find a new job. It had been a stressful time. However, I was hired by a wonderful company and started working with them in December 2015. My lovely bride Linda helped me arranged flights, so I could go to the show and not miss work. Since the last time I'd seen him, I had started my Springsteen-themed podcast, *Set Lusting Bruce*. I was excited about meeting other fans and capturing thoughts that I could share on the podcast.

Before the show, I met several fans, talked Bruce, talked life and tried to guess what David Bowie song he would play (he passed away a few days before). I made my way into the arena, found my seat and found myself in the happiest place on earth, a Bruce Springsteen concert. As the sounds of 'Meet Me in the City' started, I felt a sense of joy and contentment. After a tough year filled with challenges, heartbreak and stress, I was at peace. My family had helped me through the year, but one constant companion was Bruce and his music.

The show was wonderful. I loved hearing 'Independence Day',' Out in the Street', 'Drive all Night' and other classics from *The River*. The other songs were amazing, and the show was special as it always is when you are seeing the E Street Band. The band had a sense of joy about them as they were playing, and I got the feeling that they were very aware that the road ahead of them is shorter than the road behind them. This awareness of their mortality was not morbid. It added to the energy and joy of the music.

Seeing Bruce Springsteen and the E Street Band is always a special event. But this night it was a little something more. It was my chance to say, yes, I'm alive, I'm still standing, and I've survived the wrecking ball of life.

MADISON SQUARE GARDEN

27 JANUARY 2016 NEW YORK CITY

I WAS THERE: AUDREY HUNN

Bruce and I are going on almost 40 years together. (Not sure he knows that, but...) I've been blessed with many opportunities to meet him as well as be transformed at an E Street Band show. I was at The Carousel show with only 60 others (including the band) in Asbury Park, December 7, 2010, and after 20 years of trying finally got my air-brushed jean-jacket signed by Bruce and the band. I had Jake Clemons at my home to do a living-room show in May 2015. I felt in my bones, weeks prior, that on that warm July evening in 2015 Bruce would join his friend Joe Grushecky on stage at The Wonder Bar. What I didn't realize was that he'd do a two-hour gig and I'd be front and center. In September 2016 I was No.1 in the door at Barnes and Noble, Freehold, NJ for Bruce's first book signing. I'm still finding pictures from that day online that I never saw. I run the largest private Springsteen *Facebook* group (*Calling All Bruce Springsteen Fans*), with more than 6,500 members. I've DJ'd on E Street Radio, worked backstage at the Philadelphia Obama rally in 2008, and so much more. I have stories & pictures that go along with all of this, and then some.

I've been blessed on this road down E Street. Well over 200 shows and in the last 15 or 16 years, more times than not, it's been elbows on the stage in the pit. All of this would have been more than enough to fill a lifetime of memories, but on January 27, 2016, I was finally able to cross No.1 off of my bucket list. It was 'my' turn to take that leap of faith and join Bruce on stage at Madison Square Garden to dance. My sign read, 'Bruce, I am 52 days clean and sober and ready to come out of the dark to dance!' It wasn't fancy. It didn't light up. It was honest and real. I think he was impressed with the courage it took to put it out there in front of tens of thousands of fans. While dancing he told me how proud he was of me and that I'd better keep it up. I have! I responded that of course I would, after all he was my higher power. He liked that. I lived a dream and I was clean and sober and remember every second.

TIMES UNION CENTER

8 FEBRUARY 2016 ALBANY, NEW YORK

I WAS THERE: RON JACOBS

A tidal wave of rock. A tsunami of sound. Metaphors seem inadequate to describe the rock'n'roll assault Bruce Springsteen and the E Street Band led off their 2016 Albany show with. Beginning with an outtake from the original album, 'Meet Me in the City,' Bruce and his band barely stopped playing for the next 20 minutes. Even when there was a pause it was just enough for Bruce to trade guitars with a crew-member. The River tour featured every song from that 1980 album plus another 90 minutes or so of more classic rock tunes. As he has at every stop on the tour, Bruce prefaced the show by telling the audience what was on his mind when he wrote the songs on *The River* - life changes, wondering what made people make and drop the commitments they made to each other, and the emotions we experience in those relationships between parent and child, amongst siblings and between lovers and friends. Then the band ripped into the afore-mentioned torrent of rock.

After this energetic romp, Springsteen quietened down the crowd with one of his most heart-wrenching ballads, 'Independence Day.' This song unleashes such a sense of loss and matter-of-fact regret, I still find it hard to listen to without tears welling.

I got into Albany, New York early Monday afternoon. The show was scheduled for the evening. My bus ride from Burlington, Vermont was uneventful. Very little snow was on most of the mountains the bus drove through. I had a couple of hours to kill before I could check into my room at the motel so decided to walk and ride buses around the city.

Albany is a classic US city. At one time economically stable with decent unionized jobs, it seems to now be at best divided between working people of fewer and fewer means and the moneyed class that feeds and feeds off the state and county bureaucracies located in the town. There are still office buildings housing union bureaucracies but organized labor is not the power it was when Albany was an industrial and shipping hub. From what I could tell, this means some residential parts of town feature blocks full of boarded up row houses and signs stating the properties are now owned by banks or a public private mortgage trust. Gentrification is probably close at hand. One expects the owners of these properties see dollar signs, not people. Other residential sections seem to be doing just fine. However, in every section of the city I rode or walked around in, I saw no supermarkets and very few bank branches. However, several large banks had buildings downtown. Everywhere else, the only ATMs were those little portable ones. This means fee-less cash withdrawals are not convenient for most residents.

I've always thought the Bruce Springsteen album *The River* was one of his most depressing. Although the songs are mostly about personal relationships, they echo with heartbreak and sadness. When the album came out in 1980 I found it emotionally difficult to listen to, in part because it was about such relationships.

Springsteen started chronicling this aspect of life on his previous album *Darkness on the Edge of Town*. Many of the songs thereon were also about the compromises Jackson Browne sang in 'The Pretender' came with 'the resignation that living brings.' If one considers

Springsteen's work through this prism, virtually every album after *Born to Run* - which still held out for some hope for escape - includes songs about that resignation.

The River, though, is full of stories about events that happen to most people as they age no matter who they are. This is the album's beauty. Its songs spoke to my hard-working and already married brother and me, a hitchhiking rambler who worked only if absolutely necessary. We both related to the emotional content of songs like 'Independence Day' and 'The River.' Furthermore, the desire for freedom expressed in songs like 'Hungry Heart' ('*Got a wife and kids in Baltimore, Jack/I went out for a ride and never went back*') and 'Out in the Street' was present in our souls even as our actions in life and love determined our future. Albany has always seemed to me to be a town where lives like those in Springsteen's USA are lived. You know, working overtime lives, married and divorced loves, lives of frustration and of joy, sorrow and love.

Bruce and the band played for over three and a half hours. After finishing up with 'Wreck on the Highway,' the band took a quick breath and broke into the tune that leads off the album just prior to *The River*. 'Badlands,' is an anthem of survival from *Darkness on the Edge of Town*. Next up was 'Backstreets', a song about love, lust and boredom from *Born to Run*. The show continued in this fashion, with the band blasting out the hits, the crowd dancing and shouting, and Bruce all the time with a huge smile on his face. Every song's an anthem for the audience at a Springsteen show, so the crowd sings along, occasionally drowning out on-stage vocals.

Bruce was animated the entire show, working the crowd like Elvis and interacting with other band members, especially Stevie Van Zandt. Between Bruce and Stevie mugging at their shared microphone, Bruce sharing leads with Nils Lofgren, Max Weinberg mouthing the lyrics to every song while he played the drums and Bruce dancing with audience members, the show was truly a celebration. From the very first time I saw Bruce fall to his knees onstage at DAR Constitution Hall in March 1975 during a version of his romantic opus from *The Wild, the Innocent and The E Street Shuffle*,

'Incident on 57th Street,' I have always known Springsteen was a showman. This show proved to me he still is.

MODA CENTER

22 MARCH 2016 PORTLAND, OREGON

I WAS THERE: ROB GRIFFITHS

I am a long-time Springsteen fan, coming aboard with *Born to Run*, which was released when I was 11-years-old. While I own most of Springsteen's albums, I'd only seen him perform live three times prior to this night. But it was the memory of those performances that had us forking out $339.50 (plus the hassle/cost of finding a sitter for the kids) for two reasonably decent seats to The River tour stop in Portland.

If I have half Bruce's energy and fitness level when I'm 66-years-old, I'll be very happy. The show ran for three and a half hours, without an intermission, and barely slowed down at all during that time. Most songs transitioned directly from one to the next, with a quick guitar change the only interruption.

The show started promptly at 8pm, and as expected the first two hours were devoted to *The River*, complete and in order. This 1980 double-album contains many classics; my favourites from this night were the stark and beautiful 'Independence Day', a wonderful rendition of 'The River', and an incredibly high-energy take on 'Cadillac Ranch'.

As 'Wreck on the Highway' came to an end, so too did *The River* portion of the concert. After a half-minute or so of raucous applause, the band launched into what might be an encore at a regular show. But given this portion of the event lasted for one and a half hours; it was more like 'concert number two' than an encore.

And unlike *The River*, which has a mix of fast and slow songs, this second concert was 100% hard-and-fast rock'n'roll. Bruce and the band launched into 'Badlands', performed in a real kick-ass upbeat manner. From there, a guitar change and a 'one-two-three-four' led right into a harder-edged version of 'Lonesome Day'. And it just kept going - rocking strong song after song, even for some that had originally been slower-paced tunes.

For instance, the original version of 'Brilliant Disguise' is a moderately paced introspective look at one's partner in a relationship (written during Bruce's brief and unhappy marriage to Julianne Phillips). But that night, it was a fast-paced hard-rocking song, sung with his wife on many key parts. Different, but very cool.

Other classics we heard during the second concert included 'Thunder Road', 'Born to Run', 'Rosalita', 'Dancing in the Dark', and 'Tenth Avenue Freeze-Out'. During this song, which contains a Clarence Clemons-specific reference *('When the change was made uptown, and the Big Man joined the band')*, the screen showed a montage of Clarence images, a nice tribute to a lost band member. There were also images of Danny Federici.

After 12 back-to-back songs with nary a pause, the concert finished with a rousing rendition of The Isley Brothers' 'Shout', with multiple extended endings, as one might expect. But finally, it was over and time to head home. It was a great show, and well worth every dollar we spent on it.

AMERICAN AIRLINES CENTER

5 APRIL 2016 DALLAS, TEXAS

I WAS THERE: AUSTEN MASSEY

He played *The River* in its entirety, then all the hits after. I admittedly was unfamiliar with many of his well-known songs outside of the *Greatest Hits* and *Born in the U.S.A.* albums. But I discovered about 10 new songs that night, leading to me discovering about 20 more.

Just watching the genuine raw emotion of him performing was the best part. Also, they did a Clarence Clemons tribute. I was having a difficult semester in law school and remember just being there stayed with me for a couple of weeks then got me through the rest of the semester. I enjoyed weirding my classmates out wearing my concert t-shirt (because we're millenials and clueless about real music). He brought some kids up on the stage to sing along with him, then body-surfed. Not bad for someone in his 60s.

ETIHAD STADIUM

25 MAY 2016 MANCHESTER, UK

I WAS THERE: PAUL MCCLELLAND

I travelled down early doors, as I like to know I am there and sorted and parked up with an easy to get away route. It rained all the way down, Bruce commenting during the show, 'It must be Manchester as it's raining!'

I had seen posters for the concert on Facebook and was hoping to score one so walked over to the stadium in the rain and went to the first stall. They were £20 so no change required but they were still setting up and wouldn't sell me one, so while I was walking around looking for other stalls I saw someone dressed as Santa Claus – I didn't think much of it. It could be a stag-do or fancy-dress party making a day of it.

I got on the pitch and found a suitable spot and all this time I was getting wetter and wetter, despite the plastic poncho I was wearing. I started to question my sanity – it was so cold and wet. But I shouldn't have. As the band came on and played the opening notes to 'Atlantic City' I could feel the hairs on my arms and neck starting to tingle – an amazing feeling that I've not experienced before at a concert.

As the gig progressed, Bruce noticed Santa Claus and started to talk to him, eventually getting him on stage, asking why he was there and not in colder climes. Then he turned to the band and said, 'Are we doing this?' Then the song you would always love to hear live but never thought you would, given the time of year, and they launched into 'Santa Claus Is Coming to Town', with everyone singing along.

CROKE PARK

27 & 29 MAY 2016 DUBLIN, IRELAND

I WAS THERE: ROBERTO DI FONZO

Some time ago, I read a post by Ermanno Labianca about amongst other things the relationship between fathers and children, about the fears that we dads have and the difficulties we encounter as our children grow up, and how music (or even just one song) can offer you a sense of protection and make you feel more alive.

Reading that post reminded me of a scene with these two men I witnessed during a Bruce Springsteen concert in Dublin in May 2016, during The River tour.

We were packed in so tightly, as you are at times in concerts like that, where you find the people who were in front of you before are now behind you, and then they're next to you, and you catch each other's eye, and you smile. They were, as far as I could make out,

Roberto Di Fonzo with Raffaella (behind him) one of his best friends who passed away suddenly in October 2017

father and son (they looked so much alike).

Throughout the concert they stood close, their arms around one another as they sang. When the music got really powerful they were both jumping (well, maybe the Dad a bit less) along with all 80,000 of us, beer in hand like all the Irish there (and quite a few Italians too).

But when the harmonica signalled the start of 'Thunder Road', as I turned to my right I saw them embracing harder than ever, and when Bruce started to sing 'The screen door slams' I saw the Dad in his son's arms openly weeping. As the song played out they stayed like that – the father's tears and his son holding and comforting him. An unforgettable scene, beautiful and moving. I wonder what that song meant for that man and his son? Were they thinking of their wife and mother? Perhaps their love for her? And where was that woman now?

Or maybe it was for another son and brother who loved that particular song but who wasn't with them? And where was he now? Or what if the young guy was on the point of leaving for a long time and that concert was their way of saying goodbye? Or maybe he'd just come back and 'Thunder Road' was the song they'd vowed to listen to together after years apart? I don't know – I never will.

What I do know is that halfway through the song amongst 80,000 voices singing as one, I embraced my wife, thought about my own kids, glanced at my friends and I was moved.

As the song finished I caught his eye, wet with tears. We looked at one another for a second and then, like two old team-mates we high-fived as I yelled out to him, 'Good luck!'

I WAS THERE: JENNY FULTON

When a show starts with 'Darkness on the Edge of Town' and 'Badlands' you know it's going to be a good night. 80,000 people crammed into Croke Park, Dublin and for nearly four hours, we were one loud, strong beating heart.

I'd always wanted to see Bruce in Dublin. I think it's his Irish connection. It looks like he's at home there and having a great time. I travelled from Australia to Duncan's place in Edinburgh and we planned to see four European shows that trip. The anticipation leading up to the day in Dublin was debilitating. I tried to calm my excitement by painting a sign asking Bruce to come back to Australia - 'Bruce Springsteen Australia wants you' with lots of pictures of Aussie icons. By the time I was finished, it looked more like a product of intense therapy than a regular concert request. I had a little piece of cardboard left over so quickly painted, 'Can I jig with Jake' on it and added a cartoon of an Irish dancer doing a jig. I'll never hold that up, I thought. I'd never wanted to share my bad dancing with anyone on a stage, let alone Bruce or Jake.

Jenny Fulton (in the well-worn grey Springsteen hoodie) on stage with Bruce and other fans (Photo credit Anjali Ram)

Three days of roll-call and we had pretty good numbers on the night, getting us front-row, in front of Patti. Our pit neighbour was a great Irish girl called Bronagh. The night couldn't have been better. Bruce came out of the gates that night with a dream set-list backed up by song requests to die for and a version of 'Back In Your Arms' that still haunts me to this day. The encore started with 'Jungleland' and by then my euphoria was at 'extreme danger' levels. 'Born to Run' and then 'Dancing in the Dark'. Before I knew it, I was holding up my 'Jig with Jake' sign and singing and dancing madly.

After this it all becomes a bit of a blur. Bruce seemed to be heading for me. He picked me out and then was pulling me up on stage before security could get there to help. I think I hugged him and then ran up on stage and headed to Jake. I totally forgot where I was and was having a great time until I looked out at the crowd…. 80,000 faces looking back – I wish I'd washed my hair or worn better jeans that didn't feel like they were falling down. And what am I doing with my arms? Is this even dancing? What's the equivalent of 'Dad dancing' for women? Because I think that's what I'm doing. Just look at Jake, look at Jake and don't take your eyes off him. Sure, he'll think you're a mad woman, but it's your only hope of surviving this experience. Suddenly out of the corner of my eye I see Bruce madly gesturing to come over to him. So off I went, there's no turning back now. Some very pathetic air guitar followed, but by the look of the video, I started to forget where I was again and have fun.

Then came the moment I'd dreamed about. A kiss and a hug and the chance to tell Bruce in person how much his music means to me and how much I love the E Street Band. Of course, none of that would come out of my mouth. All I could say was 'Thank you, thank you, thank you.' That was enough… for now.

That was just one of my amazing nights with Bruce Springsteen and the E Street Band. Since 2014 I've been travelling all over the world to see them. This has become my life. I've learnt to make it happen somehow. Work is no longer number one and they seem to be coping with it. When I say I'm going to see Bruce, they laugh and let me go. My 50th time was at *Springsteen on Broadway* in January. A fitting show to bring up that milestone. Not many shows compared to most, but not bad for an Aussie. I've learnt it's not about the numbers though, it's about the feeling the music gives you and how you can hold on to that feeling when life gets shitty and there's not much to believe in. Whether you've seen him once or 300 times, you always have that feeling to hold on to. It's his gift, his magic and we are so lucky to have found him in all this madness of life. Thank you, Bruce, for your genius, your humanity and your outstanding ability to share it with all of us.

I WAS THERE: GEMMA BROWN

I went to see Bruce in May 2016 at Croke Park, Dublin with three good friends who were not Springsteen fans but agreed to go with me, as I'm most definitely his greatest fan. We queued for six hours in total, so we could get into the 'golden circle'. And it was worth every second. I met some great people and laughed all day in the sunshine.

The doll you see in the picture is one I made and waved at him when he walked past. He chuckled mid-way through 'Out on the Street', then asked for it, so I threw it. He then danced with it up on stage and kept it. That really was the highlight of our day. We'd carried that inflatable doll around from early morning and managed to keep it alive, and it clearly impressed him.

Gemma Brown and her inflatable Bruce

Best concert I've ever been to, for value for money and atmosphere. Hope to see him again before he calls it a day.

RICOH ARENA

3 JUNE 2016 COVENTRY, UK

I WAS THERE: NICK BARBER

I bought a ticket to see him in Coventry on The River anniversary tour - got a number for the pit and queued all day. The stadium security marched us around the ground and held us in a waiting area for an hour or so, then we were allowed into the pit. At no point did anyone check our tickets or bags and I walked right in with a super-zoom camera that allowed me to get some great shots.

I WAS THERE: GRAHAM BATTY

Amazing set of over 30 songs, each as good as the last. Highlights were stunning versions of 'Born to Run' and 'Born in the U.S.A.' And when you thought this couldn't get any better he took it up another level with 'Seven Nights To Rock', 'Tenth Avenue Freeze-Out', 'Dancing In The Dark', and a brilliant version of The Isley Brothers' 'Shout.'

Another highlight was when Bruce lifted nine-year-old Haydn Craven, from Dinas Powys, Wales, on to the stage to help him sing 'Hungry Heart.' The young boy had a *Born in the U.S.A.* T-shirt on and was singing away at the top of his voice.

ULLEVI STADION

25 JUNE 2016 GOTHENBURG, SWEDEN

I WAS THERE: JIM WILKINSON

My last Bruce show to date was appropriately enough a retrospective River tour celebration, Bruce's four-hour midsummer show on a Saturday night in Gothenburg in 2016. I was with my wife Lesley, who I'd taken on a nervous, tentative date to see The Jam shortly after my first Springsteen show at Birmingham's NEC in 1981.In a complicated series of twists, we never had another date until 2002, never seeing each other for 20 years. But Bruce shows punctuated those intervening years with the regularity of bank holidays or birthdays in the diaries.

In 1985 I was at St James Park, Newcastle, unrecognisably modernised since. It's strange to imagine Little Steven wasn't in the band. He made a brief guest appearance as my then-fiancée and I sat on the hill at Roundhay Park, Leeds, on an idyllic Sunday afternoon.

By 1988 the fiancée had gone and when the Tunnel of Love tour rolled into Bramall Lane, Sheffield, I knew how love could hurt. The lyrics from the album rang as true as any before or since. I took my pal, Damian, a fledgling musician and songwriter who hadn't really 'got' Bruce by then ('I just don't understand why that riff never alters all through 'Born in the U.S.A.', he'd say, looking puzzled). He got him that night. From the moment the band walked on, paying one by one at the ticket booth, carrying balloons and the like, the first and only time the E Street Band made any concession to theatricality or stunting up their entrance, he was captivated.

I felt for the first time that real thrill I've had many times since of taking someone along to see The Boss and watch the enlightenment shine through on their faces. It's like seeing the Blackpool Illuminations switch-on, never mind a light-bulb. If he hadn't to that point decided to be a career musician, he did that afternoon and has made a decent living at it since, his cruise-ship sets always sprinkled with Bruce covers. He was one of the late Keith Emerson's last collaborators.

Four gigs in seven years as a member of the E Street Nation was a modest initial effort on a clerk's wages before the days of budget travel, but I was getting a taste for it - just as Bruce broke up the band.

By mid-1993 I'd actually seen the 'Other Band' more times than Clarence and co. Not that I regarded it a problem. Now in my early 30s, they were some of the happiest times. I began to realise that being a Bruce fan made you part of a community where friendships, fleeting and lasting, were to be made. I even sampled going abroad to see my hero for the first time.

The Badlands trip to the Bruce shows in Paris in late June 1992 came at a very low point personally but I was persuaded by my parents not to miss out altogether and lose the money I had forked out. And that proved pivotal in turning things around for me. A succession of disastrous *affaires du couer* left me depressed, dependent on drink and having committed career suicide repeatedly. I was booked on the coach to Paris on my own, a little shy and worried if I'd fit in or even be able to make conversation with 70-odd people I'd never met before. I came home feeling like a new man with phone numbers and addresses from new friends, promises to supply me with bootleg tapes and a renewed determination to sort my life and myself out.

The much-criticised *Human Touch/Lucky Town* albums and what one tourist in friendly discussion on the trip called, 'A poor man's E Street Band', may not have been to everyone's taste, but in Paris, Sheffield a year later and Milton Keynes, also in 1993, Bruce's words spoke directly to me.

It would be some years until his autobiography revealed he of all people suffered from bouts of depression, but I knew from the lyrics on those albums he had overcome demons just like the ones tearing me apart. I was in deep and profound depression too.

I could tell, too, from his exuberance on stage with his new friends that he was rejoicing in throwing off the dark shackles. There was hope. Performances of songs like 'Better Days,' 'Leap of Faith,' 'Living Proof' and 'Real World' are some of my happiest in-concert Bruce moments. Transformative almost.

I was with Badlands friends too in 1996 when I caught the sombre Ghost of Tom Joad tour in Manchester, Dublin and Belfast. By now I'd got my shit together a little, changed career and was working as a journalist.

May 1999 brought the Reunion tour, two nights in Manchester and one in Birmingham as the reformed E Street Band re-asserted its omnipotence, Nils and Steve now a permanent guitar duo.

In 2002, getting on a bit to be single, I'd found the girl I needed to be with - the same sweet red-headed teenager I'd taken to see The Jam in 1981. We met again by chance with a little help from Friends Reunited and though I'd made up my mind, there was an acid test we had to make sure about. Could she put up with a Bruce fanatic as a permanent partner? I went alone to Wembley Arena in 2002 as we were becoming close, but a May 2003 afternoon at Old Trafford Cricket Club confirmed she could.

She called a few days later and said: 'Do you want to go to New Jersey to see him in July?' I replied: 'Yes! And while we're there shall we get married?' Deal sealed.

The Giants Stadium gig on July 27th, two days after we married at City Hall, Manhattan, was our last night in the States. 'At last, a hot New Jersey night,' said Bruce, walking on, 'we've been waiting for one of these.'

It was the seventh in a run of seven straight dates (the band returned later that summer for four more). Funnily enough, we saw Roxy Music at Radio City the evening before – that connection again – and got a taxi in the late afternoon from our hotel in the Meadowlands to the stadium, clearly visible from our window across a couple of lanes of freeway.

It was a terrific show, my first as a married man, but just as it was coming up for ending, during an insanely long, 'Kitty's Back,' the heavens opened. In newly-wedded bliss sauntering on the sunny 'Jersey Boardwalk' walkway erected round the stadium before the concert, gate-crashing tailgate parties and chatting to all and sundry, we'd completely omitted to book or even think about transport back.

When we found the bus shelters, they were empty, all gone. The few taxi drivers around told us they were booked up and a reservation now with the traffic at standstill would entail hours of waiting. We were saturated, top to toe. After an hour or so someone took pity on us and gave us a ride back to the Hilton. It was one of the best nights ever.

We sat at the bar with Bruce fans from far-flung places and every five minutes or so another bedraggled pair of specimens would make it back and join us for a beer or warming brandy. Many, discovering we were newly married, generously ordered us champagne.

I told the crowd that at one time we seriously thought about walking over the freeway and field to the hotel. 'Good job you didn't,' said one guy, 'the alligators are keen on a bit of supper after dark!' It wasn't our last post-Bruce gig soaking.

In 2012 in Florence, 'Siete pronte? ... OK, here we go ... the frenzy in Firenze!' exclaimed Bruce on a sunny afternoon in Fiorentina FC's Artemio Franchi Stadium. This was an extraordinarily-special night as my daughter Olivia, born in 2004 and now eight, was with us. We'd missed bumping into Steve and Maureen Van Zandt by an hour at the Leaning Tower of Pisa 24 hours earlier.

We were, incredibly under the cover of the one bit of seated stand in an otherwise open-to-the elements stadium. The show was superb, the Apollo Soul Medley still a big feature, and when Bruce threw in a rare cover of Elvis' 'Burning Love' the weather was still fine.

But before darkness fell we could see ominous clouds rolling over the mountains and it rained so torrentially I'm astonished Serie A football has been played there in the six years since. Many fans rushed to the concourses for cover and many more, with nowhere to shelter, left. Unthinkable to diehards, but this was one serious mother of a storm that only dedicated fans would have been daft enough to ride out.

A couple of visits to the toilet and refreshment huts (I hate people making beer runs at gigs but made an exception on this occasion in the Italian heat) had already rendered Olivia and I so wet it hardly mattered any more.

Despite being fortunate enough to have seats among the 2,000 or so out of the rain, Olivia saw the remaining die-hards dancing on the soggy playing area, looked at me with that look only a daughter can throw, asking if we could join them. What kind of Dad refuses his daughter a request to dance? We trooped back out of our oasis of shelter once more and were soon sloshing across the field to 'Born in the U.S.A.', 'Tenth Avenue Freeze-Out,' 'Twist and Shout,' 'Dancing in the Dark, 'and 'Who'll Stop The Rain'. That was only the start.

The pair of us couldn't have been any wetter had we dived into the River Arno. When we returned to the seats my wife was bone-dry, but 10 minutes later as it dawned on us we had no transport back, she was as soaked as us. After a two-hour trek in biblical precipitation – every bar, cafe, restaurant and point of refuge closed at 10pm on Sunday in Italy, even when the E Street Band's in town - neither of our phones could ever be revived. We lost every picture. But what a night.

Most gigs at Springsteen venues in Manchester have been hit by rain too, but who cares. Even the most recent, magical midsummer night in Gothenburg in 2016 ended with a light shower. It had been the most idyllic day. One of my greatest memories is hearing Finnish tribute Little St Band playing in the park, at first thinking it was a dodgy bootleg airing, joining fans from all over the world in the fan-zone around them. Just one of the enchanted moments.

The Bruce who walked on at the Ullevi and sat at the piano to play 'The Promise' was a different man to the burning, confident rocker who walked on at the NEC 35 years earlier. Older, wiser, more reflective and a man I admire for his humanity, compassion, ability to educate and inspire far more than I was capable of appreciating at age 22 in 1981.

But as 'The Promise' ended and his band-mates took the stage one by one, it was that same unquenchable thrill, that tear-in-eye 'I'm actually here in the same space as the legend' sense of enthrallment and anticipation in the pit of the stomach and that deep connection with the words and music I felt looking at that ripped-off album listening to the *Born to Run* tape.

'Badlands' and the 3.99 hours which followed cemented every good feeling you've ever had about yourself, your loved ones and your fandom at a Springsteen concert. In 1993, a review in now-defunct fanzine *For True Rockers Only* described the E Street fans filing out of Milton Keynes Bowl as possibly having 'their very last great Saturday night.'

I'm so glad I was still lucky enough and healthy enough to be capable of enjoying another one to the full in the company of my soulmate, 23 years burning down the road. Nothing, not even growing old, can reduce a fan's passion for the legendary E Street Band. 'The older you get, the more it means....' Now who was it said that?

ACCORHOTELS ARENA

11 JULY 2016 PARIS, FRANCE

I WAS THERE: JACK WALTERS

I was 20 years old and on my own, travelling from a town near Bath to see Bruce Springsteen and the E Street Band in Paris as part of the 2016 River tour. That summer I saw them live at Manchester, Dublin (night two), London and finally Paris, my fifth time seeing Springsteen live and my first at an indoor arena (the only indoor arena show of that tour).

I queued from 9am, surrounded by French fans and the occasional traveller from afar. All day I quietly queued, counting the hours until I could finally see the greatest frontman and band of all time doing their magic right before my very eyes.

Eventually we reached a point where we were able to enter the arena, filled with adrenaline and excited nervousness, knowing all this effort was for this. The security guard tried to make small talk but soon realised I didn't speak French and my mind was on other matters. I was soon

running down the steps, fast as I could, realising I could be front row on the rail of the general admission section. I got a front row position on the middle left, but cameras were blocking my view. I went further left. It would be another hour and a half until Bruce walked on.

The house lights dimmed and then the person who all 13,000 of us had been waiting for walked on to a darkly-lit stage and slowly headed toward the piano, starting with a sublime piano solo version of 'Incident On 57th Street.' Next, the E Street

Band came out to a mighty roar and kicked into one of my favourite tracks from *Nebraska*, 'Reason to Believe.' It was a great rock/bluesy rendition, Springsteen performing powerful harmonica parts and standing at the front of the stage like a preacher warning us all about life's disappointments. From this point onwards, I knew this concert was not only a special concert for me but a special concert for the band as well. There was energy in the air that could only be conjured up by this then-66-year-old plus his loyal bar band.

He rattled through *The River* album, and hearing tracks like the punchy 'Jackson Cage', the sombre 'Independence Day', the heart-breaking 'Drive All Night' and exquisite 'Point Blank' was a beautiful experience. Other highlights came from one of Springsteen's greatest song 'Jungleland.' When Jake Clemons was performing the famous saxophone solo during the composition, I felt the presence of the late Clarence Clemons and Danny Federici. Springsteen also performed by himself with an acoustic guitar playing the bleak 'Nebraska', another highlight.

During 'Ramrod', the PA system and lighting failed, with no sound coming out of the speakers and the arena alarms going off, telling people to exit the building. Like the master Springsteen is, he turned what could have been an embarrassing moment into one which will be remembered as funny and genuine. He continued performing for a little longer around the pit, the band unamplified, almost like silent actors. Then Springsteen went back on stage signing autographs on signs for the next 20 minutes. When the power returned, he finished the song.

It became the greatest concert of all time for me when during, 'I'm A Rocker', Springsteen was on the walkway directly between the pit and the general admission section. I was front row on the rail. He started his journey from the other side and as he descended from the slightly-raised middle part of the walkway he noticed a sign held by a young female several rows behind me that said, 'My Dad Promised Me A Hug From The Boss.'

Springsteen decided he wanted that sign and to fulfil that promise, having to lean into the crowd to help the young girl out. I saw him coming my way and he was heading towards me. The next moment was one of the most spiritual, profound incidents that's ever happened to me. Bruce was in front of me and used a step attached to the rail I was leaning on. The most important artist of my life, the human being who deeply touched me on a personal, emotional and intellectual level, within touching distance. He was far higher than me as he leaned in. That was it, I was now holding and hugging my hero, resting my face on his stomach while embracing him. All this happened just under a couple of minutes but has and will continue to live far longer than the incident itself. If it was not for that girl with that sign, who did get pulled out and got her hug, I would not have had this transcendental experience.

He ended the concert with a beautiful solo acoustic 'Thunder Road'. I experienced something greatly significant that wonderful night. That's why there are so many dedicated fans out there going to his concerts, because Springsteen is able to create moments of bliss, wonder and hope within concerts like no other musician can.

CIRCUS MAXIMUS

16 JULY 2016 ROME, ITALY

I WAS THERE: PETER SNEDDON

I've been a Springsteen fan since 1984 after seeing Bruce pull Courteney Cox out of the crowd 'During the Dancing In The Dark' video. I've seen him in concert 27 times since and pretty much have a story to tell about most of the shows, but Rome 2016 is the show I'm going to focus on.

It's always been a wish of mine and gig buddy Davie to travel a little further afield to see Bruce. I told myself it would have to be somewhere special - where the uber-fans are, at a unique venue.

I'd watched documentaries about Ancient Rome's chariot racing track and thought, 'I'm going there one day', so to say I was excited would be an understatement when the tour was announced, and it turned out that the Circus Maximus would be the preferred venue for Bruce and the band in Italy.

A phone call to Dave was made, and he was all in. There's a little saying me and my gig buddies quote to one another before during and after Springsteen tours - 'I've paid the cost to see The Boss'. And it starts with getting hands on tickets. We can all identify with trying to navigate foreign ticket sites and how challenging they can be, but I was determined and overcame. I registered. All I had to do now was buy two tickets two weeks later.

The morning of the ticket sale came all too soon. I was thinking there was no way I'd get through, amid tens of thousands of crazy Italians jamming the sites. Being in deepest, darkest Scotland I had no chance. But I bagged two tickets and quickly booked flights from Edinburgh, an early-morning flight offering a full day to explore the wonders and delights of one of the finest, oldest cities in the world. Sleeping on a floor at Edinburgh Airport in your 40s isn't a fun experience, but 'You pay the cost to see The Boss.'

Peter Sneddon on the left with his friend Davie

On the day of the show, our bags safely booked into our cheap and cheerful hostel, we saw the sights. Not too many posters in and around the city but plenty of middle-aged guys and gals with past tour shirts. We found a wee restaurant, slightly off the tourist area, where much pasta and red wine was enjoyed. All the main tourist sights were visited and absolutely enjoyed by us, taking us to just an hour before show-time.

Viewing the massive outdoor venue for the first time, I was overwhelmed by its scale and surrounding beauty. Not to mention the history. The safety aspect left something to be desired, but thankfully I didn't hear of anyone getting injured.

Finding a piece of grass to stand on, off the verge, was at a premium, but a little space next to the Heineken tent did nicely. By then the light was fading fast, with the stage lights on, and the large screens. And a loud universal roar went up from the front of the crowd as musicians walked on. Checking the screens, I noticed several musicians taking their seats towards the rear and side of the stage with what looked like violins and other string instruments. An orchestra. Surely, Bruce wouldn't start with 'New York City Serenade'. Well, Roy Bittan started running his fingers along his ivories and it dawned on me that it was indeed the most amazing and greatest intro to any rock/pop song ever. I looked at crazy Davie and our jaws dropped, 10 minutes of sheer excellence following. I would have paid 90 euros for this song alone.

'Badlands' followed, then several request signs were dragged on to the stage, with 'Summertime Blues' chosen. What a belter. It rocked. Seven songs from *The River* followed, and my second standout of the evening was 'Tougher Than The Rest' from the *Tunnel of Love*, performed by Bruce and Patti Scialfa, sung with so much emotion and passion. It brought a little tear to my tartan-tinted eye.

'Drive all Night' followed, including many emotional twists and turns, only found when heard live. Stunning. And the remaining 11 songs were a greatest-hits tour de force, full of classics. One aspect of this show that surprised and pleased me was the quality and clarity of the sound. I'm sure I'm not the only fan to complain about the sound at stadium gigs. But Rome was an exception - every chord, word and call out was PERFECTO!

I've heard varying guesses as to the capacity that night - ranging from 50,000 to 120,000. Was it the best show I've ever seen? I'm not sure. I've seen Bruce more energetic and wild, years before, that defied comprehension. But this show certainly was special.

I WAS THERE: EFRAT CHOMSKI

One November evening I read that Bruce Springsteen, my long-time life-journey friend, was to hit the road again. And I thought to it just might be my dream come true year. I'm 43, and it's been 31 years since I first listened to him. Maybe, finally, I could allow myself - financially and family-wise - to go. I consulted with my husband and he thought it was definitely my time. I picked the date and place, bought two concert tickets through a friend who lives in Rome, and started the countdown. When the tickets arrived I couldn't hold back my tears.

We got to Rome two days before and the hotel we were staying at was next to the Coliseum and Circo Massimo. The next day we went walking to check it out. I joined a line with my husband to get numbers to get into the ring. We stood two hours. No more numbers were handed out. No ring for us. OK, we thought, and went for pizza.

The next day I woke up early. All very anxious. I felt the blood run so fast in my veins and the clock didn't move! Come 5 o'clock I couldn't wait and off we went. We got inside. It was really hot and we sat down on half-grass - mostly thorns and dirt ground - had some beer with the rest of the Italians and waited.

After the opening act, it was not so hot anymore. The sun was on its way down when I heard the piano of 'New York Serenade' and then saw him, on stage, as I have always dreamt but never thought could happen. I started crying and crying. All those times he put me out of my misery, walked me through growing up, studying, marrying, having children, working, living. All the moments of joy he has given me, the essence of them all was there at that moment. The next four hours were dreamy. I was completely within the music and my memories, stories, people whom those songs accompanied my whole life. I had a meeting with the man who with my family raised and built me, and it felt like coming home.

I would like to thank you for the opportunity to tell this story and to thank Bruce Springsteen for being such an important character-builder, who helped me raise awareness, be kind, have empathy, think and read, have a critical mind of my own, be interested in other people, places and cultures, learn English through his songs, and educate myself. Along with my family, I owe him a lot and thank him for what I have become.

I'm 45 this year, happily married, have two teenagers, work as a teacher, have a master's degree and still feel I learned more from a three-minute Bruce Springsteen record than I learned in school, still imagining the Magic Rat and thinking about 'Johnny 99'. I hope everybody can be lucky enough to have inspirations like that in their lives.

CITIZENS BANK PARK

7 & 9 SEPTEMBER 2016 PHILADELPHIA, PENNSYLVANIA

I WAS THERE: TONI KAISER

I live in Coopersburg Pennsylvania and found Bruce when I was 19, thanks to my sister. I first heard Bruce on the radio, singing 'Born to Run', and then my sister got me into his first two albums. The first I bought was *Born to Run*, and 'Thunder Road' became my favourite song.

My favourite concert was on September 7, 2016. It took two hours traveling both ways but was worth it. It was his longest concert ever in Philly. It was also my son Bobby Jean's and my cousin Maria's first Springsteen concert and they both became huge fans that night. Bobby Jean loved it and was up dancing. My favourite song that night was 'Incident on 57th Street.' It was beautiful the way he sang it. It brought tears to my eyes. I went a second time with my sister, Domenica.

I am chronically ill and have spent months in hospital listening to Bruce. I still do that, it helps me stay sane.

Toni Kaiser on the left and Maria Zampirri and son Zack Kaiser Grimaldi

I WAS THERE: MATTHEW AUCOIN

I was 19 at the time, and I've been a fan since 2008's Magic tour. Dad and I travelled all the way from Houston, TX to see this show. This was our 12th Springsteen concert together. After looking at the set-list from the first night, arguably the best set-list of all time, we were extremely excited. I made the sign 'Can a College Kid play No Surrender with you?' the night before, and to make it stand out I wrote down the chords, proving to Bruce I knew how to play it.

We arrived in Philly and checked in to our hotel, but there was little downtime - we had to get to the arena early for the wristband lottery procedure, to try and get close to the stage in the pit area. The staff hand out 1,500 wristbands, and at 5pm, a random number is selected. This is where things got interesting, and this next detail proved to be the most important factor of this entire experience. We arrived at the subway station and this group of teenage guys were throwing a football around. We asked which train took us to Citizens Bank Park, and they said to hop on with them because they were going too. We proceeded, but about 10 minutes later, we realized the subway was going in the opposite direction and had got on the wrong subway. We were delayed about 20 minutes.

We get to the arena, joining a very long line of eager fans looking to get a magic wristband. Dad and I were worried we wouldn't make the cut off. We stepped in line, me carrying my sign all the way from Houston, managing to keep it in perfect condition, waiting our turn. I earlier had the pleasure to meet Tom England, a fellow fan who was lucky enough to play on stage with Bruce singing 'Working On A Highway' earlier that year. He inspired me to create my sign, and I asked him for advice, keeping his words in mind. Once we got to the front of the line, we realized we were in luck. We had made the cut-off and were dealt wristband numbers 1306 and 1307.

When the clock struck 5pm, Dad, who prides himself on having something called 'Pat Luck', had a sneaking suspicion we were going to get in. Me on the other hand, I'm just laying low, reminding myself I was lucky to even be in this position, and if I'm one of the last 1,500 to go in, I'll still get a great spot. A man appeared on top of a ladder with a bucket of 1,500 numbers. He reached in, pulled out the number, put a megaphone to his lips, and called '1,221' Which meant Dad and I would be the 84th and 85th person in. Good old 'Pat Luck'.

Think about it, had we got on the correct subway, we would

Matthew Aucoin poses on stage playing Bruce's Sunburst Takamine guitar

have been dealt a number way before and would have been one of the last to enter. I'd like to give a shout-out to those boys at the station, who played a huge role in getting us on the wrong subway. God works in mysterious ways. That mishap was all part of His plan.

The show started at 8pm and I was blown away by opening song, 'New York City Serenade' and the string section that accompanied. Bruce was open to requests right from the get go, collecting and playing rare songs like, 'I'm Goin' Down', 'Loose Ends', 'From Small Things (Big Things One Day Come)'. The show was rocking.

Then came 'Rosalita', and towards the end, Springsteen, Little Steven, and Jake Clemons were directly to my left, close enough to where I could probably touch them. As Bruce cued the end of the song, I knew this was my moment. I grabbed my sign and threw it up at the exact time he turned his head. He hesitated and started reading it with a smirk. I knew right then this was it. It was win or go home, boom or bust, take it or leave it. He turned to Dad and asked, 'Can he play it?' I'm screaming 'Bruce, I can play it!' and Dad's yelling, 'He can play it!' He grabbed my sign and I climbed on stage.

Guitar tech Kevin Buell handed me his beautiful Sunburst Takamine guitar and pick, with the capo on the third fret ready to go. I fingered the D-chord that kicked off the song, gave it a strum,

and heard its beautiful sound. I'm thinking, 'Matthew, this is the one
and only time I am ever going to do this. Don't look like an idiot, stay
focused, perform the song, and when you leave this stage, don't have
any regrets.' Bruce counted in the band, and out came the basting
sound of Nils' guitar, along with Bruce's. I began playing and looked
out at 40,000-plus fans looking right back at me as the song went into
the first verse. Once the chorus hit, I stepped closer to the mic., but
didn't want to overstep a boundary. But Bruce motioned his hand
over to me to come closer and sing into the mic. I did so and out
came the first lyrics I've ever sung to a live audience, '*No retreat, baby
no surrender.*' Bruce followed with a big grin. The next verse kicked in,
and he seemed more confident with me up there. We started trading
off chunks of the verses.

I've watched Bruce do this song for years, so had also seen all the
motions and poses he likes to do. I found myself instinctually doing
exactly what Bruce was doing. In the film, on the big hit where
the band gets quiet, Bruce and I, looking like we've rehearsed it
hundreds of times, both flung our arms back on the up-strum and
struck the exact same pose. When I see the picture of him and I in
that pose, it almost seems surreal. I still find it hard to believe that's
me next to him, with his guitar, performing his song, at his concert,
in front of his audience.

Towards the end, when the band was still quiet, he generously
gave me the entire last verse. I sang, '*I wanna sleep beneath peaceful skies
in my lover's bed, with a wide-open country in Philly tonight* (instead of 'in
my eyes') *and these romantic dreams in my head ...*' At that moment Bruce
turned to Stevie before the final chorus, with the biggest smile on
his face. It's possible at that moment maybe he was having more fun
than I was, which I couldn't believe.

As the song ended, after more synchronized motions from him and
myself, I wanted to be respectful and not overstay my welcome. I had
watched some fans in the past tend to stay way longer than needed
and wanted to make sure I was respectful to Bruce, the band, and the
fans. I thanked him and the band, then promptly got off the stage.
However, I did have to run back for a quick selfie ... cause it's still a

once in a lifetime chance, right?

I was greeted by fans with so many compliments and supportive words and showered by fans wanting a picture afterwards. Feeling like a celebrity for the first and probably the only time in my life, I was gladly willing for them to take as many as they wanted. Along with that, local news stations contacted me in the days after. I even made it to national channels - to *The Today Show, Good Morning America*, and *World News Tonight*.

In the months after the experience, I was sent thousands of messages online from people around the world. Dad, however, was probably happier for me than everybody else combined, having watched the footage more than me.

I want to thank Bruce Springsteen for giving this Texas college kid a once in a lifetime opportunity to sing on stage with the greatest rock artist and band of all time, Dad for taking the time and sacrifice to bring me to Philadelphia for the show, and God for making it all happen. For the rest of my life, Philadelphia will always hold a special place in my heart.

BARNES AND NOBLE BOOKSTORE

26 SEPTEMBER 2016 FREEHOLD, NEW JERSEY

I WAS THERE: BRANDON THOMPSON

There I was outside a Barnes and Noble bookstore, about to meet Bruce Springsteen for the first time. After driving the hour or so up from Southern New Jersey to Freehold, we arrive. It's the usual wait - a couple hours in metal banisters that keep the line in form. But it wasn't too bad, with the sun tucked away behind the clouds and E Street Radio blaring next to us.

The line started finally moving, you could feel the excitement as we pushed forward. We made it inside to pre-buy the book then get in line to get our seven seconds of fame with The Boss.

We were able to see everyone else taking pictures, anxiously waiting our turn, winding in and out of the aisles. I made my way to the front to be greeted by a lot of people making sure everything was running smoothly. I hand my phone to the nice employee and ask her to take a burst-shot. She did thankfully. 'Next up,' I hear as I walk towards the small raised stage.

Brandon Thompson with Bruce at the Barnes and Noble bookstore

'As soon as the next person goes up, step up on stage and you'll be meeting Mr. Springsteen.' It just hit me hard - I'm meeting Bruce Springsteen. There he stands in his famous leather jacket and looks my way. As I approached, I decided I didn't want to talk his ear off, just a quick handshake and a 'thanks for everything.' He was very gracious and receiving to everyone I saw meet him, myself included. Even if it was for just a quick few seconds, it was all worth it. I did what I always wanted to do. Look the man in the eye, shake his hand, and simply say thank you. Thanks, Bruce.

FREE LIBRARY OF PHILADELPHIA

29 SEPTEMBER 2016 PENNSYLVANIA

I WAS THERE: MICHAEL CAVACINI

Let me tell you about Bruce's event at the Free Library of Philadelphia promoting his autobiography: *Born to Run*. Billed as a meet-and-greet, the idea was that you could shake Bruce's hand, say a few words to him and pose for a photo with 'The Boss.' An exciting proposition. The way I see it, you can buy an autographed book on eBay if you want it badly enough but can't buy a photo of yourself with Bruce Springsteen online. At $33, it was worth way more than they were charging. Unfortunately, tickets sold out in six minutes. The site crashed and when I refreshed, it said: 'This event is sold out.' Thankfully, the library straightened things out and provided me with a ticket.

It was scheduled to take place from 12 to 2 p.m., but Bruce showed up 90 minutes early for a similar event in Freehold earlier that week, so I knew to arrive early to ensure I wouldn't miss out. I figured 10am early enough. I was wrong. There were already hundreds of fans in line. The line wrapped around the block. By the time the doors opened and people started to file in, there were 1,200 fans waiting to meet their idol, many of us clutching umbrellas, trying to make sure the constant drizzle didn't ruin our hair or outfits. Who wants to look like a drowned rat in their photo with Bruce Springsteen?

I met and spoke with several fans, many of whom had seen Bruce live numerous times. It was great hearing their stories. As I inched closer, I pulled out my ticket and got my camera ready. Crossing the threshold of the library, an employee scanned my ticket and I was given a wristband. A table of autographed copies of Bruce's book was in front and I was handed one. We were led down a hallway to a wing of the library closed off specifically.

I entered the room and peered to my right, seeing Bruce in front of a banner emblazoned with the library logo. An employee took my umbrella, bag and jacket and another took my camera. I was told to stand on a black marker, next to the person about to meet Bruce. After a few seconds I approached 'The Boss,' shook his hand and said, 'Bruce, it's a pleasure to meet you.' He said, 'Thanks, it's great to meet you too!' I put my arm around him and we faced the photographer, who snapped the photo. I turned and shook his hand, saying, 'Thanks, Bruce. I really appreciate it. Have a great day!' He replied, 'Thanks, you too!' It was incredibly fast, but I got to meet and interact with an American icon, get my photo taken with him and leave with an autographed copy of his autobiography. It doesn't get much better than that.

2017

PERTH ARENA

25 JANUARY 2017 PERTH, AUSTRALIA

I WAS THERE: ANN MCDONALD

He opened with his acoustic guitar on a beautiful orchestra-fuelled version of 'New York City Serenade'. I've always been a huge fan of Nils Lofgren and he played a blinding guitar solo in 'Because the Night', which Bruce appeared to enjoy as much as I did.

We laughed at all the homemade signs littering the crowd – some requesting songs, others a dance, and we thought the funniest one was 'Springsteen 4 President', which is an interesting thought. Mid-show, he downed a beer presented to him by an audience member.

ENTERTAINMENT CENTRE

30 JANUARY 2017 ADELAIDE, AUSTRALIA

I WAS THERE: ALISON EDDY

I was lucky enough to be front row in the pit in Adelaide Australia and experienced one of the greatest nights of my life. Seeing Bruce live is a life-changing experience and to witness what he gives to his fans up close and personal is hard to put into words. He takes you on an emotional journey with him and by the end you feel like you have seen into this amazing man's soul. During 'Thunder Road' he held my hand for a line or two whilst he was singing and I got to look into the eyes of this incredible man. I was so overcome with emotion I mouthed that I loved him. When he stood back and kept singing I just thought I was so lucky to have that experience. But it wasn't over, he pulled his harmonica that he had been playing just a minute earlier from his pocket and placed it in my hand. I have a treasured keepsake from the night I experienced such an amazing moment that only Bruce can deliver. He understands his fans, he loves what he does and words can't describe the emotion of that night.

A week later I saw him in Brisbane and had a sign on Valentine's Day, 'Bobby Jean fills my heart.' It has always been my favourite Bruce song and had never seen it live. The final song of the night and he pointed to me at 'when you hear me sing your song.' I already had tears running down my face from the time those first notes started and to see him acknowledge what that song meant to me was something I can't put into words. He is one of the biggest rock stars in the world but when you see him live and you get to feel his genuine love for his fans, that is all stripped away. That's why we all connect with him and feel like we know him and love him.

AAMI PARK

7 FEBRUARY 2017 MELBOURNE, AUSTRALIA

I WAS THERE: TRICIA O'NEILL

Following on from my husband, Tim Mullin's recollections of a Bruce Springsteen show in Baltimore show for our family on 20 November 2009, I'm sorry to say our daughter, Cameron, died at the age of 16 on an exchange trip to Australia in 2011. So when we learned that Bruce was going to Australia six years later, I decided to go and pay tribute to her.

While unable to make the shows in Perth or Adelaide, in February 2017 my pilgrimage began. I

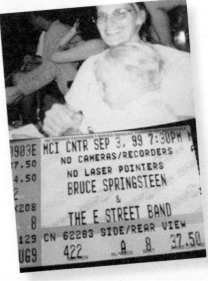

Tricia O'Neill with her daughter Cameron in Washington DC

attended all eight of the remaining Australian shows; driving solo up and down the eastern coast for two shows in Melbourne, two in Sydney, back down south to Hanging Rock, two more in Brisbane, and the final Australian show in the Hunter Valley.

All the shows were memorable, but the first at Sydney really tugs at my heart. Over there they still do multi-day roll calls (no lotteries), so after the show in Melbourne I drove through the night to Qudos Arena, Sydney, to get a good 'number' for the first show there. Then I found a hotel and resumed the familiar pattern: show up four times a day the next day and the day of the show to check in and preserve my place in the roll-call line for the pit. Along the way, I made a pink sign to mark my place as Cameron's Mom *('Got a wife and kids in Baltimore')* and honor Cameron as 'Hungry Heart' was her favourite song in 1999 at her first show and the sign she made that Bruce chose and displayed at what turned out to be her final show in November 2009. The photo in the center of my sign is from that show, propped against Bruce's microphone stand as he sang the song.

In Sydney that night, during 'My Love Will Not Let You Down', Bruce came over to where I was in the pit and asked, during a solo by an E Street Band member, 'Are you really from Baltimore?' I said yes. Here's what happened next. He started taking signs, with mine one of those chosen. OMG, I'm thinking - for me, Cameron and for all the special moments of shows (I've seen 49 to date, not counting Springsteen on Broadway). This was my magic moment – again, Cameron's 'Hungry Heart' connected with the Boss. Yet my incredible night wasn't over. After showing Stevie the sign, causing Stevie to smile, Bruce began the song with a huge shout of 'Who's from Bal-teeeee-more? Like millions of fans all over the world know, 'faith will be rewarded', and now I have my own special memory of how Cameron, her sign, and that moment in Baltimore still live on via a Sydney Springsteen show eight years and 9,000-plus miles away.

I WAS THERE: CATHY TORPY

I first saw Bruce live in Melbourne, 1985. I was 16, it was one of my first concerts, and I can honestly say, I'd never experienced anything like it. I was drawn in hook, line and sinker. Since then I've seen multiple Australian and New Zealand shows and also had the opportunity to see some US shows in 2016 with friends I met through Bruce. I've had so many highlights I could talk about, being lucky enough to meet Bruce, dance on stage with Bruce, host a Jake Clemons Living Room show at my house, and have multiple sign requests played. I would, however, like

to share one very special story, from Melbourne 2017.

Bruce seemed different during the Australian Summer Tour. He wasn't engaging as much with the crowd compared to how he did during Wrecking Ball and High Hopes. Pre-tour I wasn't aware this was going to be the case and wanted to make a sign, personalised and special to his devoted Australian fans. Bruce loves his dogs and many of my Bruce friends have dogs that we consider to be members of our family. How fun would it be to have pictures of our dogs on a sign and have it make the big screen for everyone to see?

I put my thinking cap on and decided the natural song choice was 'Promised Land.' My sign would read, 'The dogs of Oz howl, cos they understand, Promised Land.' I'd make it in the shape of Australia and have our dogs' photos floating around in balloons. Bright, colourful and fun. Melbourne was my first show of the tour, I got a great number and was right down the front of the pit.

Excitement was building as Bruce took to the stage, opening with a dig at Trump, 'Don't Hang Up', followed by 'American Land.' I briefly held the sign up a few times as he was finishing songs, but couldn't catch his eye. It was too big to hold up too long.

Then I heard the opening bars of 'Promised Land.' Argh! I'd put the sign under the stage, so close and yet so far! He started walking towards my group, stopped, leant forward and asked, 'Where's the dogs?' I fumbled around, managed to retrieve the sign and pass it to him with my shaking hand. He held it up and there was a huge cheer. Success! I was ecstatic, and his face beamed with happiness. It was perfect. He played the song and walked towards me again, finishing the song with his harmonica solo. Then he leant forward and handed it to me. A totally-unexpected gesture. I put my treasured gift straight in my pocket, where it would stay for the rest of the show. It was the only sign request he played that night. Within a couple of months, my old 'Brucehound' Monty passed away, as did two other 'Brucehounds' that graced our sign. It made it all the more special for us.

I was lucky enough to have friends capture some wonderful photos of the moment. Those along with my ticket and Bruce's harmonica make for a wonderful framed picture as a souvenir of this very special night. How many other artists manage to engage like Bruce does and even in a 40,000 stadium still manage to make it a personal experience for so many fans? Whether it's by inviting them onstage, playing song requests, crowd-surfing over their heads or just reaching out to hold their hand. I personally don't know of another. Thank you, Bruce, for being my reason to believe over so many of life's hard times.

QUDOS BANK ARENA

7 & 9 FEBRUARY 2017 SYDNEY, AUSTRALIA

I WAS THERE: MARTIN ROBBINS

Being a casual Bruce fan since I was a teenager in the Eighties, I thought it was about time to see him live. My dear friend Phil Gelormine (*Elvis*

World magazine) from New Jersey had been encouraging me to see The Boss for several years and promised it would change my life. That's a big promise, but Phil was right. Seeing Bruce Springsteen left an indelible mark on my musical soul. It wasn't just a concert. It was a glimpse into something we don't usually experience in our mundane day-to-day lives. It was the powerful force of music reaching out and leaving us all exhilarated and moved.

I just had to see the second Sydney show. If there were more I would have gone to them as well. Bruce closed his second Sydney show with a solo version of 'Thunder Road' that had me and many more in the audience moved to tears. As I walked out of the arena that night I felt ever so grateful to have been part of something so special. That's the power of music, and The Boss.

I WAS THERE: JESSICA BLOOM

My Dad Martin raised me on his music so it was huge deal for us to go together - just incredible - an unforgettable night. It was the first time I had seen Bruce Springsteen.

The selfie was an amazing piece of luck! I was at the concert with my Dad, who is a huge Boss fan, and I got up on the chair and started dancing during the encore ("Tenth Avenue Freeze Out"). Suddenly, he was singing to me, so I had to turn around and snap a picture! I didn't even look at the photo, just turned back around and kept dancing.

I posted the picture to Facebook and Instagram, and then a stranger from the Netherlands posted it to Reddit and...the rest is history!

The photo went viral and I ended up on British TV, US radio, and in newspapers around the world. The icing on the cake was going to Italy later that year and being greeted with "Hey, you're Selfie Girl - you were in la Republica!"

HANGING ROCK

11 FEBRUARY 2017 MELBOURNE, AUSTRALIA

I WAS THERE: KHAN ATKINSON

My best mate and I flew from Perth to Melbourne to go and Bruce at Hanging Rock. It was the best concert of our lives.

We had a sign made up by my fiancé, saying, 'I'm Goin' Down on someone tonight!' It's our favourite song. My friend Andy lifted me up with the sign in hand and it caught Stevie's eye. He told Bruce and I lifted Andy up on my shoulders so Bruce could see it. He cracked up laughing, yelling, 'Bring that sign up here! I'm inspired. Alright, you're next!' We sprinted through the mosh-pit to the front, where Andy handed it to Bruce. Then, after the next song, they played 'I'm Goin Down.' Unbelievable moment, unbelievable show!

I WAS THERE: MATTHEW FINN

Fans arrive dressed in a variety of tour T-shirts going back to the Seventies and Eighties, T-shirts that in many cases have got a bit tatty and tighter over the years. Many people bring large signs requesting songs from 1973 right through.

While the concert I saw at Hanging Rock included a few songs from *The River*, there were more tracks from the iconic *Born to Run* and *Born in the U.S.A.* and even three from *Greetings from Asbury Park,*

Matthew Finn with Jake Clemons

NJ. Bruce also took the stage by himself for a solo version of 'Promised Land', maybe a nod to this picturesque, country venue, surely a welcome change from all those stadia.

The E Street Band joined him and they leapt into 'American Land', a clear message to someone back in the US about the contribution that immigrants, including a New Jersey singer with Irish, Dutch and Italian ancestry, have made to building that nation.

Then, appropriately given the location, another 'land' song, 'Badlands' and the first guitar solo from Nils Lofgren, first sax solo from Jake Clemons, and Bruce off the stage and down in front of the mosh-pit as the crowd chanted over and over again.

After some River classics, during which Bruce and Steve Van Zandt admired the perfect rainbow that had formed behind the crowd, Springsteen introduced a tour first: 'Blinded by the Light', the first track on the very first album. He laughed that to this day it's still his only US No.1 single, when covered by Manfred Mann's Earth Band. He nailed the complicated lyrics, as did many in the crowd, and they aren't easy.

They also knew the opening verse of 'Hungry Heart', just as well seeing as Bruce didn't even bother to join in till the chorus.

'Can you feel the spirit?' he called to the crowd before 'Spirit in the

Night', also from that first album. By now the crowd, and the band, and Bruce, were certainly feeling the spirit and rocked and danced and sang for nearly two hours.

Including Bruce, there were just nine on stage, the brass section and backing vocalists that accompanied him on past tours Down Under not here this time. Neither were guitarist Tom Morello nor long-time band member, Patti Scialfa.

'Rosalita' wrapped up the first part of the show, Bruce suggesting to the crowd they stop the car on the way home and tell a kangaroo they've just seen 'the heart-stopping, pants-dropping, hard-rocking, booty-shaking, love-making, earth-quaking, viagra-taking, death-defying, legendary E Street Band'.

Bruce's one long dialogue (there's always a story) was about raising the cash to get his first guitar. It cost 18 dollars and he had to take on a lawn-mowing job for 50 cents an hour to get the money to buy it. He also claimed he'd, 'Never worked an honest day in my life. And it feels good!'

When he finally had enough money to buy that guitar he said he held it. then played it, 'And it sounded… terrible!' Since then, of course, he's learned how to make it talk. He's also learned how to perform live, highly-energetic concerts, night after night on long tours, capture crowds and attract an army of fans, many of whom travel vast distances to see him perform time and time again. There were fans at this concert going to all 14 shows in Australia and New Zealand, including a couple of friends who'd travelled from Yorkshire and will have notched up their 63rd and 100th Springsteen concerts by the tour's end in Auckland.

He may claim he's never done an honest day's work in his life, but Springsteen toils hard. The band returned almost immediately and stretched the show towards the three-hour mark with what's become a fairly consistent encore, with a hushed crowd during 'Jungleland', then audience members pulled up on stage for 'Dancing in the Dark', and all venue lights on full for 'Born to Run', the crowd fist-pumping, while there were photos of Clarence Clemons and Danny Federici on the large screens during 'Tenth Avenue Freeze-Out', and a cover of The Isley Brothers' 'Shout' had everyone dancing.

As the band finally left the stage, Bruce turned back to the crowd as if to suggest, 'One more?' and he ended a long night with a solo version of 'Thunder Road'.

ENTERTAINMENT CENTRE

14 FEBRUARY 2017 BRISBANE, AUSTRALIA

I WAS THERE: ADAM BROOKER

Mum and Dad got me a ticket for my birthday and I'd been waiting impatiently for the concert to happen. For the past four years, we'd been working on trying to tell Bruce how much he's helped me. The *Courier Mail* put me in the newspaper a couple of times, while Mum talked about me to people on the internet, and I finally finished my 'thank you' letter to Bruce.

Then, something amazing happened. Mum got an email from Mushroom Records to say Bruce and the band had invited us backstage before the concert. It was very exciting, knowing we would go backstage. We were told we might see the band, and maybe

Bruce. I crossed my fingers and toes.

When we got there, we were taken backstage to The E Street Lounge. Just when we got a drink and sat down, a lady called Barbara who works with Bruce came and got us and said she had a gift for me. We quickly followed her to a different room and she gave me a programme and a signed *Born to Run* book from Bruce. Then she said, 'Quick, quick' and we followed her again. We weren't sure where we were going but walked around a corner and Bruce

Adam Brooker enjoys his pre concert backstage tour (and behind the kit on previous page)

was standing there. I couldn't believe it. I didn't even have time to be nervous. He was right there!

We shook hands and I was able to say, 'Hi, Bruce', then I gave him a copy of some writing I had done. It was the lyrics to 'No Surrender'. We had photos taken and Bruce gave me a big hug.

I still couldn't believe what was happening. Then I met Kevin Buell (Springsteen's right-hand man) who I've watched in DVDs all the time. I was excited about that, because Kevin can catch guitars when Bruce throws them to him! Kevin took us backstage and showed us all Bruce's, Nils', Garry's, and Stevie's guitars. Then he let me hold Bruce's guitar - the one I love! I was so happy. Then he took me up on stage, right up to where Bruce stands, and asked the lighting people to shine a light on me, like they would on Bruce. Mum took photos, then he let me sit at Max's drum-kit and look at Jake and Soozi's instruments, and The Professor's beautiful piano.

Kevin also took us to the catering room. That was pretty cool. I'm always hungry and love buffets! But I was too overwhelmed to eat. Mum did let me have a Coke (my first ever) and Barbara told me that if Bruce ever drinks a soda, he only drinks Coke.

We talked to lots of people in the catering room and I saw Jake and

Stevie come in for dinner, which was cool. We didn't bother them, but Jake came over after he finished eating, said hello, and talked to us for a couple of minutes.

Just before the concert started, Max, who works with Bruce, asked if we'd like to move seats and watch the concert from stage-side instead. Of course, we said yes! He took us into the hall just before the band walked on stage. I was so nervous walking out in front of all the people who were in their chairs or standing in the pit. I wonder if Bruce and the band get nervous when they walk out and see all the people in the hall?

The concert started, and I loved watching Nils play guitar and go crazy during 'Youngstown' and 'Badlands'. He's so cool. We saw Kevin come on stage and give Bruce new guitars or catch the one he didn't need anymore – awesome! We saw Max go nuts on the drums, drumming so fast and so hard that a lot of the time his drumsticks were a blur! His arms must really ache.

The concert was so loud that my ears were still making noise even when we got in the car and it was quiet. I had so much fun. I want to thank my Mum for helping me have this experience and Bruce and the E Street Band, Barbara, Kevin, Max, Mushroom Records, and all my Bruce Buds who helped share my letter so Bruce would know how much he's helped me. This is the letter which made it all happen.

Dear Bruce,

My name is Adam Brooker, I am 13 years old and I live in Brisbane.

I have been listening to your music since I was about four years old (really, I've been listening since before I was born because my Mum and Dad went to one of your concerts when Mum was pregnant with me!) I listen to you every single day: sometimes on my iPad, sometimes on a CD or DVD, and now I can listen to your records because my Grandma and Pop gave me a record player for Christmas and Pop gave me his original Born in the U.S.A. album that he has had since 1984.

My Mum has been working hard to find a way to contact you to tell you how much you have helped me and lots of people on the Internet have helped her. She wrote this letter for me because I can't do it myself, but these are all my words. My Mum home-schools me now, so I don't have to go to school. School was hard because I couldn't talk properly and when I did talk most of the kids laughed at how I sounded and most of the kids and teachers couldn't understand what I was saying. But I couldn't talk at all until Mum taught me to sing along with your songs. I got to learn how to say words by singing to your music and even though I wish I could talk better I'm happy that my family understand me.

The reason I listen to your music is because it makes me feel so happy. Sometimes I don't feel very happy and I listen to your music because it helps me remember to be happy again.

The songs I really love changes every day. It's too hard to pick a favourite. When my brother, sister and I ask Mum which one of us is her favourite she says she loves us all the same and I feel the same about your songs. I love them all the same but for different reasons. But, if I had to pick my top three favourites they are 'No Surrender', 'Working on a Dream', and 'Bobby Jean'.

I love 'No Surrender' because when Mum explained it to me, I realised that it's not that important how well people do at school if they have good friends, music, and they know not to give up in life when things are hard.

I love 'Working on a Dream' because my family helps me every day to work on my dream to be able to read and write by myself and to be able to talk. Sometimes I get angry and annoyed because I can't do these things but you have taught me that if I keep working on it, I will get there. I'm 'working on a dream', though sometimes it feels so far away. I'm working on a dream, and I know it will be mine someday

And I love 'Bobby Jean' because the music makes me feel happy. I really like the way the guitars sound. Mostly I love Nils playing guitar on 'Youngstown' and Steve playing and singing on' Glory Days' because he makes me smile and laugh. My brother plays drums and bass so he loves Max and Garry. He finds everything he can about Max and has a photo of him with his hands in a bucket of icy water after a show that we all think is very cool.

Mum and Dad took me to my first concert in 2013 and I had so much fun. I couldn't believe that I got to see you and the E Street Band! We went again in 2014 and this time Mum and I sat close to the front. You played the whole The Wild, the Innocent & the E Street Shuffle album including one of my other favourite songs, 'Incident on 57th Street'. Dad and my brother and sister went too but they sat up the back and when we left we couldn't find them because Dad had to take my little sister to the ambulance tent. She had pulled a muscle in her chest from dancing so hard! She was OK though! This time, Mum and I are coming to the first Brisbane concert with my Pop (Mum's dad). It's his first ever Bruce concert even though he's been a fan of yours since before my Mum was even born! I know he is going to have so much fun.

So I wanted to say thank you because even though you don't know it, you and the E Street Band have helped me to learn how to talk and even more than that, your music has always made me very happy and taught me, and reminds me every day, that I should never give up. Because every day I am working on my dream and I know that even though it's hard I will get there eventually.

I know that you are very busy but I am wondering if you might have time to meet me in Brisbane? I would love to meet you so I can shake your hand and say thank you properly and I also have some of my writing practice (we use your song lyrics to help me learn to read and write) that I would love to give you.

Mum made a website about all of the stuff I don't really understand and she called it 'Bruce Raised An Adam' (just like your song 'Adam Raised A Cain'). And Mum let me make my own Bruce Facebook page that I write on and talk to other Bruce Buds called 365 Days of The Boss.

Love always,

Adam

AMI STADIUM

21 FEBRUARY 2017 CHRISTCHURCH, NEW ZEALAND

I WAS THERE: JEREMY PARKINSON

Bruce's first gig in Christchurch, and he played a number of songs from *The Rising*, which really suited the night. 'My City of Ruins' really suited the Christchurch earthquake, and went down a treat. Some people in the crowd had been to all the Australian shows too.

I WAS THERE: ANDREA KENNETT

I saw him on the first of two New Zealand dates, and he was amazing. The memories that stick with me most are how personal he made the concert. Christchurch has suffered some serious, deadly earthquakes in recent years, and he talked about that and how he and the band had visited sites around the city. He really cared, and I know it meant a lot to the people who were there. 'My Hometown' and 'My City of Ruins' took on whole new meanings. The memories will stay with me.

Springsteen on Broadway opened on October 12, 2017 at the Walter Kerr Theatre. The run was originally expected to close on November 26, 2017; (tickets for the initial run sold out within a day), but due to high demand additional dates were added, the run ending on June 30, 2018 and the show then extended again until December 15, 2018.

Springsteen stated; 'I wanted to do some shows that were as personal and as intimate as possible. I chose Broadway for this project because it has the beautiful old theaters, which seemed like the right setting for what I have in mind. In fact, with one or two exceptions, the 960 seats of the Walter Kerr Theatre is probably the smallest venue I've played in the last 40 years.'

Springsteen dedicated the opening show to Tom Petty, who had died the previous evening saying; 'Down here on E Street, we're devastated and heartbroken over the death of Tom Petty. Our hearts go out to his family and bandmates. I've always felt a deep kinship with his music. A great songwriter and performer, whenever we saw each other, it was like running into a long lost brother. Our world will be a sadder place without him.'

WALTER KERR THEATRE

23 DECEMBER 2017 NEW YORK CITY

I WAS THERE: JOHN C. GATTI JR

There was a dark cloud rising above Parsippany, New Jersey. My wife and I had many obstacles in our way, it was December 23, and the Christmas rush was upon us. Pregnancy had been causing my wife morning sickness, turned to afternoon sickness, along with evening sickness for good measure. This had been Christine's norm for the last six weeks. But, this was Bruce. Bruce! On Broadway! Nothing was going to stop us, not the weather, the Christmas rush, nor any sickness. And with that, we packed our bags and headed across the Hudson and straight into the storm.

After enduring the rain and finding the Walter Kerr Theater, (after getting wrong directions three times) we were inside and took our seats. My wife had no idea what to expect, but I had an idea as, like a kid on Christmas, I was way too excited and snuck a peak at the set-list. But this year Christmas came early. When the lights finally went down it felt like just the three of us, Christine, me, and… Bruuuuuuuce!

I knew the stories from the book, but quickly realized I didn't truly understand where he was coming from until I heard him speak the words. As I told my wife (and many others) this was an emotional show. There were several moments that brought tears to our eyes. That first moment was during 'My Hometown'. I always really liked this song, but it wasn't until I had a boy of my own that it really hit me. Many nights Johnny and I sit in the chair and rock and sing 'My Hometown' together. Right away my son came to mind, the connection was established, and emotions kicked in.

'My Father's House' is a song I have listened to, but never fully heard. Like most fans, I've read all of the stories and listen regularly to all the different songs Bruce sings about his father, but it wasn't until he told the story and then sang the song right after, that it hit me. The two-standout pieces were the story of him wanting to be close to his father, and because he couldn't connect emotionally he connected by wearing the clothes his father wore and dressing like the blue collar working man.

Although I'm a massive fan, the workingman persona always rang slightly hypocritical to me. But after hearing this story my feelings about that completely changed. By the end of the song when he finds out, 'No one by that name lives here anymore' I was flooded with thoughts of my wife's upbringing and how there would be no way my son would ever have to feel this way about me. It was equally difficult to listen to, and touching at the same time. Just as I know my wife felt every one of those lyrics during 'My Father's House', she also felt the feelings of joy, love, and mother-son relationship when Springsteen talked about his Mom and played 'The Wish'. The affection he has for his mother comes through not only in the lyrics, but also in the change of tone in his voice while telling their story.

As the journey continued he played our wedding song, our favourite song, and Bruce's best song, 'Thunder Road', a line-by-line tour de force. As he's said before, this is a song about taking a chance. Take a chance on me; take a chance on us, along with a real world-weariness that is unmatched in most people's clichéd choices for a wedding song. What more could I want from a song that will connect my wife and me for eternity?

A little later he played what quickly became my favourite version of 'The Promised Land' and towards the end a version of 'Dancing in the Dark', that could rival any performance he's ever put on. As you experience life and all its ups and downs, you really gain a deeper appreciation for this song. There are so many days where you have to say, 'There's a joke here somewhere and it's on me,' just to keep yourself from crying. In many ways, Bruce, and the guitar, and this theater, lent intensity to this song that I never felt before. I mean that in a literal sense. I could feel the guitar pulsating through my veins, and it seemed as if Bruce were singing to me, about me, about us.

It all ends with the story about the tree. I won't spoil it for those who haven't seen this. But it's a beautiful, spiritual story that stops you in your tracks, grounds you to your roots, and returns you to your faith. 'The Lord's Prayer' follows, a wonderful way to take this congregation to a rousing crescendo of a conclusion. And with that he played THE song that brought Bruce Springsteen and the rest of us to the dance... '*Tramps like us, baby we were Born to Run!*'

2018

WALTER KERR THEATRE

16 JANUARY 2018 NEW YORK CITY

I WAS THERE: KAREN BARTON

I'm finally coming out of my jet-lag and New York City flu fog, it's time for my review. To start, I have to say I deliberately stayed away from any form of social media related to Springsteen on Broadway. I needed to experience the show blind, to feel the excitement and anticipation of Bruce's magic. However, I did take one bit of advice with me - 'take tissues'. And I'm glad I listened.

I did enjoy seeing photos of all the Bruce Buds there before me

Karen Barton (in original 1981 t-shirt) and Gary

though, standing outside the Walter Kerr Theater. In fact, when I arrived it felt as though I was home. I had a sense of reassurance, warmth and peace. Funny how a building can do that to you.

Just after 8pm, Bruce was introduced, quite simply and matter of fact, no bells or whistles. He walked out on to the stage, said, 'Hi' and the show began.

The ultimate storyteller, through his lyrics, words and now his show, Bruce took us on his journey, one that included us, his fans. An emotional journey that touched on relationships, the sort that touch the heart and soul of all of us, the sort that last forever in life and in death. Bruce has a magical gift, he is magic, and needs to share his magic tricks. He is an actor, comic and performer, giving all and everything of himself. His generosity and selflessness exceed no boundaries; he is genuine, honest and authentic.

As Bruce delivers, we are all along for the ride, staying deathly silent when required and enthusiastically joining in during the audience participation. The sound is amazing, the acoustics as clear as glass. I will never forget the sound of Bruce's guitars as he manipulates and teases the tunes we all know so well, altered slightly but amazingly beautiful and emotional. Patti joins her husband on stage for a truly magical two-song interlude, before Bruce brings us to the end of his show in an explosive, heart-stopping, soul-driving, mind-blowing, awe-inspiring, gob-smacking, magical end. Two hours and 20 minutes of pure, unadulterated magic. Thank you, Bruce. I hope and wish all Bruce fans get to witness this amazing show.

WALTER KERR THEATRE

25 JANUARY 2018 NEW YORK CITY

I WAS THERE: PAUL BEARD

My wife Ei and myself are just about returning to some kind of normality. After a fantastic week in New York, we decided to spend an evening at home listening to the music of Bruce Springsteen while trying to remember and relive the many special moments we had both forgotten from our special night on Broadway. And by doing this it helped and underlined to us both the power Bruce has when standing in front of an audience, no matter how big or small it may be. He held us in the palm of his hand from the first DNA moment and 'Growin' Up' to the final chords of 'Born to Run', a truly inspiring evening.

All the new arrangements of songs and his guitar and piano playing were exemplary, his lightness of touch and fullness of sound on the piano during 'My Hometown' blew us away. It was time to leave home and move away, to be young and free... screen door slams, Mary's dress sways. At this moment it felt to me like you could have cut the air with a knife. Then I wiped a tear away.

The way he moved off mic. during 'Promised Land' and made it feel like he was singing to you in your own living room. His timing with all his stories was just perfect, he made us laugh and made us cry and for us every song was special and all had their place. We loved the moments shared with Patti on 'Tougher Than The Rest' and 'Brilliant Disguise', a very important part of the story.

Forty years burnin' down the road, the power of his words and slide guitar prowess achieved in 'Born in the U.S.A.' was so down and dirty, it made it feel it was the first time you'd ever heard it.

The new guitar arrangement of 'The Rising' with the poignant lighting helped create that special, ethereal atmosphere.

It was time to put on our dancin' shoes and for me the best version of 'Dancing in the Dark' I've ever heard, a song I felt had maybe passed its sell-by date and for me had lost its original meaning until this show. I loved the way he segued into one of my favourite all-time songs, 'Land of Hope and Dreams'. Perfect.

Bruce took us back to a place where the St Rose of Lima churchyard once stood and gave us his thoughts about loss and yet how we still remain surrounded by God. When Ei and I walked out at the end, we couldn't speak. We'd never felt like this before in 37 years attending Springsteen shows. We were absolutely blown away and really did see a magic trick on this night. One and one really does make three. Over in the blink of an eye, it was one of the best nights of our lives.

There were many more special moments, too many to mention them all, but three more stood out. First, stories relating to his father, Bruce telling us how after his father had died he had a dream where he was at a show sitting in an aisle seat. Bruce was sat next to him and said 'Dad, that guy up on stage is how I see you.' Heart-breaking but unconditional love.

Secondly, the special words he had for his Mom, so heartfelt. His story about his first guitar and first performance, aged eight, in his backyard, before giving us 'The Wish', the best Mom song ever written.

Finally, introducing 'Tenth Avenue Freezeout', mentioning all the band and the perfect tribute to his lost soul brother, Clarence

Clemons. As Bruce said, 'Losing Clarence was like losing the rain. See you in the next life, Big Man'.

One of the reasons all those years ago that intrigued me about the music of Bruce Springsteen, was not just his ability to write and perform a great song, but also to tell a story, even back then that related to your own life. This was a true rock'n'roll star who was really just the same as you. And he's still doing it 40 years later. It was like seeing your life pass by in front of you in the space of two-and-a-quarter-hours, watching and listening to Springsteen On Broadway.

When we first saw Bruce in 1981 at Wembley Arena, he opened with 'Born to Run', which totally blew us away. With him finishing with 'Born to Run' on this night, it was like we'd come full circle. Yes, here we are again. Does it get any better than this? I think it does. We're so glad we have tickets for another Springsteen on Broadway show, returning to NYC in May.

Keep the Fire Burnin'.

Bruce crowd
surfing during the
Australian tour
March 2013

BRUCE SPRINGSTEEN TOURS

01. Greetings From Asbury Park Tour (1972-73)
02. The Wild, the Innocent & The E Street Shuffle Tour (1973-74)
03. Born to Run Tours (1975-77), including Chicken Scratch Tour (1976) and Lawsuit Tour (1976-77) - 210 shows
04. Darkness Tour (1978) - 115 shows
05. River Tour (1980–81) - 140 shows
06. Born in the U.S.A. Tour – 156 shows (1984–85)
07. Tunnel of Love Express – 67 shows (1988)
08. Human Rights Now! – 20 shows (1988)
09. World Tour - 107 shows (1992–93)
10. Ghost of Tom Joad Tour – 128 shows (1995–97)
11. Reunion Tour – 133 shows (1999–2000)
12. Rising Tour – 120 shows (2002–03)
13. Vote for Change – 40 shows (2004)
14. Devils & Dust Solo & Acoustic Tour – 76 shows (2005)
15. Seeger Sessions Tour – 62 shows (2006)
16. Magic Tour – 100 shows (2007–08)
17. Working on a Dream Tour - 84 shows (2009)
18. Wrecking Ball Tour - 133 shows (2012-13)
19. High Hopes Tour – 34 shows (2014)
20. The River Tour - 89 shows (2016)

PHOTO CREDITS

Capital Theater 1978 photos courtesy of David Reiss, Fred Laparoas (Corinne hand photo), Hanging Rock courtesy of Matthew Finn, Point Blank Archives, Greg Turnbull for Clarence Clemons and Dan, Newcastle airport. Martin Salisbury, David J. Bernstein and Anjali Ram. Tess Parks for Alex Lipinksi photo. Getty Images.

ACKNOWLEDGEMENTS AND SOURCE NOTES

I am immensely grateful to everyone who has so generously helped with this project, giving up hours in their busy schedules to talk to me about their personal experiences and providing insights into the world of Bruce Springsteen.

There are many people to thank in the course of researching and compiling this book. Firstly a big thanks to all the Springsteen fans from around the world who very kindly took time to send me their memories of seeing Bruce live in concert as well as sending photo's, ticket stubs, flyers and posters to be included in the book.

I consulted the following television/radio networks, organisations magazines, newspapers, websites, and weeklies, some of which have now ceased publication, and in some cases I extracted previously publish material and for this I remain truly grateful to:

Best Classic Bands.com, The Irish Times, Set Lusting Bruce: The Springsteen Podcast, Jesse Jackson, http://setlustingbruce. libsyn.com/ The Orange County Register, Tom Cool Yolton, http:// www.castiles.net, L.Kirsch - TheLightinDarkness.com, Torsten Mörke, Alex Lipinski from Soulhub.co.uk, Off Camera with Sam

Jones, MusicCityMike.net, The Scotsman, Fife Today, Yorkshire Evening Post, Daily Telegraph, Hotpress, Today FM, The Sun, Wales online, Newsday, YouTube. Thanks to Mark Saleski from SomethingElseReviews.com, Chris Charlesworth from Justbackdated. blogspot.com, The Daily Record, The Guardian, Thisweekinworcester. com, Uber Rock, Theconversation-com, http://sites.google.com/ site/wildandinnocentproductions/7-river-tour.

Extra thanks to Liz Sanchez for photo research, cover images and design. Bob Young, Nigel Oakley and David Stock for all their support. Malcolm Wyatt for his editing skills and Richard Houghton for the 'The Day I Was There' concept.

And thanks to all Bruce Springsteen fan sites from around the world that helped with compiling this book including, Greasylake.org, Backstreets.com and Badlands.co.uk

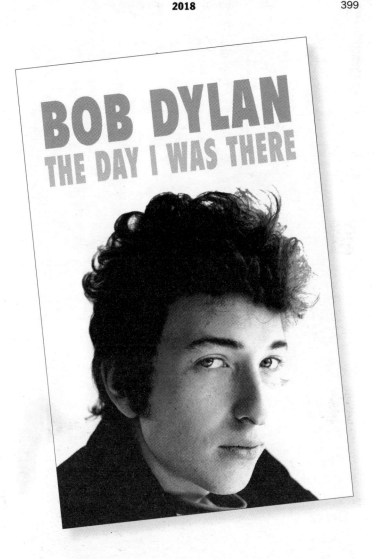

Fans, friends and colleagues tell their stories of seeing, knowing and working with Bob Dylan from his hometown of Hibbing right through to finding Jesus - with first-hand accounts of seeing him live from the smallest of venues to festivals and arenas, this book reveals a contemporary view of the younger Dylan.

During his six-decade career, he has played with all the greats. His career sky-rocketed when Crosby, Stills & Nash played only their second gig together at Woodstock in 1969. Stephen Stills is the only person to have been inducted twice in one night into The Rock and Roll Hall of Fame.